# AS / Year 1 Biology

## Exam Board: OCR A

Revising for Biology exams is stressful, that's for sure — even just getting your notes sorted out can leave you needing a lie down. But help is at hand...

This brilliant CGP book explains **everything you'll need to learn** (and nothing you won't), all in a straightforward style that's easy to get your head around. We've also included **exam questions** to test how ready you are for the real thing.

There's even a free Online Edition you can read on your computer or tablet!

## A-Level revision? It has to be CGP!

# Contents

Published by CGP

From original material by Richard Parsons.

Editors:
Charlotte Burrows, Christopher Lindle, Claire Plowman, Rachael Rogers, Hayley Thompson.

Contributors:
Gloria Barnett, James Foster, Paddy Gannon, Barbara Green, Adrian Schmit, Sophie Watkins.

ISBN: 978 1 78294 286 3

With thanks to Lauren Burns, Janet Cruse-Sawyer and Glenn Rogers for the proofreading.
With thanks to Laura Jakubowski for the copyright research.

Cover image © duncan1890/iStockphoto.com

With thanks to Science Photo Library for permission to reproduce the images on pages 17, 61, 74 and 101.

Data for graph showing glucose concentration vs absorbance on page 31 was obtained
using a Mystrica colorimeter © Mystrica Ltd. www.mystrica.com

Clipart from Corel®
Printed by Elanders Ltd, Newcastle upon Tyne.

# The Scientific Process

*'How Science Works' is all about the scientific process — how we develop and test scientific ideas. It's what scientists do all day, every day (well, except at coffee time — never come between a scientist and their coffee).*

## Scientists Come Up with **Theories** — Then **Test Them...**

Science tries to explain **how** and **why** things happen — it **answers questions**. It's all about seeking and gaining **knowledge** about the world around us. Scientists do this by **asking** questions and **suggesting** answers and then **testing** them, to see if they're correct — this is the **scientific process**.

1) **Ask** a question — make an **observation** and ask **why or how** it happens. E.g. why is trypsin (an enzyme) found in the small intestine but not in the stomach?

2) **Suggest** an answer, or part of an answer, by forming a **theory** (a possible **explanation** of the observations) e.g. pH affects the activity of enzymes. (Scientists also sometimes form a **model** too — a **simplified picture** of what's physically going on.)

3) Make a **prediction** or hypothesis — a **specific testable statement**, based on the theory, about what will happen in a test situation. E.g. trypsin will be active at pH 8 (the pH of the small intestine) but inactive at pH 2 (the pH of the stomach).

4) Carry out a **test** — to provide **evidence** that will support the prediction (or help to disprove it). E.g. measure the rate of reaction of trypsin at various pH levels.

The evidence supported Quentin's Theory of Flammable Burps.

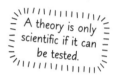

A theory is only scientific if it can be tested.

## ...Then They **Tell** Everyone About Their **Results...**

The results are **published** — scientists need to let others know about their work. Scientists publish their results in **scientific journals**. These are just like normal magazines, only they contain **scientific reports** (called papers) instead of the latest celebrity gossip.

1) Scientific reports are similar to the **lab write-ups** you do in school. And just as a lab write-up is **reviewed** (marked) by your teacher, reports in scientific journals undergo **peer review** before they're published.

2) The report is sent out to **peers** — other scientists that are experts in the **same area**. They examine the data and results, and if they think that the conclusion is reasonable it's **published**. This makes sure that work published in scientific journals is of a **good standard**.

3) But peer review **can't guarantee** the science is **correct** — other scientists still need to **reproduce** it.

4) Sometimes **mistakes** are made and bad work is published. Peer review **isn't perfect** but it's probably the best way for scientists to self-regulate their work and to publish **quality reports**.

## ...Then **Other Scientists** Will **Test** the Theory Too

Other scientists read the published theories and results, and try to **test the theory** themselves. This involves:
- Repeating the **exact same experiments**.
- Using the theory to make **new predictions** and then testing them with **new experiments**.

## If the **Evidence** Supports a Theory, It's **Accepted** — *for Now*

1) If all the experiments in all the world provide good evidence to back it up, the theory is thought of as **scientific 'fact'** (for now).

2) But it will never become **totally indisputable** fact. Scientific **breakthroughs or advances** could provide new ways to question and test the theory, which could lead to **new evidence** that **conflicts** with the current evidence. Then the testing starts all over again...

And this, my friend, is the **tentative nature of scientific knowledge** — it's always **changing** and **evolving**.

# The Scientific Process

*So scientists need evidence to back up their theories. They get it by carrying out experiments, and when that's not possible they carry out studies. But why bother with science at all? We want to know as much as possible so we can use it to try and improve our lives (and because we're nosy).*

## Evidence Comes from Lab Experiments...

1) Results from **controlled experiments** in **laboratories** are **great**.
2) A lab is the easiest place to **control variables** so that they're all **kept constant** (except for the one you're investigating).
3) This means you can draw meaningful **conclusions**.

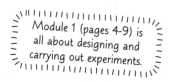
Module 1 (pages 4-9) is all about designing and carrying out experiments.

## ...and Well-Designed Studies

1) There are things you **can't** investigate in a lab, e.g. whether stress causes heart attacks. You have to do a study instead.
2) You still need to try and make the study as controlled as possible to make it **valid**. But in reality it's **very hard** to control **all the variables** that **might** be having an effect.
3) You can do things to help, e.g. have **matched groups** — **choose two groups** of people (those who have quite stressful jobs and those who don't) who are **as similar as possible** (same mix of ages, same mix of diets etc.). But you can't easily rule out every possibility.

Samantha thought her study was very well designed — especially the fitted bookshelf.

## Society Makes Decisions Based on Scientific Evidence

1) Lots of scientific work eventually leads to **important discoveries** or breakthroughs that could **benefit humankind**.
2) These results are **used by society** (that's you, me and everyone else) to **make decisions** — about the way we live, what we eat, what we drive, etc.
3) All sections of society use scientific evidence to make decisions, e.g. politicians use it to devise policies and individuals use science to make decisions about their own lives.

Other factors can **influence** decisions about science or the way science is used:

### Economic factors

- Society has to consider the **cost** of implementing changes based on scientific conclusions — e.g. the **NHS** can't afford the most expensive drugs without **sacrificing** something else.
- Scientific research is **expensive** so companies won't always develop new ideas — e.g. developing new drugs is costly, so pharmaceutical companies often only invest in drugs that are likely to make them **money**.

### Social factors

- **Decisions** affect **people's lives** — E.g. scientists may suggest **banning smoking** and **alcohol** to prevent health problems, but shouldn't **we** be able to **choose** whether **we** want to smoke and drink or not?

### Environmental factors

- Scientists believe **unexplored regions** like remote parts of rainforests might contain **untapped drug** resources. But some people think we shouldn't **exploit** these regions because any interesting finds may lead to **deforestation** and **reduced biodiversity** in these areas.

## So there you have it — how science works...

*Hopefully these pages have given you a nice intro to how science works, e.g. what scientists do to provide you with 'facts'. You need to understand this, as you're expected to know how science works — for the exam and for life.*

# Planning an Experiment

*Experiments are pretty cool — much more exciting than revising anyway. Before you start planning an experiment, you need to be really clear on what you're trying to find out — you should start off with a prediction or hypothesis (see p. 2).*

## A **Good Experiment** Gives **Results** that are:

1) **Precise** — precise results **don't vary** much **from the mean**. Precision is **reduced** by **random error**.

2) **Repeatable and reproducible** — repeatable means if the **same person** repeats the experiment using the same methods and equipment, they will get the same results. Reproducible means if **someone different** does the experiment, using a slightly different method or piece of equipment, the results will be the same.

3) **Valid** — valid results **answer the original question**. To get valid results you need to **control all the variables** to make sure you're only testing the thing you want to.

4) **Accurate** — accurate results are **really close** to the **true answer**. If you're studying a **sample** of a population (see p. 106), a **larger sample size** will increase the accuracy of your results.

*Precise results are sometimes referred to as reliable results.*

You need to be able to **design** a good experiment. Here are some things you'll need to consider:

1) **Only one variable should be changed** — Variables are **quantities** that have the **potential to change**, e.g. pH. In an experiment you usually **change one variable** and **measure its effect** on another variable.
   - The variable that you **change** is called the **independent variable**.
   - The variable that you **measure** is called the **dependent variable**.

2) **All the other variables should be controlled** — When you're investigating a variable you need to keep everything else that could affect it **constant**. This means you can be sure that **only** your **independent** variable is **affecting** the thing you're measuring (the dependent variable).

3) **Negative controls should be used** — Negative controls are used to **check** that only the independent variable is affecting the dependent variable. Negative controls **aren't expected** to have **any effect** on the experiment.

4) **The experiment should be repeated at least three times and a mean should be calculated** — this reduces the effect of **random error** on your experiment, which makes your results **more precise**. Doing repeats and getting similar results each time also shows that your data is **repeatable** and makes it more likely to be **reproducible**.

> **EXAMPLE:** Investigating the effect of **temperature** on **enzyme activity**.
> 1) Temperature is the **independent** variable.
> 2) Enzyme activity is the **dependent** variable.
> 3) pH, volume, substrate concentration and enzyme concentration should all **stay the same** (and the quantities should be recorded to allow someone else to reproduce the experiment).
> 4) The experiment should be **repeated** at least **three times** at each temperature used.
> 5) A **negative control**, containing everything used **except the enzyme**, should be measured at each temperature used. No enzyme activity should be seen with these controls.

## Select Appropriate **Apparatus**, **Equipment** and **Techniques**

1) When you're **planning** an experiment you need to decide what it is you're going to **measure** and **how often** you're going to take measurements. E.g. if you're investigating the **rate of respiration**, you could either measure the volume of **oxygen used** over time or the volume of **carbon dioxide produced** over time. You could take measurements at, e.g. 30 second intervals or 60 second intervals.

2) Then you need to choose the most **appropriate** apparatus, equipment and techniques for the experiment. E.g.

- The **measuring apparatus** you use has to be **sensitive** enough to measure the changes you're looking for. E.g. if you need to measure changes of **1 cm³** you need to use a **measuring cylinder** that can measure in **1 cm³** increments. It'd be no good trying with one that only measures 10 cm³ increments — it wouldn't be sensitive enough. And if you need to measure **small changes** in **pH**, a **pH meter** (which can measure pH to several decimal places) would be more sensitive than indicator paper.

- The **equipment** and **apparatus** you choose has to be **appropriate** for the **function** it needs to perform. E.g. if you are studying the **nuclei** of cells under the microscope you need to **stain** them with a dye that stains nuclei, e.g. methylene blue. It would be no good staining them with eosin, as this doesn't stain the nuclei.

- The **technique** you use has to be the most **appropriate** one for your **experiment**. E.g. if you want to make a series of solutions for a **calibration curve**, you'd usually use a **serial dilution technique** (see p. 31).

Examiners love getting you to **suggest improvements** to **methods** — for example, how a method could be improved to make the results more precise. So make sure you really know how to **design** a **good experiment**.

# Planning an Experiment

## Use **Apparatus** and **Techniques** Correctly to Obtain **Precise Results**

1) Once you've chosen the best apparatus and techniques to use in your experiment, you need to make sure you can **use them correctly**. In the exams, you could be asked about a **whole range** of different apparatus and techniques — make sure you know how to use all the ones you've come across in class. Here are just a few examples:

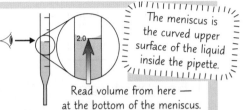

The meniscus is the curved upper surface of the liquid inside the pipette.

Read volume from here — at the bottom of the meniscus.

- **Pipettes** — Graduated pipettes have a **scale** so you can measure specific volumes — make sure you read the **meniscus** at **eye level**.

- **Water baths** — Make sure you **allow time** for water baths to **heat up** before starting your experiment. Don't forget that your **solutions** will need **time** to get to the **same temperature** as the water before you start the experiment too.

- **Data logger** — Decide **what** you are **measuring** and what **type** of **data logger** you will need, e.g. temperature, pH. Connect an **external sensor** to the data logger if you need to. Decide **how often** you want the data logger to take readings depending on the **length** of the **process** that you are measuring.

2) Make sure you're measuring things using **appropriate units**. E.g. if you're measuring time, it might be better to use seconds rather than minutes — when you come to processing your results, it'll be easier to work with a result of 73 seconds than a result of 1.217 minutes. Also, make sure you **record** your **units properly**, e.g. if you're measuring the length of something and accidently write cm instead of mm, any **calculations** you do will be **affected** and your **conclusions** may be **wrong**.

3) Make sure you **perform** all **techniques carefully** and that any **apparatus** is **set up correctly** — this will help to **minimise errors** which would affect your results.

## Risk Assessments Help You to **Work Safely**

1) When you're planning an experiment, you need to carry out a **risk assessment**. To do this, you need to identify:
   - All the **dangers** in the experiment, e.g. any hazardous chemicals, microorganisms or naked flames.
   - **Who** is at **risk** from these dangers.
   - What can be done to **reduce** the **risk**, such as wearing goggles or gloves or working in a fume cupboard.

2) You also need to consider any **ethical issues** in your experiment. For example, if you're using **living animals** (e.g. insects) you must treat them with **respect**. This means **handling them carefully** and keeping them away from **harmful chemicals**, **extreme heat sources** and other things that might cause them **physical discomfort**.

## Record Your **Data** in a **Table**

It's a good idea to draw a table to **record** the **results** of your experiment in.

1) When you draw a table, make sure you **include** enough **rows** and **columns** to **record all of the data** you need to. You might also need to include a column for **processing** your data (e.g. working out an average).

2) Make sure each **column** has a **heading** so you know what's going to be recorded where.

3) The **units** should be in the **column** heading, not the table itself.

heading · data · units · column

| Farm | Length of hedgerows (km) | Number of species |
|------|--------------------------|-------------------|
| 1 | 49 | 21 |
| 2 | 90 | 28 |
| 3 | 155 | 30 |

row

### Watch Out for **Anomalous Results**

Doing repeats makes it easier to spot anomalous results.

When you look at all the **data** in your **table**, you may notice that you have a result that **doesn't seem to fit in** with the rest at all. These results are called **anomalous results**. You should **investigate** anomalous results — if you can work out what happened (e.g. you measured something totally wrong) you can **ignore** them when **processing** your results.

## My best apparatus is the pommel horse...

*It's not really, I just like the word pommel. Scientists are rightfully fussy about methods and equipment — I mean if you're going to bother doing an experiment, you should at least make sure it's going to give you results you can trust.*

# Processing and Presenting Data

*Once you've collected your data you really need to do something with it so you can use it....*

## Processing the Data Helps You to Interpret it

### You Need to be Able to Calculate Percentage Change

Calculating **percentage change** helps to **quantify** how much something has changed, e.g. the percentage of plants that were killed with a herbicide in a particular year compared to the previous year.
To **calculate** it you use this equation:

$$\text{Percentage change} = \frac{\text{final value} - \text{original value}}{\text{original value}} \times 100$$

A **positive** value shows an **increase** and a **negative** value shows a **decrease**.

### Averages and the Range Summarise Your Data

When you've done **repeats** of an experiment you should always calculate the **mean**. To do this **add together** all the data values and **divide** by the **total** number of values in the sample.

*You could also be asked to calculate the median (the middle number when you put all your data in numerical order) or the mode (the number that appears most often in a set of data).*

| Test tube | Repeat (g) 1 | Repeat (g) 2 | Repeat (g) 3 | Mean (g) | Range (g) |
|-----------|---|---|---|----------|-----------|
| A | 28 | 37 | 32 | $(28 + 37 + 32) \div 3 = 32.3$ | $37 - 28 = 9$ |
| B | 47 | 51 | 60 | $(47 + 51 + 60) \div 3 = 52.7$ | $60 - 47 = 13$ |
| C | 68 | 70 | 70 | $(68 + 70 + 70) \div 3 = 69.3$ | $70 - 68 = 2$ |

You might also need to calculate the **range** (how **spread out** the data is). To do this find the **largest** data value and **subtract** the **smallest** data value from it.

**Standard deviation** can be more useful than the **range** because it tells you how **values** are spread about the **mean** rather than just the **total spread** of data. A **small standard deviation** means the repeated results are all **similar** and **close** to the mean, i.e. **precise**. There's more on standard deviation on pages 119-120.

## Statistical Tests Tell You Whether to Accept or Reject Your Hypothesis

**Statistical tests** are used to **analyse** data **mathematically**. They can be used to analyse **quantitative** (numerical) or **qualitative** (non-numerical) results. For example:

1) The **Student's t-test** — you can use the Student's t-test when you have two sets of **data** that you want to **compare**, e.g. whether males and females performed differently in the same test. It tests whether there is a **significant difference** in the **means** of the two data sets. The value obtained is compared to the **theoretical expected** value, which helps you decide **how likely** it is that the results or 'differences in the means' were **due to chance**.

2) **Spearman's rank correlation coefficient** — this tells you the **degree** to which **two sets** of **data** are **related**. It is given as value between 1 and –1. A value of 1 indicates a **strong positive correlation**, 0 means there is **no correlation** and –1 is a **strong negative correlation** (see page 8 for more on correlation).

### Watch Out For Significant Figures

When you're processing your data you may well want to round any **really long numbers** to a certain number of **significant figures**. E.g. **0.6878976** rounds to **0.69** to 2 s.f..

*The first significant figure of a number is the first digit that isn't a zero. The second, third and fourth significant figures follow on immediately after the first (even if they're zeros).*

When you're doing **calculations** using numbers given to a certain number of significant figures, you should always give your **answer** to the **lowest number** of significant figures that was used in the calculation.
For example:

$$1.2 \div 1.85 = 0.648648648... \quad = 0.65$$

2 s.f.    3 s.f.    Answer should be rounded to 2 s.f.    Round the last digit up to 5.

This is because the **fewer digits** a measurement has, the less **accurate** it is.
Your answer can only be as accurate as the **least accurate measurement** in the calculation.

# Processing and Presenting Data

## Choose a Suitable **Graph** or **Chart** to Present Your Data

Graphs and charts are a great way of **presenting data** — they can make results much **easier to interpret**.

1) When you have **qualitative** data (non-numerical data, e.g. blood group) or **discrete** data (numerical data that can only take certain values in a range, e.g. shoe size) you can use **bar charts** or **pie charts**.

2) When you have **continuous** data (data that can take any value in a range, e.g. height or weight) you can use **histograms** or **line graphs.**

3) When you want to plot **one variable against the other** you can use a **scatter graph.**

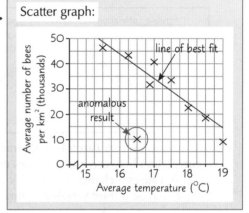

Scatter graph:

Whatever type of graph you use, you should make sure that:

- The **dependent variable** goes on the **y-axis** (the vertical axis) and the **independent** on the **x-axis** (the horizontal axis).
- You always **label** the **axes**, include the quantity and **units**, and choose a **sensible scale**.
- The graph covers **at least half** of the **graph paper**.

If you need to draw a **line** (or curve) **of best fit** on a **scatter graph**, draw the line through or as near to as many points as possible, **ignoring** any **anomalous** results.

## Find the **Rate** By Finding the **Gradient**

Rate is a **measure** of how much something is **changing over time**. Calculating a rate can be useful when analysing your data, e.g. you might want to the find the **rate of a reaction**. Rates are easy to work out from a graph:

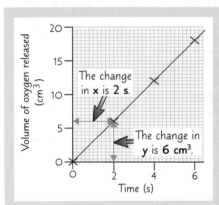

For a **linear** graph you can calculate the **rate** by finding the **gradient of the line**: $\Longrightarrow$ 

$$\text{Gradient} = \frac{\text{Change in Y}}{\text{Change in X}}$$

So in this **example**: $\quad \text{rate} = \dfrac{6 \text{ cm}^3}{2 \text{ s}} = \mathbf{3 \text{ cm}^3 \text{ s}^{-1}}$ $\quad$ cm³ s⁻¹ means the same as cm³/s (centimetres per second)

The **equation** of a **straight line** can always be written in the form $y = mx + c$, where $m$ is the **gradient** and $c$ is the **y-intercept** (this is the **value of y** when the line crosses the y-axis). In this example, the equation of the line is $y = 3x + 0$ (or just $y = 3x$). Knowing the equation of the line allows you to estimate results not plotted on the graph. E.g. in this case, when x (the time) is **20 s**, y (the volume of oxygen released) will be $3x = 3 \times 20 = \mathbf{60 \text{ cm}^3}$.

For a **curved** (non-linear) graph you can find the **rate** by drawing a **tangent**:

1) Position a ruler on the graph at the **point** where you want to know the **rate**.

2) **Angle** the **ruler** so there is **equal space** between the **ruler** and the **curve** on **either** side of the point.

3) **Draw a line** along the ruler to make the tangent.

   **Extend** the line right across the graph — it'll help to make your **gradient calculation easier** as you'll have **more points** to choose from.

4) **Calculate** the **gradient** of the **tangent** to find the **rate**.

$$\text{Gradient} = 55 \text{ m}^2 \div 4.4 \text{ years} = \mathbf{12.5 \text{ m}^2 \text{ year}^{-1}}$$

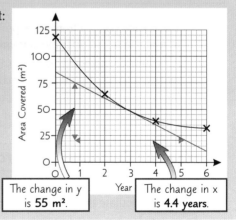

The change in y is **55 m²**. | Year | The change in x is **4.4 years**.

---

## *Significant figures — a result of far too many cream cakes...*

*Graphs and charts are great for seeing what's going on in your results. Don't get confused if you need to find the rate of something from a graph — you just have to find the gradient of the line. And if you haven't got a straight line, draw one.*

# Drawing Conclusions and Evaluating

*So once you've processed your data you'll want to see what conclusions you can come to. Evaluations are important too so you can assess your experiment and think about how you could do things differently next time.*

## You Need to **Draw Conclusions** From Your **Data**

1) Conclusions need to be **valid**. A conclusion can only be considered as valid if it answers the original question (see page 4).

2) You can often draw conclusions by looking at the relationship (**correlation**) between two variables:

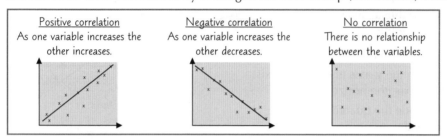

Positive correlation
As one variable increases the other increases.

Negative correlation
As one variable increases the other decreases.

No correlation
There is no relationship between the variables.

There is no correlation between the colour of your tights and the proportion of your life you spend upside down.

3) You have to be very **careful** when **drawing conclusions** from data like this because a **correlation** between two variables **doesn't** always mean that a **change** in one variable **causes** a **change** in the other (the correlation could be due to **chance** or there could be a **third variable** having an effect).

4) If there's a relationship between two variables and a change in one variable **does** cause a change in the other it's called a **causal relationship**.

5) It can be **concluded** that a **correlation** is a **causal relationship** if every other variable that could possibly affect the result is **controlled**.

*In reality this is very hard to do — correlations are generally accepted to be causal relationships if lots of studies have found the same thing, and scientists have figured out exactly how one factor causes the other.*

6) When you're making a conclusion you **can't** make broad **generalisations** from data — you have to be very **specific**. You can only **conclude** what the results show and **no more**.

> **Example**
> The graph shows the results from a study into the effect of penicillin dosage on the duration of fever in men. The only **conclusion** you can draw is that as the **dosage** of **penicillin increases**, the **duration** of **fever** in **men decreases**. You **can't** conclude that this is true for any other antibiotic, any other symptom or even for female patients — the **results** could be **completely different**.

*Duration of fever in men*

*Penicillin dosage*

## Uncertainty is the Amount of Error Your Measurements Might Have

1) The results you get from an experiment won't be completely perfect — there'll always be a **degree of uncertainty** in your measurements due to limits in the **sensitivity** of the apparatus you're using.

2) For example, an electronic mass balance might measure to the **nearest 0.01 g**, but the real mass could be up to **0.005 g smaller or larger**. It has an **uncertainty value** of ± **0.005g**.

3) The ± sign tells you the **range** in which the **true value** lies (to within a certain probability). The range is called the **margin of error**.

### You Can **Calculate** The **Percentage Error** of Your **Measurements**

If you know the **uncertainty value** of your measurements, you can calculate the **percentage error** using this formula:

$$\text{percentage error} = \frac{\text{uncertainty}}{\text{reading}} \times 100$$

**Example**

50 cm³ of HCl is measured with an uncertainty value of ± 0.05 cm³.

percentage error = $\frac{0.05}{50} \times 100 = \mathbf{0.1\%}$

# Drawing Conclusions and Evaluating

## You Can *Minimise* the *Errors* in Your *Measurements*

1) One obvious way to **reduce errors** in your measurements is to buy the most **sensitive equipment** available. In real life there's not much you can do about this one — you're stuck with whatever your school or college has got. But there are other ways to **lower the uncertainty** in experiments.

2) For example, you can plan your experiment so you **measure** a **greater amount** of something:

> If you use a **500 cm³** cylinder that goes up in **5 cm³** increments, each reading has an uncertainty of ± **2.5 cm³**.
>
> So using a 500 cm³ cylinder to measure **100 cm³** of liquid will give you a percentage error of:
>
> But if you measure **200 cm³** in the same cylinder, the percentage error is:
>
> $$\frac{2.5}{100} \times 100 = \mathbf{2.5\%}$$
>
> $$\frac{2.5}{200} \times 100 = \mathbf{1.25\%}$$
>
> Hey presto — you've just **halved** the uncertainty.

## You Need to *Sum Up* Your Experiment in an *Evaluation*

1) In an **evaluation** you need to assess the following things about your **experiment** and the **data** you gathered:
   - **Repeatability**: Did you take enough repeat readings of the measurements? Would you do more repeats if you were to do the experiment again? Do you think you'd get similar data if you did the experiment again?
   - **Reproducibility**: Have you compared your results with other people's results? Were your results similar? Could other scientists gain data showing the same relationships that are shown in your data?
   - **Validity**: Does your data answer the question you set out to investigate?

2) Make sure you **evaluate** your **method**. Is there anything you could have done to make your results more **precise** or **accurate**? Were there any **limitations** in your method, e.g. should you have taken measurements more **frequently**? Were there any **sources** of **error** in your experiment? Could you have used more sensitive **apparatus** or **equipment**? Think about how you could **refine** and **improve** your experiment if you did it again.

3) Once you've thought about these points you can decide how much **confidence** you have in your **conclusion**. For example, if your results are **repeatable**, **reproducible** and **valid** and they back up your conclusion then you can have a **high degree** of **confidence** in your conclusion.

## Practice Questions

Q1 What is a dependent variable?

Q2 Why is it important to repeat an experiment at least three times?

Q3 Describe how you would find the rate at a specific point on a curved graph.

Q4 Give one way that you could minimise error in an experiment.

**Exam Question**

Q1 Amylase is an enzyme that catalyses the breakdown of starch into simple sugars. The presence of starch can be detected with iodine solution — it turns from a browny-orange colour to blue-black when starch is present. An experiment was done to investigate the effect of temperature on the action of amylase. In the experiment amylase solution and starch solution were added to a boiling tube and mixed together. The boiling tube was then placed in a water bath set to the required temperature. At the start of the experiment and every minute afterwards, a small sample of the solution was taken from the boiling tube and added to a spot tile. Iodine solution was added to the sample and the time at which the solution remained browny-orange was recorded. The experiment was repeated at six different temperatures. The graph above shows the results.

    a) Give three variables that should have been controlled in this experiment.     [3 marks]

    b) Suggest why the result at 30 °C has not been included on the graph's curve of best fit.     [1 mark]

    c) Give two limitations of the method used and suggest how these could be improved.     [4 marks]

    d) What conclusions can be drawn from the results of the experiment?     [2 marks]

---

## *Correlation Street — my favourite programme...*

*Don't ever, ever assume that correlation means cause. There, I've told you again. No excuses now. A good evaluation is a sign that you really understand what makes a good experiment, so make sure your evaluation-writing-skills are top notch.*

# Eukaryotic Cells and Organelles

*Ah, cells. Where would we be without them? There are two types of cell — prokaryotic and eukaryotic. This topic is about eukaryotic cells and their organelles (all the tiny bits and bobs that you can only see in detail with a fancy microscope)...*

## Organisms can be **Prokaryotes** or **Eukaryotes**

1) Prokaryotic organisms are **prokaryotic cells** (i.e. they're single-celled organisms) and eukaryotic organisms are made up of **eukaryotic cells**.

2) Both types of cells contain **organelles**. Organelles are **parts** of cells — each one has a **specific function**.

1) Eukaryotic cells are **complex** and include all **animal** and **plant cells**.

2) Prokaryotic cells are **smaller** and **simpler**, e.g. bacteria. See page 15 for more.

## *Plant* and *Animal* Cells are Both *Eukaryotic*

Eukaryotic cells are generally a **bit more complicated** than prokaryotic cells. You've probably been looking at **animal** and **plant cell** diagrams for years, so hopefully you'll be familiar with some of the bits and pieces...

**Animal Cell**

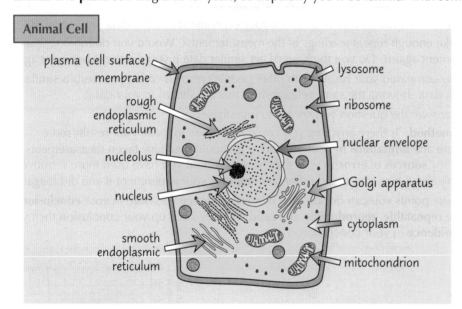

plasma (cell surface) membrane

rough endoplasmic reticulum

nucleolus

nucleus

smooth endoplasmic reticulum

lysosome

ribosome

nuclear envelope

Golgi apparatus

cytoplasm

mitochondrion

You're expected to be able to interpret photos of cells and their organelles, taken through different types of microscope — so make sure you learn to recognise all the structures on pages 11-13.

**Plant Cell**

Plant cells have all the **same organelles** as animal cells, but with a few **added extras**:

• a **cell wall** with **plasmodesmata** ('channels' for exchanging substances with adjacent cells),

• a **vacuole** (compartment that contains cell sap),

• and of course good old **chloroplasts**.

plasma (cell surface) membrane

chloroplast

rough endoplasmic reticulum

plasmodesma

mitochondrion

Golgi apparatus

vacuole

smooth endoplasmic reticulum

cytoplasm

nucleolus

nucleus

ribosome

cell wall

# Eukaryotic Cells and Organelles

## Different Organelles have Different Functions

This giant table contains a big list of organelles — you need to know the **structure** and **function** of them all.  Sorry.
Most organelles are surrounded by **membranes**, which sometimes causes confusion — don't make the mistake of
thinking that a diagram of an organelle is a diagram of a whole cell.  They're not cells — they're **parts of** cells.

| ORGANELLE | DIAGRAM | DESCRIPTION | FUNCTION |
|---|---|---|---|
| **Plasma (cell surface) membrane** | plasma membrane / cytoplasm | The membrane found on the **surface** of **animal cells** and just inside the cell wall of **plant cells** and **prokaryotic cells**.  It's made mainly of **lipids** and **protein**. | **Regulates the movement** of substances into and out of the cell.  It also has **receptor molecules** on it, which allow it to respond to chemicals like hormones. |
| **Cell wall** | plasma membrane / cell wall / cytoplasm | A rigid structure that surrounds **plant cells**.  It's made mainly of the carbohydrate **cellulose**. | **Supports** plant cells. |
| **Nucleus** | nuclear envelope / nucleolus / nuclear pore / chromatin | A large organelle surrounded by a **nuclear envelope** (double membrane), which contains many **pores**.  The nucleus contains **chromatin** (which is made from **DNA** and proteins) and a structure called the **nucleolus**. | The nucleus **controls the cell's activities** (by controlling the transcription of DNA — see page 40).  **DNA** contains instructions to make proteins — see page 38.  The **pores** allow substances (e.g. RNA) to move between the nucleus and the cytoplasm.  The **nucleolus** makes **ribosomes** (see below). |
| **Lysosome** | | A **round organelle** surrounded by a **membrane**, with no clear internal structure. | Contains **digestive enzymes**. These are kept separate from the cytoplasm by the surrounding membrane, and can be used to **digest invading cells** or to **break down** worn out components of the cell. |
| **Ribosome** | small subunit / large subunit | A **very small organelle** that either **floats free** in the cytoplasm or is attached to the **rough endoplasmic reticulum**. It's made up of **proteins and RNA** (see page 34).  It's **not** surrounded by a membrane. | The site where **proteins** are made. |

# Eukaryotic Cells and Organelles

| ORGANELLE | DIAGRAM | DESCRIPTION | FUNCTION |
|---|---|---|---|
| Rough Endoplasmic Reticulum (RER) | ribosome / fluid | A system of membranes enclosing a fluid-filled space. The surface is **covered with ribosomes.** | **Folds** and **processes proteins** that have been made at the ribosomes. |
| Smooth Endoplasmic Reticulum (SER) | | Similar to rough endoplasmic reticulum, but with no **ribosomes.** | **Synthesises** and **processes lipids.** |
| Vesicle | cell's plasma membrane / vesicle | A small **fluid-filled** sac in the cytoplasm, surrounded by a membrane. | **Transports substances** in and out of the cell (via the plasma membrane) and between organelles. Some are formed by the Golgi apparatus or the endoplasmic reticulum, while others are formed at the cell surface. |
| Golgi Apparatus | vesicle | A group of fluid-filled, membrane-bound, **flattened sacs.** Vesicles are often seen at the edges of the sacs. | It **processes** and **packages** new lipids and proteins. It also **makes lysosomes.** |
| Mitochondrion | outer membrane / inner membrane / crista / matrix | They're usually oval-shaped. They have a **double membrane** — the inner one is folded to form structures called **cristae.** Inside is the **matrix**, which contains enzymes involved in respiration. | The **site of aerobic respiration**, where **ATP** is produced. They're found in large numbers in cells that are very **active** and require a lot of **energy.** |
| Chloroplast | stroma / two membranes / granum (plural = grana) / lamella (plural = lamellae) | A small, **flattened** structure found in **plant cells.** It's surrounded by a **double membrane**, and also has membranes inside called **thylakoid membranes.** These membranes are stacked up in some parts of the chloroplast to form **grana.** Grana are linked together by lamellae — thin, flat pieces of thylakoid membrane. | The **site** where **photosynthesis** takes place. Some parts of photosynthesis happen in the **grana**, and other parts happen in the **stroma** (a thick fluid found in chloroplasts). |

# Eukaryotic Cells and Organelles

| ORGANELLE | DIAGRAM | DESCRIPTION | FUNCTION |
|---|---|---|---|
| Centriole | microtubule | Small, **hollow cylinders**, made of **microtubules** (tiny protein cylinders). Found in animal cells, but only some plant cells. | Involved with the **separation of chromosomes** during cell division (see p. 60-62). |
| Cilia | side    cross-section | Small, **hair-like structures** found on the surface membrane of some **animal cells**. In cross-section, they have an outer membrane and a ring of nine pairs of **protein microtubules** inside, with two microtubules in the middle. *This is known as the '9 + 2' formation.* | The microtubules allow the cilia to **move**. This movement is used by the cell to **move substances along the cell surface**. |
| Flagellum | | Flagella on eukaryotic cells are **like cilia** but longer. They **stick out** from the cell surface and are surrounded by the plasma membrane. Inside they're like cilia too — two **microtubules** in the centre and nine pairs around the edge. | The microtubules **contract** to make the flagellum **move**. Flagella are used like **outboard motors** to propel cells forward (e.g. when a **sperm cell** swims). |

## Practice Questions

Q1 How does the structure of rough endoplasmic reticulum differ from that of smooth endoplasmic reticulum?

Q2 Describe the function of vesicles.

Q3 What is the function of chloroplasts?

Q4 What is the function of the centrioles?

### Exam Questions

Q1 Which of the following describes a structure found in plant cells but not in animal cells?

  A  A system of membranes enclosing a fluid-filled space.

  B  A flattened structure surrounded by a double membrane. Internal membranes are stacked up in places to form grana.

  C  A small organelle consisting of two subunits. It is not surrounded by a membrane.

  D  A round, membrane-bound organelle containing digestive enzymes.   [1 mark]

Q2 a) Identify these two organelles from their descriptions as seen in an electron micrograph.

    i)  An oval-shaped organelle surrounded by a double membrane. The inner membrane is folded and projects into the inner space, which is filled with a grainy material.   [1 mark]

    ii)  A collection of flattened membrane 'sacs' arranged roughly parallel to one another. Small, circular structures are seen at the edges of these 'sacs'.   [1 mark]

  b)  State the function of the two organelles that you have identified.   [2 marks]

## That's enough talk of fluid-filled sacs for my liking. Scientists eh...

*'Organelle' is a very pretty-sounding name for all those blobs. Actually, under a microscope some of them are really quite fetching — well I think so anyway, but then my mate finds sheep fetching, so there's no accounting for taste. Anyway, you need to know the names and functions of all the organelles and also what they look like.*

# Organelles Working Together

*After that endless list of organelles, you might need a few minutes to regain consciousness... Then you can read this lovely page about how they work together to produce proteins. And there's some stuff on cytoskeletons too...*

## Organelles are Involved in Protein Production

1) Proteins are made at the **ribosomes**.

2) The ribosomes on the **rough endoplasmic reticulum (ER)** make proteins that are **excreted** or attached to the **cell membrane**. The free ribosomes in the **cytoplasm** make proteins that **stay in the cytoplasm**.

3) New proteins produced at the rough ER are **folded** and **processed** (e.g. sugar chains are added) in the rough ER.

4) Then they're **transported** from the ER to the **Golgi apparatus** in **vesicles**.

5) At the Golgi apparatus, the proteins may undergo **further processing** (e.g. sugar chains are trimmed or more are added).

6) The proteins enter more **vesicles** to be transported around the cell. E.g. glycoproteins (found in **mucus**) move to the cell surface and are **secreted**.

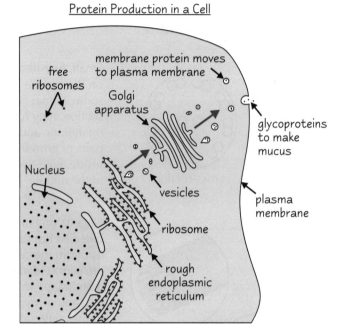

Protein Production in a Cell

free ribosomes

membrane protein moves to plasma membrane

Golgi apparatus

glycoproteins to make mucus

Nucleus

vesicles

plasma membrane

ribosome

rough endoplasmic reticulum

## The Cytoskeleton has Several Functions

1) The organelles in cells are surrounded by the **cytoplasm**. The cytoplasm is more than just a solution of chemicals though — it's got a **network of protein threads** running through it. These protein threads are called the **cytoskeleton**.

2) In eukaryotic cells the protein threads are arranged as **microfilaments** (small solid strands) and **microtubules** (tiny protein cylinders).

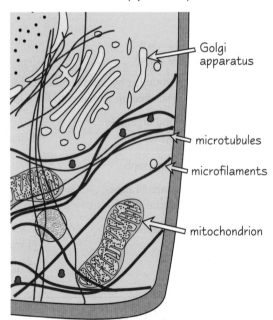

Golgi apparatus

microtubules

microfilaments

mitochondrion

The cytoskeleton has **four main functions**:

1) The microtubules and microfilaments **support** the cell's organelles, keeping them **in position**.

2) They also help to **strengthen the cell** and **maintain its shape**.

3) As well as this, they're responsible for the **movement of materials** within the cell. For example, the movement of **chromosomes** when they separate during cell division depends on contraction of microtubules in the spindle (see pages 60-62 for more on cell division).

4) The proteins of the cytoskeleton can also cause the cell to **move**. For example, the movement of **cilia** and **flagella** is caused by the cytoskeletal protein filaments that run through them. So in the case of single cells that have a flagellum (e.g. sperm cells), the cytoskeleton propels the **whole cell**.

The assembly of microtubules and microfilaments, and the movement of materials along them, requires energy from respiration. So microtubules and microfilaments can be prevented from functioning using respiratory inhibitors.

# Prokaryotic Cells

## Prokaryotes are a Different Kind of Cell

You need to be able to compare and contrast prokaryotic and eukaryotic cells. This big orange table should help...

A micrometre (μm) is one millionth of a metre, or 0.001 mm.

| PROKARYOTES | EUKARYOTES |
|---|---|
| Extremely small cells (less than 2 μm diameter) | Larger cells (about 10-100 μm diameter) |
| DNA is circular | DNA is linear |
| No nucleus — DNA free in cytoplasm | Nucleus present — DNA is inside nucleus |
| Cell wall made of a polysaccharide, but not cellulose or chitin | No cell wall (in animals), cellulose cell wall (in plants) or chitin cell wall (in fungi) |
| Few organelles and no membrane-bound organelles, e.g. no mitochondria | Many organelles — mitochondria and other membrane-bound organelles present |
| Flagella (when present) made of the protein flagellin, arranged in a helix | Flagella (when present) made of microtubule proteins arranged in a '9 + 2' formation |
| Small ribosomes | Larger ribosomes |
| **Example:** *E. coli* bacterium | **Example:** Human liver cell |

## Bacterial Cells are Prokaryotic

1) Prokaryotes like bacteria are roughly a **tenth the size** of eukaryotic cells.

2) This means that normal microscopes aren't really powerful enough to look at their **internal structure**.

3) The diagram shows a bacterial cell as seen under an **electron microscope** (see page 17).

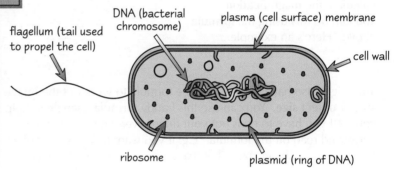

flagellum (tail used to propel the cell)

DNA (bacterial chromosome)

plasma (cell surface) membrane

cell wall

ribosome

plasmid (ring of DNA)

## Practice Questions

Q1 An unidentified cell is found to contain mitochondria. Is it prokaryotic or eukaryotic?

Q2 How is a prokaryotic cell wall different to a eukaryotic cell wall?

### Exam Questions

Q1 Some mucus-secreting cells were immersed in a solution of radioactive amino acids.
Every five seconds, some of the cells were removed and their organelles were separated and analysed.
The radioactivity in the different organelles was measured for each five second interval.

When answering the first two questions below, use organelles from this list —
Golgi apparatus, ribosomes, rough endoplasmic reticulum, vesicles.

a) In which of these organelles would you expect radioactivity to appear first? Explain your answer. [2 marks]

b) After 5 minutes, the Golgi apparatus had become radioactive.
Which other organelle(s) would be radioactive by this time? [2 marks]

c) The researchers were particularly interested in the cells' vesicles. What is the function of vesicles? [1 mark]

Q2 Give three functions of a cell's cytoskeleton. [3 marks]

## A cell without a nucleus — it's like Posh without Becks...

*Prokaryotes are way, way older than eukaryotes. In fact, most cellular biologists think that mitochondria and chloroplasts are remnants of ancient prokaryotes that lived inside the first eukaryotes and eventually just became part of them. Mad.*

# Studying Cells — How Microscopes Work

*If you were born over a century ago then you wouldn't have had to learn all this stuff about organelles because people wouldn't have known anything about them. But then better microscopes were invented and here we are.*

## Magnification *is* Size, Resolution *is* Detail

We all know that microscopes produce a **magnified image** of a sample, but **resolution** is just as important...

1) MAGNIFICATION is how much **bigger** the image is than the specimen (the sample you're looking at). It's calculated using this formula:

$$\text{magnification} = \frac{\text{image size}}{\text{object size}}$$

2) RESOLUTION is how **detailed** the image is. More specifically, it's how well a microscope **distinguishes** between **two points** that are **close together**. If a microscope lens can't separate two objects, then increasing the magnification won't help.

Georgina didn't believe in the need for microscopes — she had her trusty varifocals.

## You Need to be Able to *Calculate* the *Magnification* of an Image

In the exam, you might be told the actual and magnified size of an object and then be asked to calculate the **magnification**. You can do this using the **formula** above. Here's an example...

5 mm

You have a magnified image that's 5 mm wide.
Your specimen is 50 μm wide.
First, get everything into the same units:
   1 mm = 1000 μm
   so 50 μm ÷ 1000 = 0.05 mm
Now calculate the magnification:
   5 ÷ 0.05 = **× 100**

÷1000
μm → mm
× 1000

You might also have to rearrange the formula to work out the **image size** or **object size**. You can use this handy **formula triangle** to help you. All you have to do is put your finger over what you want to know and read off the formula. E.g. if you want to know the object size, cover up object size. That leaves image size ÷ magnification.

image size
magnification × object size

## You Need to Know About *Three Types* of Microscope

### 1) Light microscopes

1) **Light microscopes** use light (no surprises there).
2) They have a **lower resolution** than electron microscopes — they have a maximum resolution of about **0.2 micrometres** (μm). So they're usually used to look at **whole cells** or **tissues**.
3) The maximum useful **magnification** of a light microscope is about **× 1500**.

### 2) Laser Scanning Confocal Microscopes (a special type of light microscope)

1) **Laser Scanning Confocal Microscopes** use **laser beams** (intense beams of light) to **scan** a specimen, which is usually tagged with a **fluorescent** dye.
2) The laser causes the dye to **fluoresce — give off light**. This light is then **focused** through a **pinhole** onto a **detector**. The detector is hooked up to a computer, which generates an image. The image can be **3D**.
3) The pinhole means that any **out-of-focus light** is **blocked**, so these microscopes produce a much **clearer image** than a normal light microscope.
4) They can be used to look at objects at **different depths** in **thick specimens**.

This is not how a Laser Scanning Confocal Microscope works. Sadly.

# Studying Cells — How Microscopes Work

## 3) Electron microscopes

**Electron microscopes** use **electrons** instead of light to form an image. They have a **higher resolution** than light microscopes so give **more detailed images**. There are two kinds of electron microscope:

1) **Transmission electron microscope (TEM)** — use **electromagnets** to focus a **beam of electrons**, which is then transmitted **through** the specimen. **Denser** parts of the specimen absorb **more electrons**, which makes them look **darker** on the image you end up with. TEMs are good because they provide **high resolution images** (so they can be used to look at a range of **organelles**) but they can only be used on **thin specimens**. A TEM image of a mitochondrion is shown above on the right.

2) **Scanning electron microscope (SEM)** — **scan** a beam of electrons across the specimen. This **knocks off** electrons from the specimen, which are gathered in a **cathode ray tube** to form an **image**. The images produced show the **surface** of the specimen and can be **3D**. But they give **lower resolution images** than TEMs. Here's an SEM image of a mitochondrion.

TEM image of a mitochondrion — crista, matrix
K.R. PORTER/SCIENCE PHOTO LIBRARY

SEM image of a mitochondrion — surface of mitochondrion, crista
PROFESSORS P. MOTTA & T. NAGURO/SCIENCE PHOTO LIBRARY

*The angle at which specimens are cut can affect how they appear (e.g. a mitochondrion cut at a different angle might appear circular).*

## You Need to be Able to **Compare Magnification** and **Resolution**

There are quite a lot of facts and figures about microscopes here. You need to know about the **magnification** and **resolution** of **light microscopes** and both types of **electron microscope**. So I've put all the important numbers in this table 'cos I'm nice like that.

| | light microscope | TEM | SEM |
|---|---|---|---|
| maximum resolution | 0.2 μm | 0.0002 μm | 0.002 μm |
| maximum magnification | × 1500 | can be more than × 1 000 000 | usually less than × 500 000 |

*TEMs have the highest resolution because they can distinguish between the smallest objects (or objects that are only 0.0002 μm apart).*

## Practice Questions

Q1 What is the formula for calculating the magnification of an image?

Q2 What is meant by a microscope's resolution?

Q3 Which has a higher resolution: a light microscope, TEM or SEM?

## Exam Questions

Q1 An insect is 0.5 mm long. In a book, a picture of the insect is 8 cm long. Calculate the magnification of the image. [2 marks]

Q2 A light micrograph shows a human cheek cell at × 100 magnification. The actual diameter of the cell is 59 μm. What is the diameter of the cell in the image? [2 marks]

Q3 The table shows the dimensions of some different organelles found in animal cells.

a) Name those organelles in the table that would be visible using a good quality light microscope. Explain your answer. [3 marks]

b) Which organelles would be visible using an SEM? Explain your answer. [2 marks]

| organelle | diameter / μm |
|---|---|
| lysosome | 0.1 |
| mitochondrion | 2 |
| nucleus | 5 |
| ribosome | 0.02 |
| vesicle | 0.05 |

## *A light microscope is better than a heavy one — for your back anyway...*

*OK, there's quite a bit of info on these pages, but the whole magnification thing isn't all that bad once you've given it a go. Make sure you can define resolution — that's a bit trickier. You also need to have a good grasp of the images produced by each of the different types of microscope — light, Laser Scanning Confocal, TEM and SEM. Phew.*

# Studying Cells — Using Microscopes

*The thing about Biology is — it's a practical subject. Not only do you need to know how microscopes work in theory, you also have to know how to actually use one. Time to roll up your sleeves and get stuck in...*

## You Need to *Stain* Your *Samples*

1) In light microscopes and TEMs, the beam of light (or electrons) **passes through the object** being viewed. An image is produced because some parts of the object **absorb more light** (or electrons) than others.

2) Sometimes the object being viewed is completely **transparent**. This makes the whole thing look **white** because the light rays (or electrons) just pass **straight through**.

3) To get round this, the object can be **stained**:

---

**Staining samples for light microscopes:**

- For the light microscope, this means using some kind of **dye**. Common stains include **methylene blue** and **eosin**.

- The stain is taken up by some parts of the object more than others — the **contrast** makes the different parts show up.

- **Different stains** are used to make **different things** show up. For example, **eosin** is used to stain **cell cytoplasms**. **Methylene blue** stains DNA.

- **More than one** stain can be used at once.

An eosin stained specimen, as seen through a light microscope.

---

**Staining samples for electron microscopes:**

For the electron microscope, objects are dipped in a solution of **heavy metals** (like **lead**). The metal ions scatter the electrons, again creating **contrast** — some parts of the object show up **darker** than others.

*Electron micrograph images are always black and white even when stained, but colour can be added artificially after the image has been made.*

---

## You Need to Know How to *Prepare* a *Microscope Slide*

1) If you want to look at a specimen under a **light microscope**, you need to stick it on a **slide** first.

2) A slide is a strip of **clear glass** or **plastic**. Slides are usually **flat**, but some of them have a small **dip** or **well** in the centre (useful if your specimen's particularly big or a liquid).

3) There are **two main ways** of preparing a microscope slide:

---

**Dry Mount**

- Your specimen needs to let **light** through it for you to be able to see it clearly under the microscope. So if you've got quite a **thick specimen**, you'll need to take a **thin slice** to use on your slide.

- Use **tweezers** to pick up your specimen and put it in the **middle** of a clean slide.

- Pop a **cover slip** (a square of thin, transparent plastic or glass) **on top**.

Cover slip
Specimen
Slide

---

**Wet Mount**

- Start by pipetting a small **drop of water** onto the slide. Then use **tweezers** to place your specimen on top of the water drop.

- To put the **cover slip** on, stand the slip **upright** on the slide, next to the water droplet. Then carefully **tilt** and lower it so it covers the specimen. Try **not** to get any **air bubbles** under there — they'll obstruct your view of the specimen.

- Once the cover slip is in position, you can add a **stain**. Put a drop of stain next to one edge of the cover slip. Then put a bit of **paper towel** next to the opposite edge. The stain will get **drawn** under the slip, **across** the **specimen**.

Cover slip
Water droplet

*Wet mounts are good for looking at tiny organisms that live in water.*

# Studying Cells — Using Microscopes

## Here's How to Use a **Light Microscope**...

You're expected to be able to use a light microscope to view a specimen.

1) Start by clipping the slide containing the specimen you want to look at onto the stage.

2) Select the lowest-powered objective lens (i.e. the one that produces the lowest magnification).

3) Use the coarse adjustment knob to move the objective lens down to just above the slide.

4) Look down the eyepiece (which contains the ocular lens) and adjust the focus with the fine adjustment knob, until you get a clear image of whatever's on the slide.

5) If you need to see the slide with greater magnification, swap to a higher-powered objective lens and refocus.

> If you're asked to draw what you can see under the microscope, make sure you write down the magnification the specimen was viewed under. You'll also need to label your drawing.

## ...and an **Eyepiece Graticule** and **Stage Micrometer**

1) Sometimes, you might want to know the **size** of your specimen. And that's where the **eyepiece graticule** and **stage micrometer** come in — they're a bit like **rulers**.

2) An **eyepiece graticule** is fitted onto the **eyepiece**. It's like a transparent ruler with **numbers**, but **no units**.

3) The **stage micrometer** is placed on the **stage** — it is a microscope slide with an **accurate scale** (it has units) and it's used to work out the **value** of the divisions on the **eyepiece graticule** at a **particular magnification**.

4) This means that when you take the stage micrometer away and replace it with the slide containing your specimen, you'll be able to **measure** the size of the specimen. Here's an **example**:

1) **Line up** the eyepiece graticule and the stage micrometer.

2) Each **division** on the stage micrometer is **0.1 mm** long.

3) At this magnification, **1 division** on the **stage micrometer** is the same as **4.5 divisions** on the **eyepiece graticule**.

4) To work out the size of **1 division** on the **eyepiece graticule**, you need to divide 0.1 by 4.5:

1 division on eyepiece graticule = 0.1 ÷ 4.5 = **0.022 mm**

5) So if you look at an object under the microscope at this magnification and it's **20 eyepiece divisions** long, you know it measures:

20 × 0.022 = **0.44 mm**

> Remember: at a different magnification, 1 division on the stage micrometer will be equal to a different number of divisions on the eyepiece graticule — so the eyepiece graticule will need to be re-calibrated.

## Practice Question

Q1 Why is it sometimes necessary to stain an object before viewing it through a microscope?

**Exam Question**

Q1 a) A microscope is set up with an eyepiece graticule and a stage micrometer. Each division on a stage micrometer is 10 μm long. At ×10 magnification, 1 division of the stage micrometer is equal to 6.5 divisions on the eyepiece graticule. Calculate the size of 1 division on the eyepiece graticule. Give your answer to the nearest 0.1 μm.

[2 marks]

b) A specimen is viewed under this microscope at ×10 magnification. It is 14 eyepiece divisions long. Use your answer to part a) to calculate the specimen's length. Give your answer to the nearest μm. [2 marks]

---

## *'Staining your samples' — a common problem at the start of exams...*

*Wow — I bet you never realised there was so much to know about using a microscope. Still, staining is straightforward and so's preparing a slide. Using a graticule, etc. is trickier, but once you get your head round it you'll be fine.*

# Water

*Your body needs all sorts of different molecules to stay alive, and this section covers all the major groups.*
*Life can't exist without water — in fact, everyday water is one of the most important substances on the planet.*

## Water is Vital to Living Organisms

Water makes up about 80% of a cell's contents. It has loads of important **functions**, inside and outside cells:

1) Water is a **reactant** in loads of important **chemical reactions**, including **hydrolysis reactions** (see page 22).

2) Water is a **solvent**, which means some substances **dissolve** in it. Most biological reactions take place **in solution** (e.g. in the **cytoplasm** of eukaryotic and prokaryotic cells) so water's pretty essential.

3) Water **transports** substances. The fact that it's a **liquid** and a **solvent** means it can easily transport all sorts of materials, like glucose and oxygen, around plants and animals.

4) Water helps with **temperature control** because it has a **high specific heat capacity** and a **high latent heat of evaporation** (see below).

5) Water is a **habitat**. The fact that it helps with **temperature control**, is a **solvent** and becomes **less dense** when it **freezes** (see next page) means many organisms can survive and reproduce in it.

## Water Molecules have a Simple Structure

Examiners like asking you to relate **structure** to **properties** and **function**, so make sure you know the structure of water.

1) A molecule of **water ($H_2O$)** is **one atom** of **oxygen (O)** joined to **two atoms** of **hydrogen ($H_2$)** by **shared electrons**.

2) Because the **shared negative** hydrogen electrons are **pulled towards** the oxygen atom, the other side of each hydrogen atom is left with a **slight positive charge**.

3) The **unshared** negative electrons on the oxygen atom give it a **slight negative charge**.

4) This makes water a **polar** molecule — it has a **partial negative ($\delta-$)** charge on one side and a **partial positive ($\delta+$)** charge on the other.

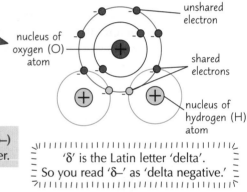

'$\delta$' is the Latin letter 'delta'.
So you read '$\delta-$' as 'delta negative.'

slightly negatively charged side

slightly positively charged side

hydrogen bonds

5) The slightly negatively-charged **oxygen atoms attract** the slightly positively-charged **hydrogen atoms** of other water molecules.

6) This attraction is called **hydrogen bonding** and it gives water some of its useful properties.

## Water's Structure is Related to its Properties and Functions

### Hydrogen Bonds Give Water a High Specific Heat Capacity

1) Specific heat capacity is the **energy** needed to **raise the temperature** of 1 gram of a substance by 1 °C.

2) The **hydrogen bonds** between water molecules can **absorb** a **lot** of energy. So water has a **high** specific heat capacity — it takes a lot of energy to heat it up.

3) This means water **doesn't** experience **rapid temperature changes**, which is one of the properties that makes it a **good habitat** — the temperature under water is likely to be more stable than it is on land.

### Hydrogen Bonds Also Give Water a High Latent Heat of Evaporation

1) It takes a lot of **energy (heat)** to **break** the hydrogen bonds between water molecules.

2) So water has a **high latent heat of evaporation** — a lot of energy is used up when water **evaporates**.

3) This is useful for living organisms because it means water's great for **cooling** things. This is why some **mammals**, like us, **sweat** when they're **too hot**. When sweat evaporates, it **cools** the **surface** of the **skin**.

# Water

## Water's *Polarity* Makes it *Very Cohesive*

1) Cohesion is the **attraction** between molecules of the same type (e.g. two water molecules). Water molecules are **very cohesive** (they tend to stick together) because they're **polar**.

2) This helps water to **flow**, making it great for **transporting substances**. It also helps water to be transported up **plant stems** in the **transpiration stream** (see page 89).

## Water's *Polarity* Also Makes it a *Good Solvent*

1) A lot of important substances in biological reactions are **ionic** (like **salt**, for example). This means they're made from **one positively-charged** atom or molecule and **one negatively-charged** atom or molecule (e.g. salt is made from a positive sodium ion and a negative chloride ion).

2) Because water is polar, the **slightly positive end** of a water molecule will be attracted to the **negative ion**, and the **slightly negative end** of a water molecule will be attracted to the **positive ion**.

3) This means the ions will get **totally surrounded** by water molecules — in other words, they'll **dissolve**.

Positive ion dissolved in water     Negative ion dissolved in water

water molecules

The polar nature of bears sometimes results in unexpected hydrogen bonding.

4) Water's **polarity** makes it useful as a **solvent** in living organisms. E.g. in **humans**, important **ions** (see p. 29) can dissolve in the water in **blood** and then be transported around the body.

## Water's *Less Dense When it's Solid*

1) At **low temperatures** water **freezes** — it turns from a liquid to a solid.

2) Water molecules are held **further apart** in **ice** than they are in liquid water because each water molecule forms **four hydrogen bonds** to other water molecules, making a **lattice** shape. This makes ice **less dense** than liquid water — which is why **ice floats**.

3) This is useful for living organisms because, in cold temperatures, ice forms an **insulating layer** on top of water — the water below **doesn't freeze**. So organisms that live in water, like **fish**, **don't freeze** and can still **move around**.

## Practice Questions

Q1 Briefly describe the structure of a water molecule.

Q2 Briefly describe what is meant by a polar molecule.

Q3 State five properties of water that make it useful for living organisms.

Q4 Why is water's high specific heat capacity useful for living organisms?

**Exam Question**

Q1 In hot temperatures, elephants commonly spray themselves with water. With reference to the structure of water, explain why this behaviour acts as a cooling mechanism for the elephant. [3 marks]

## Pssssssssssssssssssssssssssssssssssssssssssssss — *need the loo yet?*

*Water is pretty darn useful really. It looks so, well, dull — but in fact it's scientifically amazing. It's essential for all kinds of jobs — keeping cool, transporting things, enabling reactions, etc. You need to learn all of its properties and functions, and be able to say how they relate to its structure. Right, I'm off — when you gotta go, you gotta go.*

# Carbohydrates

*Carbohydrates are important biological molecules — for a start they're the main energy supply in living organisms.*

## Carbohydrates are Made from Monosaccharides

1) Most carbohydrates are **polymers**. A polymer is a molecule made up of **many similar, smaller molecules** (called **monomers**) bonded together.

*Although most carbohydrates are polymers, single monosaccharides are also called carbohydrates.*

2) The monomers that make up carbohydrates are called **monosaccharides**.

3) **Glucose** is a monosaccharide with **six carbon** atoms — this means it's a **hexose** monosaccharide.

4) There are **two forms** of glucose — **alpha** (α) and **beta** (β). They both have a **ring structure**:

The two types of glucose have these groups reversed.

5) Glucose's **structure** is related to its **function** as the main **energy source** in animals and plants. Its structure makes it **soluble** so it can be **easily transported**. Its chemical bonds contain **lots of energy**.

*Ribose is the sugar component of RNA nucleotides (see p. 34).*

6) **Ribose** is a monosaccharide with **five carbon** atoms — this means it's a **pentose** monosaccharide.

7) You need to know its **structure**:

8) All carbohydrates are made up of the same **three chemical elements** — **carbon (C)**, **hydrogen (H)** and **oxygen (O)**. For every **carbon atom** in the carbohydrate there are usually **two hydrogen atoms** and **one oxygen atom**.

## Monosaccharides Join Together to Form Disaccharides and Polysaccharides

1) Monosaccharides are **joined together** by **glycosidic bonds**.

2) During **synthesis**, a **hydrogen** atom on one monosaccharide bonds to a **hydroxyl (OH)** group on the other, **releasing** a molecule of **water**. This is called a **condensation** reaction.

3) The **reverse** of this synthesis reaction is **hydrolysis**. A molecule of water reacts with the glycosidic bond, **breaking it apart**.

*Sugar is a general term for monosaccharides and disaccharides.*

4) A **disaccharide** is formed when **two monosaccharides** join together:

For example, two α-**glucose** molecules are joined together by a **glycosidic bond** to form **maltose**:

α-glucose + α-glucose ⇌ (synthesis / hydrolysis) maltose + H₂O

H₂O is removed

glycosidic bond

Other disaccharides are formed in a similar way. **Sucrose** is a disaccharide formed when α–**glucose** and **fructose** join together. **Lactose** is a disaccharide formed by the joining together of β–**glucose** and **galactose**.

5) A **polysaccharide** is formed when **more than two monosaccharides** join together:

Lots of α-glucose molecules are joined together by **glycosidic bonds** to form **amylose**.

glycosidic bonds

α-glucose   α-glucose   α-glucose   α-glucose   α-glucose

# Carbohydrates

## You Need to Learn About **Three Polysaccharides**

You need to know about the relationship between the **structure** and **function** of three polysaccharides:

Amylose

### 1 Starch — the main **energy storage material** in **plants**

1) Cells get **energy** from **glucose**. Plants **store** excess glucose as **starch** (when a plant **needs more glucose** for energy it **breaks down** starch to release the glucose).

2) Starch is a mixture of **two** polysaccharides of **alpha-glucose** — **amylose** and **amylopectin**:

- **Amylose** — a long, **unbranched chain** of α–glucose. The angles of the glycosidic bonds give it a **coiled structure**, almost like a cylinder. This makes it **compact**, so it's really **good for storage** because you can **fit more in** to a small space.

one alpha-glucose molecule

- **Amylopectin** — a long, **branched chain** of α–glucose. Its **side branches** allow the **enzymes** that break down the molecule to get at the **glycosidic bonds easily**. This means that the glucose can be **released quickly**.

Amylopectin

3) Starch is **insoluble** in water, so it **doesn't** cause water to enter cells by **osmosis** (see p. 58) which would make them swell. This makes it good for **storage**.

Glycogen

### 2 Glycogen — the main **energy storage material** in **animals**

1) Animal cells get **energy** from **glucose** too. But animals **store** excess glucose as **glycogen** — another polysaccharide of **alpha-glucose**.

2) Its structure is very similar to amylopectin, except that it has **loads** more **side branches** coming off it. Loads of branches means that stored glucose can be **released quickly**, which is **important for energy release** in animals.

3) It's also a very **compact** molecule, so it's good for storage.

### 3 Cellulose — the major component of **cell walls** in **plants**

1) Cellulose is made of **long, unbranched** chains of **beta-glucose**.

2) When beta–glucose molecules **bond**, they form **straight** cellulose chains.

3) The cellulose chains are linked together by **hydrogen bonds** to form strong fibres called **microfibrils**. The strong fibres mean cellulose provides **structural support** for cells (e.g. in plant cell walls).

one cellulose molecule

weak hydrogen bonds    one beta-glucose molecule

## Practice Questions

Q1 What is the structural difference between an alpha-glucose molecule and a beta-glucose molecule?

Q2 Describe how glycosidic bonds are formed and broken in living organisms.

Q3 Briefly describe the structure of starch.

Q4 What is the function of cellulose?

### Exam Questions

Q1 Mannose is a hexose monosaccharide.
Which of the following is most likely to give the chemical formula of a mannose molecule?

A $C_5H_{10}O_5$         B $C_6H_{12}O_6$         C $C_6H_{12}N_6$         D $C_5H_5O_{10}$         [1 mark]

Q2 State the function of glycogen and explain how the structure of glycogen is linked to its function.         [3 marks]

---

## _Mmmm, starch... Tasty, tasty chips and beans... *dribble*. Ahem, sorry._

_Remember that condensation and hydrolysis reactions are the reverse of each other. You need to learn how maltose, sucrose and lactose are formed and broken down by these reactions. And don't forget that starch is composed of two different polysaccharides... and that glucose exists in two forms... so many reminders, so little space..._

# Lipids

*On to lipids, or 'fatty oily things' to you and me. Some of them are just straightforward fats, but others have extra bits stuck to them. You need to know about three types of lipid — triglycerides, phospholipids and cholesterol.*

## Triglycerides are a Kind of Lipid

1) Triglycerides are **macromolecules** — they're **complex molecules** with a relatively **large molecular mass**.

2) Like **all lipids**, they contain the chemical elements **carbon**, **hydrogen** and **oxygen**.

3) Triglycerides have **one** molecule of **glycerol** with **three fatty acids** attached to it.

Structure of a Triglyceride

Fatty acid molecules have long 'tails' made of **hydrocarbons** (compounds that contain only carbon and hydrogen atoms).

The tails are '**hydrophobic**' (they repel water molecules). These tails make lipids insoluble in water. All **fatty acids** have the same basic structure, but the **hydrocarbon tail varies**.

Basic Structure of a Fatty Acid

variable 'R' group hydrocarbon tail

## Triglycerides Contain Ester Bonds

1) Triglycerides are **synthesised** by the formation of an **ester bond** between each **fatty acid** and the **glycerol molecule**.

2) Each ester bond is formed by a **condensation reaction** (in which a water molecule is released).

3) The process in which triglycerides are synthesised is called **esterification**.

4) Triglycerides **break down** when the ester bonds are **broken**. Each ester bond is broken in a **hydrolysis reaction** (in which a water molecule is used up).

## Fatty Acids can be Saturated or Unsaturated

There are **two** kinds of fatty acids — **saturated** and **unsaturated**. The difference is in their **hydrocarbon tails**.

**Saturated** fatty acids **don't** have any **double bonds** between their **carbon atoms**. The fatty acid is 'saturated' with hydrogen.

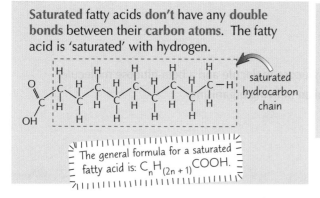

saturated hydrocarbon chain

The general formula for a saturated fatty acid is: $C_nH_{(2n+1)}COOH$.

**Unsaturated** fatty acids have **at least one** double bond between **carbon atoms**, which cause the chain to kink.

unsaturated hydrocarbon chain

## Phospholipids are Similar to Triglycerides

1) **Phospholipids** are also **macromolecules**. They're pretty similar to triglycerides except one of the fatty acid molecules is replaced by a **phosphate group**.

2) The phosphate group is **hydrophilic** (it attracts water molecules) and the fatty acid tails are **hydrophobic**.

Structure of a Phospholipid

phosphate group

Glycerol

Fatty Acid

Fatty Acid

# Lipids

## The **Structures** of Lipids Relate to Their **Functions**

You need to know how the **properties** of **triglycerides**, **phospholipids** and **cholesterol** are related to their **functions**:

**TRIGLYCERIDES**

In **animals** and **plants**, triglycerides are mainly used as **energy storage molecules**.
Some **bacteria** (e.g. *Mycobacterium tuberculosis*) use triglycerides to store both **energy** and **carbon**.
Triglycerides are good for storage because:

1)  The **long hydrocarbon tails** of the fatty acids contain lots of **chemical energy** — a load of energy is **released** when they're **broken down**. Because of these tails, lipids contain about **twice** as much energy per gram as carbohydrates.

2)  They're **insoluble**, so they don't cause water to enter the cells by **osmosis** (see p. 58) which would make them swell. The triglycerides bundle together as **insoluble droplets** in cells because the fatty acid tails are **hydrophobic** (water-repelling) — the tails **face inwards**, shielding themselves from water with their glycerol heads.

**PHOSPHOLIPIDS**

Phospholipids are found in the **cell membranes** of all eukaryotes and prokaryotes.
They make up what's known as the **phospholipid bilayer** (see p. 50).
Cell membranes **control** what **enters and leaves a cell**.

1)  Phospholipid heads are **hydrophilic** and their tails are **hydrophobic**, so they form a **double** layer with their heads facing **out** towards the water on either side.

2)  The **centre** of the bilayer is **hydrophobic**, so water-soluble substances **can't** easily pass through it — the membrane acts as a **barrier** to those substances.

**CHOLESTEROL**

Cholesterol is another type of lipid — it has a **hydrocarbon ring** structure attached to a **hydrocarbon tail**. The ring structure has a **polar hydroxyl (OH) group** attached to it. In **eukaryotic cells**, cholesterol molecules help **strengthen** the cell membrane by **interacting** with the **phospholipid bilayer**.

> 'Polar' means it has a slightly negatively charged bit and a slightly positively charged bit — see p. 20.

1)  Cholesterol has a **small size** and **flattened shape** — this allows cholesterol to fit **in between** the phospholipid molecules in the membrane.

2)  They bind to the hydrophobic tails of the phospholipids, causing them to **pack more closely together**. This helps to make the membrane **less fluid** and **more rigid**.

cholesterol

## Practice Questions

Q1  What are triglycerides composed of?

Q2  What is the difference between a saturated fatty acid and an unsaturated fatty acid?

Q3  Sketch the structure of a phospholipid.

**Exam Questions**

Q1  Explain how phospholipid molecules arrange themselves in cell membranes and relate this to their structure. [3 marks]

Q2  Explain how each of these features of lipids is important for their function in living things:

a)  Cholesterol molecules have a flattened shape. [2 marks]

b)  Triglycerides have a hydrophobic tail. [2 marks]

---

## *Hydrocarbon tails, phospho-thingies... Whatever happened to just lard?*

*You don't get far in life without extensive lard knowledge, so learn all the details on this page good and proper. Lipids pop up in other sections, so make sure you know the basics about how their structure gives them some quite groovy properties. Right, all this lipids talk is making me hungry — chips time...*

# Proteins

*There are millions of different proteins. They're the most abundant molecules in cells, making up 50% or more of a cell's dry mass — now that's just plain greedy. Like carbohydrates and lipids, proteins are essential for life.*

## Proteins are Made from Long Chains of Amino Acids

1) Just like carbohydrates (see page 22), proteins are **polymers**.

2) Amino acids are the **monomers** in proteins.

3) A **dipeptide** is formed when **two** amino acids join together.

4) A **polypeptide** is formed when **more than two** amino acids join together.

5) **Proteins** are made up of **one or more polypeptides**.

*Grant's cries of "die peptide, die" could be heard for miles around. He'd never forgiven it for sleeping with his wife.*

## Different Amino Acids Have Different Variable Groups

1) All amino acids have the same general structure — a **carboxyl group** (-COOH) and an **amino group** (-NH$_2$) attached to a **carbon** atom. The **difference** between different amino acids is the **variable** group (**R** on diagram) they contain.

Structure of an Amino Acid

R ◄— variable group

$H_2N — C — COOH$

amino group ▲ H ◄ carboxyl group

E.g. Structure of Glycine

H

$H_2N — C — COOH$

H

Glycine is the smallest amino acid — the R group is a hydrogen atom.

2) All amino acids contain the chemical elements **carbon**, **oxygen**, **hydrogen** and **nitrogen**. Some also contain **sulfur**.

## Amino Acids are Joined Together by Peptide Bonds

1) Amino acids are linked together by **peptide bonds** to form dipeptides and polypeptides.

2) A molecule of **water** is **released** during the reaction — it's a **condensation** reaction.

3) The **reverse** of this reaction **adds** a molecule of water to **break** the peptide bond — it's a **hydrolysis** reaction.

amino acid 1     amino acid 2                                          dipeptide

H     R          H     R                              H   R   O   H   R
 \    |           \    |         condensation          \  |   ||  |   |
  N — C — COOH  +  N — C — COOH   ⇌                      N—C—C—N—C — COOH
 /    |          /    |          hydrolysis            /  |       |   |
H     H         H     H                               H   H       H   H

$H_2O$ — a molecule of water is formed during synthesis.

peptide bond

# Proteins

## Proteins Have Four Structural Levels

Proteins are **big, complicated** molecules. They're much easier to explain if you describe their structure in four 'levels'. These levels are a protein's **primary**, **secondary**, **tertiary** and **quaternary** structures.

<u>Primary Structure</u> — this is the **sequence** of **amino acids** in the **polypeptide chain**. Different proteins have **different sequences** of amino acids in their primary structure. A change in just one amino acid may change the structure of the whole protein.

amino acid

<u>Secondary Structure</u> — the polypeptide chain doesn't remain flat and straight. **Hydrogen bonds** form between nearby amino acids in the chain. This makes it automatically **coil** into an **alpha (α) helix** or **fold** into a **beta (β) pleated sheet** — this is the secondary structure.

α-helix          β-pleated sheet

<u>Tertiary Structure</u> — the coiled or folded chain of amino acids is often **coiled** and **folded further**. **More bonds** form between different parts of the polypeptide chain. For proteins made from a **single** polypeptide chain, the tertiary structure forms their **final 3D structure**.

<u>Quaternary Structure</u> — some proteins are made of **several different polypeptide chains** held together by **bonds**. The **quaternary structure** is the way these polypeptide chains are assembled together. E.g. **haemoglobin** is made of **four** polypeptide chains, bonded together. For proteins made from **more than one** polypeptide chain, the quaternary structure is the protein's **final 3D structure**.

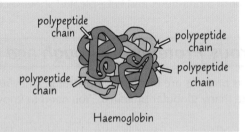

polypeptide chain

polypeptide chain

polypeptide chain

polypeptide chain

Haemoglobin

**Computer modelling** can create **3D interactive images** of proteins. This is really handy for **investigating** the **different levels of structure** in a protein molecule.

## Different Bonds Hold Different Structural Levels Together

The four structural levels of a protein are held together by **different kinds** of **bonds**:

1) **Primary structure** — held together by the **peptide bonds** between amino acids.

2) **Secondary structure** — held together by **hydrogen bonds** (see above).

3) **Tertiary structure** — this is affected by a few different kinds of bonds:

   - **Ionic interactions.** These are **weak attractions** between **negatively-charged** R groups and **positively-charged** R groups on different parts of the molecule.

   - **Disulfide bonds.** Whenever two molecules of the amino acid **cysteine** come close together, the **sulfur atom** in one cysteine bonds to the sulfur in the other cysteine, forming a disulfide bond.

   - **Hydrophobic** and **hydrophilic interactions.** When **hydrophobic** (water-repelling) R groups are close together in the protein, they tend to **clump together**. This means that **hydrophilic** (water-attracting) R groups are more likely to be pushed to the **outside**, which affects how the protein **folds up** into its final structure.

   > Heating a protein to a high temperature will break up its ionic and hydrophobic/hydrophilic interactions and hydrogen bonds. In turn this will cause a change in the protein's 3D shape.

   - **Hydrogen bonds** — these weak bonds form between slightly **positively-charged hydrogen atoms** in some R groups and **slightly negatively-charged** atoms in other R groups on the polypeptide chain.

4) **Quaternary structure** — this tends to be determined by the **tertiary structure** of the individual polypeptide chains being bonded together. Because of this, it can be influenced by **all the bonds** mentioned above.

# Proteins

## Globular Proteins Are Round and Compact

1) In a globular protein, the **hydrophilic R groups** on the amino acids tend to be pushed to the **outside** of the molecule. This is caused by the **hydrophobic** and **hydrophilic interactions** in the protein's **tertiary structure** (see previous page).

2) This makes globular proteins **soluble**, so they're **easily transported** in fluids.

3) Globular proteins have a **range of functions** in living organisms. For example:

*Dean did a great impression of a globular protein.*

**HAEMOGLOBIN** is a globular protein that carries **oxygen** around the body in **red blood cells** (see page 84). It's known as a **conjugated protein** — this means it's a protein with a **non-protein group** attached. The non-protein part is called a **prosthetic group**. Each of the four polypeptide chains in haemoglobin has a prosthetic group called **haem**. A haem group contains **iron**, which oxygen binds to.

haem group

**INSULIN** is a **hormone** secreted by the **pancreas**. It helps to regulate the **blood glucose level**. Its **solubility** is important — it means it can be **transported** in the **blood** to the tissues where it acts. An insulin molecule consists of **two polypeptide chains**, which are held together by **disulfide bonds**.

**AMYLASE** is an **enzyme** (see page 42) that catalyses the breakdown of **starch** in the digestive system. It is made of a **single chain** of amino acids. Its secondary structure contains **both** alpha-helix and beta-pleated sheet sections. **Most enzymes** are **globular proteins**.

## Fibrous Proteins Are Tough and Rope-Shaped

Fibrous proteins are **insoluble** and **strong**. They're **structural** proteins and are fairly **unreactive** (unlike many globular proteins). You need to know about these **three** fibrous proteins:

- **Collagen** — found in animal **connective tissues**, such as bone, skin and muscle. It is a very **strong** molecule. **Minerals** can bind to the protein to increase its **rigidity**, e.g. in bone.

  *The Structure of a Collagen Molecule*

- **Keratin** — found in many of the **external structures** of animals, such as skin, hair, nails, feathers and horns. It can either be **flexible** (as it is in skin) or **hard and tough** (as it is in nails).
- **Elastin** — found in **elastic connective tissue**, such as skin, large blood vessels and some ligaments. It is **elastic**, so it allows tissues to return to their original shape after they have been stretched.

## Practice Questions

Q1 Describe the general structure of an amino acid.

Q2 Name the bond that joins amino acids together in proteins.

Q3 What is a conjugated protein?

**Exam Questions**

Q1 Suggest which of the following proteins is most abundant in a tortoise's shell.

    A Collagen      B Elastin      C Alpha-amylase      D Keratin      [1 mark]

Q2* HSA is a globular protein, which transports other molecules such as fatty acids around the bloodstream. The molecule consists of 585 amino acids, several of which are cysteine.

Describe the bonds that could be present in the tertiary structure of HSA and suggest how its structure makes it suited for its role of transporting molecules in the blood.      [6 marks]

\* You will be assessed on the quality of your written response in this question.

## The name's Bond — Peptide Bond...

*Quite a lot to learn on these pages — proteins are annoyingly complicated. Not happy with one, or even two structural levels, they can have four of the things — and you need to learn 'em all. Remember that condensation and hydrolysis reactions are the reverse of each other. And as for all that nasty stuff about disulfide bonds and ionic interactions... Urgh.*

# Inorganic Ions

*Inorganic ions are just teeny tiny little things, but they're essential for many biological processes.*

## Inorganic Ions Have an Electric Charge

1) An **ion** is an atom (or group of atoms) that has an **electric charge**.
2) An ion with a **positive charge** is called a **cation**.
3) An ion with a **negative charge** is called an **anion**.
4) An **inorganic** ion is one which **doesn't contain carbon** (although there are a few exceptions to this rule).
5) Inorganic ions are really important in **biological processes**. Here are the ones you need to know about:

| | Name of ion | Chemical Symbol | Example(s) of roles in biological processes |
|---|---|---|---|
| **Cations** | Calcium | $Ca^{2+}$ | Involved in the transmission of **nerve impulses** and the release of **insulin** from the pancreas. Acts as a **cofactor** for many **enzymes** (see p. 47), e.g. those involved in blood clotting. Is important for **bone formation**. |
| | Sodium | $Na^+$ | Important for generating **nerve impulses**, for **muscle contraction** and for **regulating fluid balance** in the body. |
| | Potassium | $K^+$ | Important for generating **nerve impulses**, for **muscle contraction** and for **regulating fluid balance** in the body. Activates essential **enzymes** needed for **photosynthesis** in plant cells. |
| | Hydrogen | $H^+$ | Affects the **pH** of substances (**more $H^+$ ions** than $OH^-$ ions in a solution creates an **acid**). Also important for **photosynthesis reactions** that occur in the thylakoid membranes inside chloroplasts (see p. 12). |
| | Ammonium | $NH_4^+$ | Absorbed from the **soil** by **plants** and is an important source of **nitrogen** (which is then used to make, e.g. amino acids, nucleic acids). |
| **Anions** | Nitrate | $NO_3^-$ | Absorbed from the **soil** by **plants** and is an important source of **nitrogen** (which is then used to make, e.g. amino acids, nucleic acids). |
| | Hydrogencarbonate | $HCO_3^-$ | Acts as a **buffer**, which helps to maintain the **pH** of the blood. |
| | Chloride | $Cl^-$ | Involved in the 'chloride shift' which helps to maintain the **pH** of the blood during **gas exchange** (see p. 85). Acts as a **cofactor** for the enzyme **amylase** (see p. 47). Also involved in some **nerve impulses**. |
| | Phosphate | $PO_4^{3-}$ | Involved in **photosynthesis** and **respiration** reactions. Needed for the synthesis of many biological molecules, such as **nucleotides** (including **ATP**), **phospholipids**, and **calcium phosphate** (which strengthens bones). |
| | Hydroxide | $OH^-$ | Affects the **pH** of substances (**more $OH^-$ ions** than $H^+$ ions in a solution creates an **alkali**). |

## Practice Questions

Q1 What is the difference between a cation and an anion?

Q2 Write the chemical symbols for the following ions: calcium, ammonium, nitrate, phosphate, hydroxide.

**Exam Question**

Q1 Carbonic acid ($H_2CO_3$) is a weak acid present in the blood.
A reaction with water causes a hydrogen ion to dissociate from the carbonic acid molecule.
Name the anion that's formed in this reaction and write its chemical symbol. [2 marks]

## Stop all that texting and get revising — I've got my ion you...

*Well, who doesn't love a big table to brighten up Biology? Make sure you know the difference between a cation and an anion for starters. Then get learning all the names and chemical symbols from the table — you'll definitely meet some of these inorganic ions again in your Biology studies, so it's a good idea to make friends with them now.*

# Biochemical Tests for Molecules

*Here's a bit of light relief for you — two pages on how you test for the different molecules you've just read about...*

## Use the **Benedict's Test** for **Sugars**

**Sugar** is a general term for **monosaccharides** and **disaccharides**. All sugars can be classified as **reducing** or **non-reducing**. The **Benedict's test** tests for sugars — it **differs** depending on the **type** of sugar you are testing for.

**REDUCING SUGARS**

1) Reducing sugars include **all monosaccharides** (e.g. glucose) and **some disaccharides** (e.g. maltose and lactose).

2) You add **Benedict's reagent** (which is **blue**) to a sample and **heat it** in a water bath that's been brought to the **boil**.

Always use an excess of Benedict's solution — this makes sure that all the sugar reacts.

The colour of the precipitate changes from:  blue ⟹ green ⟹ yellow ⟹ orange ⟹ brick red

3) If the test's **positive** it will form a **coloured precipitate** (solid particles suspended in the solution).

4) The higher the concentration of reducing sugar, the further the colour change goes — you can use this to **compare** the amount of reducing sugar in different solutions. A more accurate way of doing this is to **filter** the solution and **weigh the precipitate**.

**NON-REDUCING SUGARS**

1) If the result of the reducing sugars test is **negative**, there could still be a non-reducing sugar present. To test for **non-reducing sugars**, like sucrose, first you have to break them down into monosaccharides.

2) You do this by getting a new sample of the test solution, adding **dilute hydrochloric acid** and carefully heating it in a water bath that's been brought to the **boil**. You then **neutralise** it with **sodium hydrogencarbonate**. Then just carry out the **Benedict's test** as you would for a reducing sugar.

3) If the test's **positive** it will form a **coloured precipitate** (as for the reducing sugars test). If the test's **negative** the solution will **stay blue**, which means it **doesn't contain any sugar** (either reducing or non-reducing).

## Use **Test Strips** for **Glucose**

Glucose can also be tested for using **test strips** coated in a **reagent**. The strips are dipped in a test solution and **change colour** if glucose is **present**. The colour change can be compared to a **chart** to give an indication of the concentration of glucose present. The strips are useful for testing a person's **urine** for glucose, which may indicate they have **diabetes**.

## Use the **Iodine Test** for **Starch**

Just add **iodine dissolved in potassium iodide solution** to the test sample.

Make sure you always talk about iodine in potassium iodide solution, not just iodine.

- If starch **is present**, the sample changes from **browny-orange** to a dark, **blue-black** colour.
- If there's **no starch**, it stays browny-orange.

## Use the **Biuret Test** for **Proteins**

There are **two stages** to this test.

1) The test solution needs to be **alkaline**, so first you add a few drops of **sodium hydroxide solution**.

2) Then you add some **copper(II) sulfate solution**.
- If protein **is** present the solution turns **purple**.
- If there's **no protein**, the solution will stay blue.

Negative result          Positive result

test solution, sodium hydroxide and copper(II) sulfate solution

The colours are pale, so you need to look carefully.

solution staying blue indicates no protein

purple colour indicates protein

## Use the **Emulsion Test** for **Lipids**

**Shake** the test substance with **ethanol** for about a minute, then **pour** the solution into **water**.

- If lipid **is present**, the solution will turn **milky**.
- The **more lipid** there is, the **more noticeable** the milky colour will be.
- If there's **no lipid**, the solution will **stay clear**.

Test substance and ethanol    Shake    Add to water    Milky colour indicates lipid

# Biochemical Tests for Molecules

## Colorimetry is Used to Determine the Concentration of a Glucose Solution

1) You can use **Benedict's reagent** and a **colorimeter** to get a **quantitative estimate** of **how much** glucose (or other reducing sugar) there is in a solution.

2) A colorimeter is a device that measures the **strength** of a **coloured solution** by seeing how much **light** passes through it.

3) A colorimeter measures **absorbance** (the amount of light absorbed by the solution). The **more concentrated** the **colour** of the solution, the **higher** the **absorbance** is.

4) It's easiest to measure the concentration of the **blue Benedict's solution** that's **left** after the test (the **paler** the solution, the **more glucose** there was). So, the **higher** the glucose concentration, the **lower** the absorbance of the solution.

### This is How You Do it:

Initially you need to make up several glucose solutions of **different, known concentrations**. You can do this using a **serial dilution** technique:

This is how you'd make **five serial dilutions** with a **dilution factor of 2**, starting with an initial glucose concentration of **40 mM**...

1) Line up five **test tubes** in a rack.

2) Add **10 cm³** of the initial **40 mM glucose solution** to the first test tube and **5 cm³ of distilled water** to the other four test tubes.

3) Then, using a pipette, draw **5 cm³** of the solution from the **first** test tube, add it to the distilled water in the **second** test tube and **mix** the solution **thoroughly**. You now have **10 cm³** of solution that's **half as concentrated** as the solution in the first test tube (it's **20 mM**).

4) Repeat this process **three more times** to create solutions of **10 mM, 5 mM** and **2.5 mM**.

*You don't have to dilute solutions by a factor of 2. E.g. to dilute by a factor of 10, take 1 cm³ from your original sample and add it to 9 cm³ of water.*

Once you've got your glucose solutions, you need to make a **calibration curve**. Here's how:

1) Do a **Benedict's test** on each solution (plus a **negative control** of **pure water**). Use the **same amount** of Benedict's solution in each case.

2) **Remove** any **precipitate** — either leave for **24 hours** (so that the precipitate **settles out**) or **centrifuge** them.

3) Use a **colorimeter** (with a **red filter**) to measure the **absorbance** of the Benedict's solution **remaining** in each tube.

4) Use the results to make the **calibration curve**, showing absorbance against glucose concentration.

Then you can test the **unknown solution** in the same way as the known concentrations and use the calibration curve to find its concentration.

An unknown solution with an absorbance value of 0.5 has a glucose concentration of 8 mM.

### Practice Questions

Q1 Describe how you would test a solution for starch.

Q2 Describe how you would test for lipids in a solution.

**Exam Question**

Q1 Equal volumes of three different sugar solutions (A, B and C) were each tested with the same large volume of Benedict's solution. Later, the concentrations of Benedict's solution in each test tube were compared, using a colorimeter. The table shows the absorbance of each solution.

| solution | absorbance |
|---|---|
| A | 1.22 |
| B | 0.68 |
| C | 0.37 |

a) Which original solution contained the highest concentration of reducing sugar? [1 mark]

b) Suggest two factors that should be kept constant when carrying out this test. [2 marks]

## The Anger Test — annoy test subject. If it goes red, anger is present...

*Make sure you know the ins and outs of all the biochemical tests on the previous page — don't get mixed up between the different colour changes. Then get your head round this colorimetry thingy-me-bob too — that's a bit more exciting.*

# Biochemical Tests and Separating Molecules

*If you haven't had enough of finding out what biochemical molecules solutions contain, you're in luck. Biosensors and chromatography now — you've probably tried chromatography before with a spot of ink on a piece of filter paper.*

## Biosensors Can Detect Chemicals in a Solution

1) A **biosensor** is a device that uses a **biological molecule**, such as an **enzyme** (see page 42) to detect a **chemical**.

2) The biological molecule produces a **signal** (e.g. a **chemical** signal), which is converted to an **electrical signal** by a **transducer** (another part of the **biosensor**).

3) The electrical signal is then **processed** and can be used to work out other information.

### Example: Glucose Biosensors

1) A **glucose biosensor** is used to determine the **concentration** of **glucose** in a solution.

2) It does this using the enzyme **glucose oxidase** and **electrodes**.

3) The enzyme catalyses the **oxidation** of **glucose** at the electrodes — this creates a **charge**, which is converted into an **electrical signal** by the electrodes (the transducer).

4) The electrical signal is then **processed** to work out the **initial glucose concentration**.

## Chromatography is Good for Separating and Identifying Things

1) Chromatography is used to **separate** stuff in a mixture — once it's separated out, you can often **identify** the components.

2) For example, chromatography can be used to separate out and identify biological molecules such as **amino acids**, **carbohydrates**, **vitamins** and **nucleic acids**.

3) There are quite a few different types of chromatography — you only need to know about **paper chromatography** and **thin-layer chromatography**.

### You Need to Understand How Chromatography Works

1) All types of chromatography (including paper and thin-layer) have the same **basic set up**:

Example: paper chromatography

stationary phase (chromatography paper)

mobile phase (solvent)

spots where different molecules have separated out

> 1) A **MOBILE PHASE** — where the molecules **can move**.
>    - In both paper and thin-layer chromatography the mobile phase is a **liquid solvent**, such as ethanol or water.
> 2) A **STATIONARY PHASE** — where the molecules **can't move**.
>    - In paper chromatography the stationary phase is a piece of **chromatography paper**.
>    - In thin-layer chromatography the stationary phase is a **thin** (0.1-0.3 mm) **layer of solid**, e.g. silica gel, on a **glass or plastic plate**.

2) And they all use the same basic principle:

- The mobile phase **moves through** or **over** the stationary phase.

- The components in the mixture spend **different amounts of time** in the mobile phase and the stationary phase.

- The components that spend longer in the **mobile phase** travel **faster** or **further**.

- The time spent in the different phases is what **separates out** the components of the mixture.

*The pattern of spots you end up with is called a chromatogram.*

# Biochemical Tests and Separating Molecules

## Paper Chromatography is used to Identify Unknown Amino Acids

In the exam you might be asked how chromatography can be used to identify the **biological molecules in a mixture**. Below is an example of how **paper chromatography** can be used to identify **amino acids** in a **mixture**. If you're trying to identify **different biological molecules**, the **method** will **vary slightly** (e.g. a different solvent might be used) but the basic principle will be the same.

Here's what you'd do:

1) Draw a **pencil line** near the bottom of a piece of **chromatography paper** and put a **concentrated spot** of the mixture of amino acids on it. It's best to carefully roll the paper into a **cylinder** with the spot on the outside so it'll stand up.

2) Add a small amount of prepared **solvent** (a mixture of **butan-1-ol**, **glacial ethanoic acid** and **water** is usually used for amino acids) to a beaker and dip the **bottom** of the **paper** into it (not the spot). This should be done in a **fume cupboard**. Cover with a **lid** to stop the solvent evaporating.

3) As the solvent spreads up the paper, the different amino acids move with it, but at **different rates**, so they separate out.

4) When the solvent's **nearly** reached the top, take the paper out and **mark** the **solvent front** with pencil. Then you can leave the paper to **dry out** before you analyse it (see below).

5) Amino acids **aren't coloured**, which means you **won't be able to see them** on the paper. So before you can analyse them, you have to spray the paper with **ninhydrin solution** to turn the amino acids **purple**. This should also be done in a **fume cupboard** and **gloves** should be worn. (Note: you can't use ninhydrin to detect all biological molecules, only proteins and amino acids.)

6) You can then use **$R_f$ values** to **identify** the separated molecules:

An **$R_f$ value** is the ratio of the distance travelled by a spot to the distance travelled by the solvent. You can calculate it using this formula:

$$R_f \text{ value of amino acid} = \frac{B}{A} = \frac{\text{distance travelled by spot}}{\text{distance travelled by solvent}}$$

When you're measuring how far a spot has travelled, you measure from the **point of origin** to the **vertical centre** of the spot.

You can work out what was in a mixture by calculating an $R_f$ value for each spot and looking each $R_f$ value up in a **database**, or **table**, of **known values**.

> You could also compare your chromatogram to the chromatogram of a known mixture and identify the components that way — if two spots have travelled the same distance in the solvent, they will be the same molecule.

## Practice Questions

Q1 What is a biosensor?

Q2 What is chromatography used for?

Q3 Why would you use ninhydrin solution when using chromatography to identify amino acids in a mixture?

| Sugar | $R_f$ value |
|---|---|
| Glucose | 0.20 |
| Fructose | 0.24 |
| Xylose | 0.30 |

**Exam Question**

Q1 The paper chromatogram above shows the separation of three sugars from a solution.

a) Briefly describe the method used to produce this chromatogram. [3 marks]

b) Explain why the spots have ended up in different positions on the chromatogram. [1 mark]

c) Calculate the $R_f$ value of spot X and use your answer to identify the sugar it contains. [3 marks]

## *I'm afraid you can't read anymore of this page — it's been bio-censored...*

*Well, these two pages aren't that bad really. There's all that clever, technical biosensor gubbins at the beginning and then the rest is fun stuff about spots appearing in chromatography. And even better, it's the end of another section.*

# Nucleotides

*You might not of heard of them, but nucleotides are pretty vital for life. These two pages will tell you more.*

## Nucleotides are Used to Make Nucleic Acids

1) A **nucleotide** is a type of biological molecule. It's made from:

> • a **pentose sugar** (that's a sugar with **5** carbon atoms),
> • a **nitrogenous** (nitrogen-containing) **base**,
> • a **phosphate** group.

Nucleotide

phosphate

pentose sugar — base

All nucleotides contain the elements **C, H, O, N** and **P**.

2) Nucleotides are really **important**. For a start, they're the **monomers** (see p. 22) that make up **DNA** and **RNA**. DNA and RNA are both types of **nucleic acid**. **DNA** is used to **store genetic information** — the instructions an organism needs to grow and develop. **RNA** is used to make **proteins** from the instructions in DNA.

3) **ADP** and **ATP** are **special types** of nucleotide (see next page). They're used to **store** and **transport energy** in **cells**.

## The Sugar in DNA is Called Deoxyribose

1) The **pentose sugar** in a **DNA nucleotide** is called **deoxyribose**. (DNA stands for **d**eoxyribo**n**ucleic **a**cid.)

2) Each DNA nucleotide has the **same sugar** and a **phosphate group**. The **base** on each nucleotide can **vary** though.

3) There are **four** possible bases — adenine (**A**), thymine (**T**), cytosine (**C**) and guanine (**G**).

4) **A**denine and **g**uanine are a type of base called a **purine**. **C**ytosine and **t**hymine are a type of base called a **pyrimidine**.

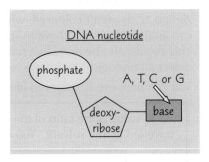

DNA nucleotide

phosphate

A, T, C or G

deoxy-ribose — base

> • A **purine** base contains **two carbon-nitrogen rings** joined together.
> • A **pyrimidine** base only has **one carbon-nitrogen ring**. So a pyrimidine base is **smaller** than a purine base.

Purine

Pyrimidine

5) A **molecule** of DNA contains two **polynucleotide** chains — each chain is made up of lots of **nucleotides** joined together. There's more on how polynucleotides form on page 36.

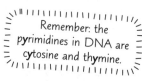

*Remember: the pyrimidines in DNA are cytosine and thymine.*

## The Sugar in RNA is Called Ribose

1) **RNA** (ribonucleic acid) contains nucleotides with a **ribose sugar** (not deoxyribose).

2) Like DNA, an RNA nucleotide also has a **phosphate group** and one of **four** different **bases**.

3) In RNA though, **uracil** (a **pyrimidine**) replaces **thymine** as a base.

RNA nucleotide

phosphate

A, U, C or G

ribose — base

*Mary didn't care if it was ribose or deoxyribose, she just wanted her cuppa.*

4) An RNA molecule is made up of a **single polynucleotide chain**.

# Nucleotides

## ADP and ATP are Phosphorylated Nucleotides

1) To **phosphorylate** a nucleotide, you **add** one or more **phosphate** groups to it.
2) **ADP** (adenosine **di**phosphate) contains the base **adenine**, the sugar **ribose** and **two phosphate groups**.
3) **ATP** (adenosine **tri**phosphate) contains the base adenine, the sugar ribose and **three** phosphate groups.

- **ATP** provides **energy** for **chemical reactions** in the cell.
- ATP is **synthesised** from **ADP** and **inorganic phosphate** ($P_i$) using the **energy** from an energy-releasing reaction, e.g. the breakdown of glucose in respiration. The **ADP** is **phosphorylated** to form **ATP** and a **phosphate bond** is formed.
- Energy is **stored** in the phosphate bond. When this energy is needed by a cell, ATP is **broken back down** into ADP and inorganic phosphate ($P_i$). **Energy** is **released** from the phosphate bond and used by the cell.

## Practice Questions

Q1 What are the three main components of nucleotides?

Q2 What sugar is found in DNA nucleotides?

Q3 Which sugar do RNA nucleotides contain?

Q4 What is the name of the base in ATP?

**Exam Questions**

Q1 The structures of two nitrogen-containing bases are shown on the right.
a) Which base, **A** or **B**, is adenine and which is cytosine? Explain your answer. [3 marks]
b) Apart from nitrogen, name a chemical element present in base **A**. [1 mark]

Q2 ADP is made up of the molecule AMP and an inorganic phosphate.
a) Suggest the chemical composition of AMP. [3 marks]
b) Name the process by which one or more phosphate groups are added to a molecule. [1 mark]

Q3 After a heart attack ATP levels in the heart are low. Studies have been carried out to find whether ribose supplements could help the heart to replenish ATP supplies after a heart attack.
Suggest why scientists think ribose supplements have the potential to be used in this way. [2 marks]

## I prefer my tides on a beach...

*There are a lot of long, dull scientific words in this topic, but all-in-all it's not too bad. It's really just a case of making sure you learn all the facts (including all the long, dull scientific words) so you can reproduce them in the exam. So go on then. Get a highlighter out. Make some notes. Or better yet, flashcards. Just make sure you learn it all.*

# Polynucleotides and DNA

*Right, by now you should know what a nucleotide is (see the previous two pages if not).*
*Well now you need to learn how they come together to form polynucleotides — like DNA.*

## Nucleotides Join Together to Form Polynucleotides

Part of a single
polynucleotide strand

1) The nucleotides join up between the **phosphate** group of one nucleotide and the **sugar** of another.

2) The bond between the phosphate group and the sugar is called a **phosphodiester bond**. The chain of sugars and phosphates is known as the **sugar-phosphate backbone**.

3) **Polynucleotides** can be **broken down** into nucleotides again by breaking the phosphodiester bonds.

Phosphodiester bond

Sugar-phosphate
backbone

## Two Polynucleotide Strands Join Together to Form a Double-Helix

1) **Two DNA** polynucleotide strands join together by **hydrogen bonding** between the bases.

2) Each base can only join with one particular partner — this is called **complementary base pairing**.

3) **Adenine** always pairs with **thymine** (**A - T**) and **cytosine** always pairs with **guanine** (**C - G**). A **purine** (A or G) always pairs with a **pyrimidine** (T or C).

4) **Two** hydrogen bonds form between **A and T**, and **three** hydrogen bonds form between **C and G**.

5) Two **antiparallel** (running in opposite directions) polynucleotide strands **twist** to form the **DNA double-helix**.

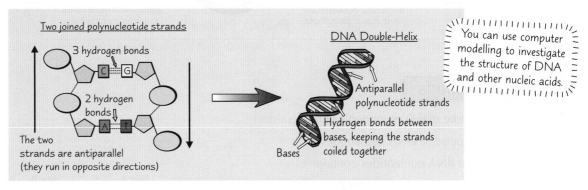

Two joined polynucleotide strands

3 hydrogen bonds

2 hydrogen bonds

The two strands are antiparallel (they run in opposite directions)

DNA Double-Helix

You can use computer modelling to investigate the structure of DNA and other nucleic acids.

Antiparallel polynucleotide strands

Hydrogen bonds between bases, keeping the strands coiled together

Bases

## You Can Purify DNA Using a Precipitation Reaction

I really like this investigation. It's **proper science**, with **green bubbly stuff** (detergent) and everything...

1) **Break up the cells** in your sample (probably a bit of **onion** or something). You can do this using a **blender**.

2) Make up a solution of **detergent** (a dilute washing-up liquid will do), **salt** (sodium chloride) and **distilled water**.

3) Add the broken-up cells to a beaker containing the detergent solution. Incubate the beaker in a **water bath** at **60 °C** for **15 minutes**.

> The detergent in the mixture breaks down the cell membranes. The salt binds to the DNA and causes it to clump together. The temperature of the water bath should stop enzymes in the cells from working properly and breaking down the DNA.

4) Once incubated, put your beaker in an **ice bath** to **cool** the mixture down. When it's cooled, **filter** the mixture. Transfer a sample of your mixture to a clean boiling tube.

5) Add **protease enzymes** to the filtered mixture. These will **break down** some **proteins** in the mixture, e.g. proteins bound to the DNA. Adding **RNase enzymes** will break down any **RNA** in the mixture.

There's more on enzymes on pages 42 - 49.

boiling tube

ethanol

DNA precipitate

detergent mixture

6) Slowly dribble some **cold ethanol** down the side of the tube, so that it forms a **layer** on top of the DNA-detergent mixture.

7) If you leave the tube for a few minutes, the DNA will form a **white precipitate** (solid), which you can remove from the tube using a glass rod.

*MODULE 2: SECTION 3 — NUCLEOTIDES AND NUCLEIC ACIDS*

# Polynucleotides and DNA

## DNA can Copy Itself — Self-Replication

**DNA copies itself** before **cell division** (see page 60) so that each new cell has the full amount of DNA.

1) **DNA helicase** (an enzyme) **breaks** the **hydrogen bonds** between the two **polynucleotide** DNA strands. The helix **unzips** to form two single strands.

Helicase breaks hydrogen bonds
DNA helix

2) Each **original** single strand acts as a **template** for a new strand. Free-floating DNA nucleotides join to the **exposed bases** on each original template strand by **complementary base pairing** — A with T and C with G.

Bases match up using complementary base pairing.

3) The nucleotides of the new strand are **joined together** by the enzyme **DNA polymerase**. This forms the **sugar-phosphate backbone**. **Hydrogen bonds** form between the bases on the original and new strand. The strands twist to form a **double-helix**.

DNA polymerase joins the nucleotides. Hydrogen bonds form between the strands.

4) Each new DNA molecule contains **one strand** from the **original** DNA molecule and **one new strand**.

New strand
Original DNA strand

1) This type of copying is called **semi-conservative replication** because **half** of the strands in each new DNA molecule are from the **original** piece of DNA (i.e. the new molecule contains one **old** strand and one **new** strand).

2) DNA replication is really **accurate** — it has to be, to make sure **genetic information** is **conserved** (stays the same) **each time** the DNA in a cell is replicated.

3) Every so often though, a **random, spontaneous mutation** occurs. A mutation is any **change** to the **DNA base sequence**. Mutations don't always have an effect, but they can **alter** the **sequence of amino acids** in a **protein** (see next page). This can cause an **abnormal protein** to be produced. The abnormal protein might function **better** than the normal protein — or it might **not work at all**.

## Practice Questions

Q1 Name the type of bond formed between nucleotides in a polynucleotide chain.

Q2 Which DNA bases pair together in complementary base pairing?

**Exam Questions**

Q1 a) Describe how nucleotides are joined together in DNA. [3 marks]

b) Describe how two single polynucleotide strands are joined to make a double helix. [3 marks]

Q2 A student is extracting DNA from peas. He adds ground-up peas to a solution containing detergent and salt.

a) Explain the purpose of the detergent. [1 mark]

b) The student incubates the mixture, then cools it. He adds cold ethanol to a sample of the mixture and a white precipitate is formed. His teacher tells him that the precipitate will be a mixture of nucleic acids and not pure DNA. Suggest what the student could have done to obtain a pure sample of DNA. [2 marks]

Q3* Describe the method of semi-conservative DNA replication. [6 marks]

* You will be assessed on the quality of your written response in this question.

## Give me a D, give me an N, give me an A! What d'you get? Confused...

*So now you know all the DNA basics — what it's made from, its structure, how to get it out of a biological sample and how it goes about making more of itself. Phew. You still need to know what it does though. Time to turn over...*

# Genes and Protein Synthesis

*You need to know how DNA is used to carry information — and how that information gets turned into proteins.*
*Luckily for you, it's all here over the next few pages...*

## DNA Contains **Genes** Which are **Instructions** for **Making Proteins**

1) A **gene** is a sequence of **DNA nucleotides** that codes for a **polypeptide** — the sequence of **amino acids** in a polypeptide forms the **primary structure** of a **protein** (see page 27).

2) Different proteins have a **different number** and **order** of amino acids.

3) It's the **order of nucleotide bases** in a gene that determines the **order of amino acids** in a particular **protein**.

4) Each amino acid is coded for by a sequence of **three bases** (called a **triplet**) in a gene.

bases on DNA

C A T T C A

DNA triplet

5) **Different sequences** of bases code for **different amino acids**. So the **sequence of bases** in a section of DNA is a **template** that's used to make **proteins** during **protein synthesis**.

## DNA is **Copied** into **RNA** for **Protein Synthesis**

1) DNA molecules are found in the **nucleus** of the cell, but the organelles that make proteins (**ribosomes**, see page 11) are found in the **cytoplasm**.

2) DNA is **too large** to move out of the nucleus, so a section is **copied** into **mRNA** (see below). This process is called **transcription** (see page 40).

3) The mRNA **leaves** the nucleus and joins with a ribosome in the cytoplasm, where it can be used to synthesise a protein. This process is called **translation** (see page 41).

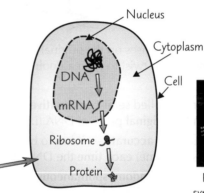

Nucleus

Cytoplasm

Cell

DNA

mRNA

Ribosome

Protein

*Rita Some knew how to synthesise some great tunes.*

## There are **Three Main Types** of RNA

Remember, RNA is a **single** polynucleotide strand and it contains **uracil (U)** as a base instead of thymine (see page 34). Uracil **always pairs** with **adenine** during protein synthesis. RNA isn't all the same though. You need to know about:

### Messenger RNA (mRNA)

- Made in the **nucleus**.
- **Three adjacent bases** are called a **codon**.
- It **carries the genetic code** from the DNA in the **nucleus** to the **cytoplasm**, where it's used to make a **protein** during **translation**.

### Transfer RNA (tRNA)

- Found in the **cytoplasm**.
- It has an **amino acid binding site** at one end and a **sequence of three bases** at the other end called an **anticodon**.
- It **carries** the amino acids that are used to make proteins to the **ribosomes** during **translation**.

Binding site

amino acid

Anticodon

U A G

*Codons and anticodons are sometimes referred to as triplets.*

### Ribosomal RNA (rRNA)

- Forms the two **subunits** in a **ribosome** (along with proteins).
- The ribosome **moves along the mRNA strand** during protein synthesis. The rRNA in the ribosome helps to **catalyse** the formation of **peptide bonds** between the amino acids.

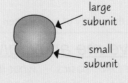

large subunit

small subunit

# Genes and Protein Synthesis

## The **Genetic Code** is **Non-Overlapping**, **Degenerate** and **Universal**

1) The genetic code is the **sequence of base triplets (codons)** in DNA or mRNA, which **codes** for **specific amino acids**.

2) In the genetic code, each base triplet is **read** in sequence, **separate** from the triplet **before** it and **after** it. Base triplets **don't share** their bases — the code is **non-overlapping**.

3) The genetic code is also **degenerate** — there are **more** possible combinations of **triplets** than there are amino acids (20 amino acids but 64 possible triplets). This means that some **amino acids** are coded for by **more than one** base triplet, e.g. tyrosine can be coded for by UAU or UAC.

4) Some triplets are used to tell the cell when to **start** and **stop** production of the protein — these are called **start** and **stop** signals (or start and stop **codons**). They're found at the **beginning** and **end** of the gene. E.g. UAG is a stop signal.

5) The genetic code is also **universal** — the **same** specific base triplets code for the **same** amino acids in **all living things**. E.g. UAU codes for tyrosine in all organisms.

## Practice Questions

Q1 What is a gene?

Q2 What is the function of mRNA?

Q3 Why is the genetic code described as degenerate?

Q4 Why is the genetic code described as universal?

### Exam Questions

Q1 Which of the following is **not** a correct description of tRNA?

   A   It has an amino acid binding site.

   B   It contains the bases adenine, guanine, cytosine and uracil.

   C   It catalyses the formation of peptide bonds between amino acids.

   D   It carries amino acids to the ribosomes during translation.      [1 mark]

Q2 A piece of mRNA has the sequence: GUGUGUCGCGCA.

| mRNA codon | amino acid |
|---|---|
| UGU | Cysteine |
| CGC | Arginine |
| GGG | Glycine |
| GUG | Valine |
| GCA | Alanine |
| UUG | Leucine |
| UUU | Phenylalanine |

   a)  How many amino acids does this sequence code for?   [1 mark]

   b)  Using the table on the right, write down the amino acid sequence it codes for.   [2 marks]

Q3 An artificial mRNA was synthesized to code for a particular protein. Part of the mRNA sequence was: UUGUGUGGGUUUGCAGCA. This produced the following sequence of amino acids: Leucine–Cysteine–Glycine–Phenylalanine–Alanine–Alanine. Use the table above to help you answer the following questions.

   a)  Explain how the result suggests that the genetic code is based on triplets of nucleotides in mRNA.   [2 marks]

   b)  Explain how the result suggests that the genetic code is non-overlapping.   [2 marks]

## Genes contain instructions — wash at 40 °C...

*You really need to get your head around how DNA and RNA work together to produce proteins or the next two pages are going to be a teeeny weeny bit tricky. Don't say I didn't warn you. Turn over too quickly at your own peril...*

# Transcription and Translation

*Time to find out how RNA works its magic to make proteins. It gets a bit complicated but bear with it.*

## First Stage of Protein Synthesis — Transcription

During transcription an **mRNA copy** of a gene
(a section of DNA) is made in the **nucleus**:

1) Transcription starts when **RNA polymerase** (an **enzyme**) **attaches** to the **DNA** double-helix at the **beginning** of a **gene**.

2) The **hydrogen bonds** between the two DNA strands in the gene **break**, **separating** the strands, and the DNA molecule **uncoils** at that point.

3) One of the strands is then used as a **template** to make an **mRNA copy**.

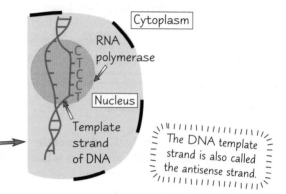

The DNA template strand is also called the antisense strand.

4) The RNA polymerase **lines up** free **RNA nucleotides** alongside the template strand. **Complementary base pairing** means that the mRNA strand ends up being a **complementary copy** of the DNA template strand (except the base **T** is replaced by **U** in **RNA**).

5) Once the RNA nucleotides have **paired up** with their **specific bases** on the DNA strand they're **joined together**, forming an **mRNA** molecule.

RNA nucleotides joined together

Free RNA nucleotides

DNA triplet A T C
codon on mRNA U A G

6) The RNA polymerase moves **along** the DNA, separating the strands and **assembling** the mRNA strand.

7) The **hydrogen bonds** between the uncoiled strands of DNA **re-form** once the RNA polymerase has passed by and the strands **coil back into a double-helix**.

Direction RNA polymerase is moving

8) When RNA polymerase reaches a **stop codon** (see previous page) it stops making mRNA and **detaches** from the DNA.

9) The **mRNA** moves **out** of the **nucleus** through a **nuclear pore** and attaches to a **ribosome** in the cytoplasm, where the next stage of protein synthesis takes place (see next page).

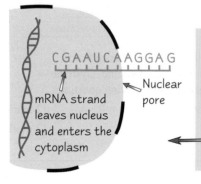

CGAAUCAAGGAG

mRNA strand leaves nucleus and enters the cytoplasm

Nuclear pore

# Transcription and Translation

## Second Stage of Protein Synthesis — Translation

Translation occurs at the **ribosomes** in the **cytoplasm**. During **translation**, amino acids are **joined together** to make a **polypeptide chain** (protein), following the sequence of **codons** carried by the mRNA.

1) The **mRNA attaches** itself to a **ribosome** and **transfer RNA (tRNA)** molecules **carry amino acids** to the ribosome.

2) A tRNA molecule, with an **anticodon** that's **complementary** to the **start codon** on the mRNA, attaches itself to the mRNA by **complementary base pairing**.

3) A second tRNA molecule attaches itself to the **next codon** on the mRNA in the **same way**.

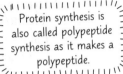

4) **Ribosomal RNA (rRNA)** in the ribosome **catalyses** the formation of a **peptide bond** between the two amino acids attached to the tRNA molecules. This **joins** the amino acids together. The first tRNA molecule **moves away**, leaving its amino acid behind.

5) A third tRNA molecule binds to the **next codon** on the mRNA. Its amino acid **binds** to the first two and the second tRNA molecule **moves away**.

Protein synthesis is also called polypeptide synthesis as it makes a polypeptide.

6) This process continues, producing a chain of linked amino acids (a **polypeptide chain**), until there's a **stop codon** on the mRNA molecule.

7) The polypeptide chain **moves away** from the ribosome and translation is complete.

## Practice Questions

Q1 What are the two stages of protein synthesis called?
Q2 Where does the first stage of protein synthesis take place?
Q3 When does RNA polymerase stop making mRNA?
Q4 Where does the second stage of protein synthesis take place?

**Exam Questions**

Q1 A DNA sequence is GCGAAGTCCATG.
  a) Write down the complementary mRNA sequence. [1 mark]
  b) Write down the sequence of the tRNA anticodons. [1 mark]

Q2 A drug that inhibits cell growth is found to be able to bind to DNA, preventing RNA polymerase from binding. Explain how this drug will affect protein synthesis. [2 marks]

Q3 A polypeptide chain (protein) from a eukaryotic cell is 10 amino acids long. Predict how long the mRNA for this protein would be in nucleotides. Explain your answer. [2 marks]

## *I could do with a translation for this page...*

*So you start off with DNA, lots of cleverness happens and bingo... you've got a protein. Only problem is you need to know the cleverness bit in quite a lot of detail. So scribble it down, recite it to yourself, explain it to your best mate or do whatever else helps you remember the joys of protein synthesis. And then think how clever you are to know it all.*

# Action of Enzymes

*Enzymes crop up loads in Biology — they're really useful 'cos they make reactions work more quickly.*

## Enzymes are Biological Catalysts

> A catalyst is a substance that speeds up a chemical reaction without being used up in the reaction itself.

1) Enzymes **speed up chemical reactions** by acting as **biological catalysts**. They catalyse **metabolic reactions** — both at a **cellular level** (e.g. **respiration**) and for the **organism** as a **whole** (e.g. **digestion** in mammals).

2) Enzymes can affect **structures** in an organism (e.g. enzymes are involved in the production of **collagen**, an important protein in the **connective tissues** of animals) as well as **functions** (like **respiration**).

3) Enzyme action can be **intracellular** — **within** cells, or **extracellular** — **outside** cells.

### Intracellular Enzyme Example — Catalase

1) **Hydrogen peroxide** ($H_2O_2$) is the **toxic by-product** of several cellular reactions. If left to build up, it can **kill cells**.

2) **Catalase** is an enzyme that works **inside cells** to catalyse the breakdown of hydrogen peroxide to **harmless oxygen** ($O_2$) and **water** ($H_2O$).

### Extracellular Enzyme Examples — Amylase and Trypsin

1) Amylase and trypsin both work **outside cells** in the human **digestive system**.

2) **Amylase** is found in **saliva**. It's **secreted** into the **mouth** by cells in the **salivary glands**. It catalyses the **hydrolysis** (breakdown, see p. 22) of **starch** into **maltose** (a sugar) in the mouth.

3) **Trypsin** catalyses the hydrolysis of **peptide bonds** — turning **big polypeptides** into **smaller ones** (which then get broken down into amino acids by other enzymes). Trypsin is produced by cells in the **pancreas** and secreted into the **small intestine**.

4) Enzymes are **globular proteins** (see p. 28).

5) Enzymes have an **active site**, which has a **specific shape**. The active site is the part of the enzyme that the **substrate** molecules (the substance that the enzyme interacts with) **bind to**.

6) The specific shape of the active site is determined by the enzyme's **tertiary structure** (see p. 27).

7) For the enzyme to work, the substrate has to **fit into** the **active site** (its shape has to be **complementary**). If the substrate shape doesn't match the active site, the reaction won't be catalysed. This means that enzymes work with very few substrates — usually only one.

## Enzymes Reduce Activation Energy

1) In a chemical reaction, a certain amount of energy needs to be supplied to the chemicals before the reaction will start. This is called the **activation energy** — it's often provided as **heat**.

2) Enzymes **reduce** the amount of activation energy that's needed, often making reactions happen at a **lower temperature** than they could without an enzyme. This **speeds** up the **rate of reaction**.

3) When a substance binds to an enzyme's active site, an **enzyme-substrate complex** is formed. It's the formation of the enzyme-substrate complex that **lowers** the **activation energy**. Here are two reasons why:

1) If two substrate molecules need to be **joined**, attaching to the enzyme holds them **close together**, **reducing** any **repulsion** between the molecules so they can bond more easily.

2) If the enzyme is catalysing a **breakdown reaction**, fitting into the active site puts a **strain** on bonds in the substrate. This strain means the substrate molecule **breaks up** more easily.

# Action of Enzymes

## The 'Lock and Key' Model is a Good Start...

Enzymes are a bit picky. They only work with **substrates** that fit their active site. Early scientists studying the action of enzymes came up with the 'lock and key' model. This is where the **substrate fits** into the **enzyme** in the same way that a **key fits** into a **lock**.

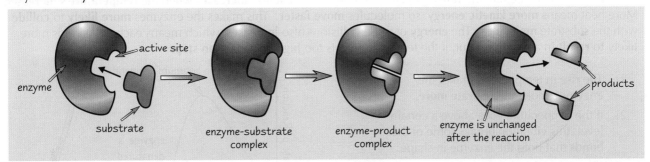

Scientists soon realised that the lock and key model didn't give the full story. The enzyme and substrate do have to fit together in the first place, but new evidence showed that the **enzyme-substrate complex changed shape** slightly to complete the fit. This **locks** the substrate even more tightly to the enzyme. Scientists modified the old lock and key model and came up with the 'induced fit' model.

## ...but the 'Induced Fit' Model is a Better Theory

The '**induced fit**' model helps to explain why enzymes are so **specific** and only bond to one particular substrate.

The substrate doesn't only have to be the right shape to fit the active site, it has to make the active site **change shape** in the right way as well. This is a prime example of how a widely accepted theory can **change** when **new evidence** comes along. The 'induced fit' model is still widely accepted — for now, anyway.

## Practice Questions

Q1 What is an enzyme?

Q2 What is the name given to the amount of energy needed to start a reaction?

Q3 What is an enzyme-substrate complex?

Q4 Explain why enzymes are specific.

**Exam Question**

Q1 Dextranase is an enzyme that catalyses the breakdown of specific bonds in dextran (a polysaccharide).

Use the induced fit model of enzyme action to explain why dextranase catalyses the breakdown of dextran, but not amylose (another polysaccharide). [3 marks]

---

## But why is the enzyme-substrate complex?

*OK, nothing too tricky here. The main thing to remember is that every enzyme has a specific shape, so it only works with specific substrates that fit the active site. The induced fit model is a newer theory that explains this.*

# Factors Affecting Enzyme Activity

44

Now you know what enzymes are and how they work, it's time to take a look at what makes them tick. There are four main factors affecting enzyme activity that you need to know about...

## 1) Temperature has a Big Influence on Enzyme Activity

Like any chemical reaction, the **rate** of an enzyme-controlled reaction **increases** when the **temperature's increased**. More heat means **more kinetic energy**, so molecules **move faster**. This makes the enzymes **more likely** to **collide** with the substrate molecules. The **energy** of these collisions also **increases**, which means each collision is more likely to **result** in a **reaction**. But, if the temperature gets too high, the **reaction stops**.

1) The rise in temperature makes the enzyme's molecules **vibrate more**.
2) If the temperature goes above a certain level, this vibration **breaks** some of the **bonds** that hold the enzyme in shape.
3) The **active site changes shape** and the enzyme and substrate **no longer fit together**.
4) At this point, the enzyme is **denatured** — it no longer functions as a catalyst.

Every enzyme has an optimum temperature. For most human enzymes it's around 37 °C but some enzymes, like those used in biological washing powders, can work well at 60 °C.

### The Temperature Coefficient (Q₁₀) Shows How Rate Changes with Temperature

1) The **temperature coefficient** or $Q_{10}$ value for a reaction shows **how much** the **rate** of a **reaction changes** when the **temperature** is **raised** by **10 °C**.
2) At temperatures **before** the **optimum**, a $Q_{10}$ value of **2** means that the **rate doubles** when the temperature is raised by 10 °C. A $Q_{10}$ value of **3** would mean that the **rate trebles**.
3) Most **enzyme-controlled reactions** have a $Q_{10}$ value of **around 2**.

## 2) pH Also Affects Enzyme Activity

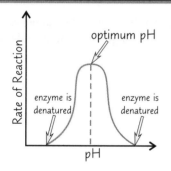

1) All enzymes have an **optimum pH value**. Most human enzymes work best at pH 7 (neutral), but there are exceptions. **Pepsin**, for example, works best at acidic pH 2, which is useful because it's found in the stomach.
2) Above and below the optimum pH, the $H^+$ and $OH^-$ ions found in acids and alkalis can mess up the **ionic bonds** and **hydrogen bonds** that hold the enzyme's tertiary structure in place. This makes the active site change shape, so the enzyme is **denatured**.

## 3) Enzyme Concentration Affects the Rate of Reaction

1) The **more enzyme molecules** there are in a solution, the more likely a substrate molecule is to **collide** with one and form an **enzyme-substrate complex**. So increasing the concentration of the enzyme **increases** the **rate of reaction**.
2) But, if the amount of **substrate** is **limited**, there comes a point when there's more than enough enzyme molecules to deal with all the available substrate, so adding more enzyme has **no further effect**.

# Factors Affecting Enzyme Activity

## 4) *Substrate Concentration* Affects the Rate of Reaction *Up to a Point*

1) The **higher** the substrate concentration, the **faster** the reaction — more substrate molecules means a **collision** between substrate and enzyme is **more likely** and so more active sites will be used.

2) This is only true up until a **'saturation'** point though. After that, there are so many substrate molecules that the enzymes have about as much as they can cope with (all the **active sites are full**), and adding more substrate **makes no difference** to the rate of reaction.

3) Substrate concentration **decreases** with **time** during a reaction (unless more substrate is added to the reaction mixture), so if no other variables are changed, the **rate of reaction will decrease over time** too. This makes the **initial** rate of reaction (the reaction rate right at the start of the reaction, close to **time 0**) the **highest** rate of reaction.

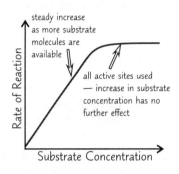

steady increase as more substrate molecules are available

all active sites used — increase in substrate concentration has no further effect

Rate of Reaction

Substrate Concentration

In the exams, you might be asked to calculate the rate of an enzyme-controlled reaction from a graph — see page 7 for more.

## You can *Measure* the *Rate* of an *Enzyme-Controlled* Reaction

You need to know how the effects of **pH**, **temperature**, **enzyme concentration** and **substrate concentration** can be investigated **experimentally**. Here are two ways of measuring the **rate** of an enzyme-controlled reaction:

### Example 1

You can measure **how fast** the **product** of the reaction **appears**. The diagram on the right shows how to measure this with the enzyme **catalase**. Catalase catalyses the **breakdown** of **hydrogen peroxide** into **water** and **oxygen**. It's easy to collect the oxygen produced and measure **how fast** it's given off.

upside down measuring cylinder

delivery tube

amount of oxygen produced per minute is measured

hydrogen peroxide solution and catalase enzyme

mixture sampled each minute

dropping pipette

drop of iodine in potassium iodide

starch solution and amylase enzyme

spotting tile

Time when iodine solution no longer turns blue-black is noted — starch has then been broken down.

### Example 2

You can also measure the **disappearance** of the **substrate** rather than the appearance of the product and use this to **compare the rate** of reaction under different conditions. For example, the enzyme **amylase** catalyses the breakdown of **starch** to **maltose** (see p. 42). It's easy to detect starch using a solution of potassium iodide and iodine. You can **time** how long it takes for the starch to disappear by **regularly sampling** the starch solution. You can then **alter** the **conditions** of the reaction and compare rates.

# Factors Affecting Enzyme Activity

## Example: Investigating the Effect of Temperature on Catalase Activity

1) In this investigation, **temperature** is the **independent variable** — the thing you **change**.

2) The **dependent variable** (the thing you **measure**) will be the **volume of oxygen** produced.

3) You need to **control** all the **other variables** that could affect the outcome of the investigation (i.e. keep them constant). That includes the **pH**, the **enzyme concentration**, the **substrate concentration**, etc.

Here's what you do:

1) Set up boiling tubes containing the **same volume** and **concentration** of **hydrogen peroxide**. To keep the pH constant, add **equal volumes** of a **buffer solution** to each tube. (A buffer solution is able to resist changes in pH when small amounts of acid or alkali are added.)

*Different buffer solutions have different pHs. You'd need to use one with the optimum pH for the enzyme you're testing here.*

2) Set up the **apparatus** to measure the **volume** of oxygen produced from each boiling tube. For example, use a delivery tube and upside down measuring cylinder, as shown on the previous page.

3) Put each boiling tube in a **water bath** set to a different temperature (e.g. 10 °C, 20 °C, 30 °C and 40 °C) along with another tube containing **catalase** (wait 5 minutes before moving on to the next step to allow the enzyme to reach the set temperature).

4) Use a pipette to add the **same volume** and **concentration** of **catalase** to each boiling tube.

5) **Record** how much oxygen is produced in the **first 60 seconds** of the reaction. Use a **stopwatch** to measure the time.

6) **Repeat** the experiment at each temperature three times, and use the results to find the **mean volume of oxygen produced** at each temperature.

*A negative control reaction, i.e. a boiling tube not containing catalase, should also be carried out at each temperature.*

7) **Calculate** the **mean rate of reaction** at each temperature by dividing the volume of oxygen produced by the time taken (i.e. 60 s). The **unit** for the **rate of reaction** here will be $cm^3$/second or $cm^3 s^{-1}$.

It's easy to **alter** this experiment to investigate the effect of a **different variable** on catalase activity. E.g. if you wanted to investigate the effect of **substrate concentration**, you'd keep the **temperature** of the reaction the **same**, but prepare boiling tubes with **different concentrations** of **hydrogen peroxide** (this could be done using **serial dilutions** — see page 31). To investigate the effect of **pH**, you could add a **buffer solution** with a **different pH** to each tube.

## Practice Questions

Q1 What does it mean if an enzyme is denatured?

Q2 Explain why increasing the concentration of an enzyme doesn't always increase the rate of reaction.

Q3 Explain the effect of increasing substrate concentration on the rate of an enzyme-catalysed reaction.

Q4 Suggest two methods of measuring the rate of an enzyme-catalysed reaction.

**Exam Questions**

Q1 An enzyme-controlled reaction has a $Q_{10}$ value of 2 between 10 °C and 30 °C.
What does the $Q_{10}$ value tell you about the reaction between these two temperatures?

A The rate of reaction halves.       C The rate of reaction doubles.

B The amount of product made doubles.   D The amount of product made halves.       [1 mark]

Q2 Casein is a protein found in milk powder. A student wants to investigate the effect of varying pH on the rate of casein breakdown by the enzyme trypsin. She intends to add trypsin to a series of solutions containing milk powder at different pHs and time how long it takes for each solution to turn from cloudy to translucent.

a) Suggest how the student could vary the pH of the milk powder solutions.       [1 mark]

b) Give one variable that the student will need to control in this experiment.       [1 mark]

c) The student has read that the optimum pH for trypsin is pH 8.
Describe and explain what will happen to the rate of the reaction above this pH.       [4 marks]

## *Factors affecting my activity — laziness, lack of sleep...*

*Enzymes are pretty fussy — they'll only work best when they are nice and comfortable. Which, come to think of it, is when I work best too. Make sure you're comfortable, then learn how temperature, pH, enzyme concentration and substrate concentration affect enzyme activity — and how to investigate their effects on the rate of a reaction.*

MODULE 2: SECTION 4 — ENZYMES

# Cofactors and Enzyme Inhibition

*Cofactors are substances that enzymes need to work. Enzyme inhibitors, yep you guessed it, inhibit their action. Some inhibitors are poisons, but they're not all bad — we use some of them as medicinal drugs.*

## Cofactors and **Coenzymes** are **Essential** for Enzymes to **Work**

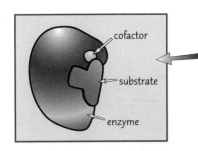

Some enzymes will only work if there is another **non-protein** substance bound to them. These non-protein substances are called **cofactors**.

1) Some cofactors are **inorganic** molecules or ions. They work by helping the enzyme and substrate to **bind together**. They don't directly participate in the reaction so aren't **used up** or **changed** in any way. For example, **chloride ions (Cl⁻)** are **cofactors** for the enzyme **amylase**.

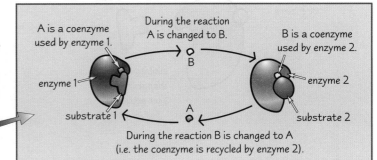

2) Some cofactors are **organic** molecules — these are called **coenzymes**. They participate in the reaction and are **changed** by it (they're just like a second substrate, but they aren't called that). They often act as **carriers**, moving **chemical groups** between different enzymes. They're **continually recycled** during this process. **Vitamins** are often **sources** of coenzymes.

3) If a cofactor is **tightly bound** to the enzyme, it's known as a **prosthetic group**. For example, **zinc ions (Zn²⁺)** are a prosthetic group for **carbonic anhydrase** (an enzyme in red blood cells, which catalyses the production of carbonic acid from water and carbon dioxide). The zinc ions are a **permanent part** of the enzyme's **active site**.

*You need to learn the Cl⁻ and Zn²⁺ examples for the exam.*

## Enzyme **Activity** can be **Inhibited**

Enzyme activity can be prevented by **enzyme inhibitors** — molecules that **bind to the enzyme** that they inhibit. Inhibition can be **competitive** (see below) or **non-competitive** (see next page).

### COMPETITIVE INHIBITION

1) **Competitive inhibitor** molecules have a **similar shape** to that of the **substrate** molecules.
2) They **compete** with the substrate molecules to **bind** to the **active site**, but **no reaction** takes place.
3) Instead they **block** the active site, so **no substrate** molecules can **fit** in it.

inhibitor molecule fits into active site because it is a similar shape to the substrate molecule

4) How much the enzyme is inhibited depends on the **relative concentrations** of the inhibitor and the substrate.
5) If there's a **high concentration** of the **inhibitor**, it'll take up **nearly all** the **active sites** and hardly any of the substrate will get to the enzyme.
6) But if there's a **higher concentration** of **substrate**, then the substrate's chances of getting to an active site before the inhibitor **increase**. So **increasing** the concentration of **substrate** will **increase** the **rate of reaction** (up to a point).

# Cofactors and Enzyme Inhibition

## NON-COMPETITIVE INHIBITION

1) **Non-competitive inhibitor** molecules bind to the enzyme **away from its active site**. The site they bind to is known as the enzyme's **allosteric site**.

2) This causes the active site to **change shape** so the substrate molecules can **no longer bind** to it.

3) They **don't** 'compete' with the substrate molecules to bind to the active site because they are a **different shape**.

4) **Increasing** the concentration of **substrate won't** make any difference to the reaction rate — enzyme activity will still be inhibited.

inhibitor molecules fits into allosteric site of enzyme

substrate molecule can no longer fit into active site

enzyme

inhibitor causes changes that alter active site

enzyme-controlled reaction without an inhibitor

same reaction with a non-competitive inhibitor — increasing the substrate conc. has little effect on rate

Rate of Reaction

Substrate Concentration

## Inhibitors *Can Be* Reversible *or* Non-Reversible

Which one they are depends on the **strength of the bonds** between the enzyme and the inhibitor.

1) If they're **strong, covalent bonds**, the inhibitor can't be removed easily and the inhibition is **irreversible**.

2) If they're **weaker hydrogen bonds** or weak **ionic bonds**, the inhibitor can be removed and the inhibition is **reversible**.

The hockey team had strong bonds. Especially after they accidentally glued their kits together.

## Some *Drugs* and *Metabolic Poisons* are *Enzyme Inhibitors*

Some **medicinal drugs** are **enzyme inhibitors**, for example:

1) Some **antiviral** drugs (drugs that stop **viruses** like **HIV**) — e.g. **reverse transcriptase inhibitors** inhibit the enzyme **reverse transcriptase**, which catalyses the **replication** of **viral DNA**. This **prevents** the virus from **replicating**.

2) Some **antibiotics** — e.g. **penicillin** inhibits the enzyme **transpeptidase**, which **catalyses** the **formation** of **proteins** in bacterial cell walls. This **weakens the cell wall** and prevents the bacterium from regulating its osmotic pressure. As a result the cell **bursts** and the bacterium is **killed**.

Metabolic **poisons interfere** with **metabolic reactions** (the reactions that occur in cells), causing **damage**, **illness** or **death** — they're often **enzyme inhibitors**. For example:

1) **Cyanide** is an **irreversible** inhibitor of **cytochrome c oxidase**, an enzyme that catalyses **respiration** reactions. Cells that can't respire **die**.

2) **Malonate** inhibits **succinate dehydrogenase** (which also catalyses respiration reactions).

3) **Arsenic** inhibits the action of **pyruvate dehydrogenase**, another enzyme that catalyses **respiration** reactions.

# Cofactors and Enzyme Inhibition

## Metabolic Pathways are Regulated by End-Product Inhibition

1) A **metabolic pathway** is a series of **connected metabolic reactions**. The **product** of the **first reaction** takes part in the **second reaction** — and so on. Each reaction is catalysed by a **different enzyme**.

2) Many enzymes are **inhibited** by the **product** of the reaction they catalyse. This is known as **product inhibition**.

3) **End-product inhibition** is when the **final product** in a **metabolic pathway** inhibits an enzyme that acts **earlier on** in the pathway.

Substance 4 inhibits Enzyme 1

Enzyme 1 — Enzyme 2 — Enzyme 3

Substance 1 → Substance 2 → Substance 3 → Substance 4

4) End-product inhibition is a nifty way of **regulating** the pathway and **controlling** the amount of end-product that gets made. For example:

- **Phosphofructokinase** is an enzyme involved in the metabolic pathway that **breaks down glucose** to make **ATP**.
- ATP **inhibits** the action of phosphofructokinase — so a **high level** of ATP **prevents** more ATP from being made.

5) Both product and end-product inhibition are **reversible**. So when the level of product starts to **drop**, the level of inhibition will start to fall and the enzyme can start to **function again** — this means that **more product** can be made.

## Enzyme Inhibition Can Help to Protect Cells

1) Enzymes are sometimes synthesised as **inactive precursors** in **metabolic pathways** to prevent them causing damage to cells. For example, some **proteases** (which **break down proteins**) are synthesised as inactive precursors to stop them **damaging proteins** in the cell in which they're made.

2) Part of the precursor molecule **inhibits** its action as an enzyme. Once this part is **removed** (e.g. via a chemical reaction) the enzyme becomes **active**.

A sense of inhibition might have protected Dan from his dress sense.

## Practice Questions

Q1 What are cofactors, coenzymes and prosthetic groups?

Q2 What's the difference between competitive and non-competitive enzyme inhibitors?

Q3 Name one metabolic poison and describe how it works.

Q4 Why are some enzymes synthesised as inactive precursors?

**Exam Questions**

Q1 In bacteria, lactose is broken down into glucose and galactose by the enzyme ß-galactosidase. Galactose inhibits ß-galactosidase by binding to the active site. Which one of the following statements is correct?

   A    Galactose is a cofactor of ß-galactosidase.      C    Galactose binds to ß-galactosidase via weak hydrogen bonds.

   B    The inhibition of ß-galactosidase              D    Galactose is a non-competitive inhibitor
         by galactose is irreversible.                     of ß-galactosidase.          [1 mark]

Q2 During an experiment hexokinase (an enzyme that catalyses reactions important in respiration) was found to work only in the presence of magnesium ions and to work slower when aluminium ions were also present.

   a)   Suggest a possible reason why hexokinase only works when magnesium ions are present.      [2 marks]

   b)   Suggest a possible reason why hexokinase works slower when aluminium ions are present.      [2 marks]

   c)   Explain why aluminium ions are a metabolic poison.      [1 mark]

Q3 HIV uses protease enzymes to catalyse the breakdown of proteins. It uses the products of the reaction to replicate new viruses. Ritonavir is a drug used to treat HIV. Its molecules have a similar shape to the protein molecules which are the substrate for HIV protease. Suggest how Ritonavir will affect HIV. Explain your answer.      [3 marks]

## Enzymes are easily inhibited — they're very shy you know...

*Crikey, it's like a rubbish soap or something — one minute the enzymes are trying to kill us, the next they're bringing us back to life, and all the while there are some things trying to stop them, and others trying to help them — if you can follow the ins, outs, ups and downs of some crazy soap then you can follow this. Everybody needs good en-zymes...*

# Cell Membranes

*You might remember a bit about cell membranes from that giant pink table of fun back in Module 2 Section 1. Well now it's time to delve a little deeper and see exactly what they do — lucky you.*

## Membranes Control What Passes Through Them

**Cells**, and many of the **organelles** inside them, are surrounded by **membranes**, which have a **range of functions**:

### Membranes at the **surface of cells** (PLASMA membranes)

1) They are a **barrier** between the **cell** and its **environment**, controlling **which substances enter and leave** the cell. They're **partially permeable** — they let some molecules through but not others. Substances can move across the plasma membrane by **diffusion**, **osmosis** or **active transport** (see pages 54-59).

2) They allow **recognition** by other cells, e.g. the cells of the **immune system** (see p. 98).

3) They allow **cell communication** (sometimes called **cell signalling**) — see p. 52.

Partially permeable membranes can be useful at sea.

### Membranes **within cells**

1) The membranes around **organelles divide** the cell into different **compartments** — they act as a **barrier** between the **organelle** and the **cytoplasm**. This makes different **functions more efficient**, e.g. the substances needed for **respiration** (like enzymes) are kept together inside **mitochondria**.

2) They can form **vesicles** to **transport** substances between different areas of the cell (see p. 57).

3) They control **which substances enter and leave** the organelle, e.g. RNA (see p. 38) leaves the nucleus via the nuclear membrane. They are also **partially permeable**.

4) You can also get membranes **within organelles** — these act as **barriers** between the membrane contents and the rest of the organelle, e.g. thylakoid membranes in chloroplasts (see p. 12).

5) Membranes within cells can be the **site** of **chemical reactions**, e.g. the **inner membrane** of a mitochondrion contains **enzymes** needed for **respiration**.

## Cell Membranes have a 'Fluid Mosaic' Structure

The **structure** of all membranes is basically the same. They're composed of **lipids** (mainly phospholipids), **proteins** and **carbohydrates** (usually attached to proteins or lipids).

*See pages 22-28 or more about lipids, proteins and carbohydrates.*

1) In 1972, the **fluid mosaic model** was suggested to describe the **arrangement** of **molecules** in the membrane.

2) In the model, **phospholipid molecules** form a continuous, double layer (**bilayer**).

3) This bilayer is '**fluid**' because the phospholipids are **constantly moving**.

4) **Cholesterol** molecules are present within the bilayer (see next page).

5) **Protein molecules** are scattered through the bilayer, like tiles in a **mosaic**.

6) Some **proteins** have a **polysaccharide** (carbohydrate) **chain** attached — these are called **glycoproteins**.

7) Some **lipids** also have a **polysaccharide chain** attached — these are called **glycolipids**.

*The phospholipid bilayer is about 7 nm thick.*

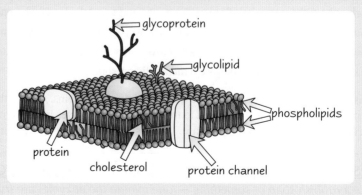

glycoprotein

glycolipid

phospholipids

protein

cholesterol

protein channel

# Cell Membranes

## The **Different Components** of Cell Membranes have **Different Roles**

### Phospholipids Form a Barrier to Dissolved Substances

1) **Phospholipid molecules** have a 'head' and a 'tail'.
2) The **head** is hydrophilic — it **attracts water**.
3) The **tail** is hydrophobic — it **repels water**.
4) The molecules automatically **arrange** themselves into a **bilayer** — the **heads face out** towards the water on either side of the membrane.
5) The **centre** of the bilayer is **hydrophobic** so the membrane **doesn't** allow **water-soluble substances** (like ions) through it — it acts as a **barrier** to these dissolved substances. (But **fat-soluble substances**, e.g. fat-soluble vitamins, can **dissolve** in the bilayer and pass directly through the membrane.)

### Cholesterol Gives the Membrane Stability

1) **Cholesterol** is a type of lipid.
2) It's present in **all** cell membranes (except bacterial cell membranes).
3) Cholesterol molecules fit **between** the phospholipids. They bind to the hydrophobic tails of the phospholipids, causing them to pack **more closely together**. This makes the membrane **less fluid** and **more rigid**.

See p. 25 for more on phospholipids and cholesterol.

### Proteins Control What Enters and Leaves the Cell

1) Some proteins form **channels** in the membrane (see p. 56) — these allow **small** or **charged** particles **through**.
2) Other proteins (called **carrier proteins**) **transport molecules** and **ions** across the membrane by **active transport** and **facilitated diffusion** (see p. 56).
3) Proteins also act as **receptors** for molecules (e.g. hormones) in **cell signalling** (see next page). When a molecule **binds** to the protein, a **chemical reaction** is triggered inside the cell.

### Glycolipids and Glycoproteins act as Receptors for Messenger Molecules

1) Glycolipids and glycoproteins **stabilise** the membrane by forming **hydrogen bonds** with surrounding **water molecules**.
2) They're also sites where **drugs**, **hormones** and **antibodies** bind.
3) They act as **receptors** for **cell signalling** (see next page).
4) They're also **antigens** — cell surface molecules involved in the immune response (see p. 98).

## Practice Questions

Q1 Give two functions of membranes at the cell surface and two functions of membranes within the cell.

Q2 Give three molecules that are present in animal cell membranes.

### Exam Questions

Q1 Explain why the plasma membrane can be described as having a fluid mosaic structure. [2 marks]

Q2 State two functions of proteins in cell membranes. [2 marks]

## *Fluid Mosaic Model — think I saw one being sold at a craft fair...*

*It's weird to think that cells are surrounded by a layer that's 'fluid' — it's a good job it is though, 'cause if cell membranes were rigid a cell wouldn't be able to change shape or stretch without bursting. It's also a good job that the membrane's partially permeable — so that it can let oxygen into the cell and carbon dioxide out of the cell. Phew.*

# Cell Membranes

*Cells like to have a good chat with one another every so often. To do this they use a process called cell signalling.*

## Cell Signalling is How Cells Communicate with Each Other

Cells need to communicate with each other to **control processes** inside the body and to **respond** to **changes** in the **environment**.

Cells communicate with each other using **messenger molecules**:
1) One cell **releases** a messenger molecule (e.g. a **hormone**).
2) This molecule **travels** (e.g. in the blood) to another cell.
3) The messenger molecule is detected by the cell because it **binds** to a **receptor** on its **cell membrane**.

## Cell Membrane Receptors Play an Important Role in Cell Signalling

1) **Proteins** in the cell membrane act as **receptors** for messenger molecules. These are called 'membrane-bound receptors'.
2) Receptor proteins have **specific shapes** — only **messenger molecules** with a **complementary shape** can **bind** to them.
3) **Different cells** have **different types** of receptors — they respond to **different messenger molecules**.
4) A cell that responds to a particular messenger molecule is called a **target cell**. The diagram below shows how messenger molecules bind to target cells.

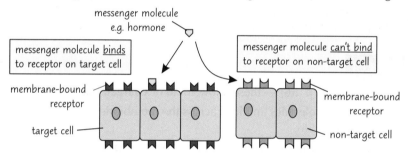

messenger molecule e.g. hormone

messenger molecule **binds** to receptor on target cell

messenger molecule **can't bind** to receptor on non-target cell

membrane-bound receptor

membrane-bound receptor

target cell

non-target cell

**Example: Glucagon**

**Glucagon** is a **hormone** that's **released** when there **isn't enough glucose** in the **blood**. It **binds** to **receptors** on **liver cells**, causing the liver cells to **break down** stores of **glycogen** to glucose.

### Drugs Also Bind to Cell Membrane Receptors

1) Many **drugs** work by **binding** to **receptors** in cell membranes.
2) They either **trigger** a **response** in the cell, or **block** the receptor and **prevent** it from **working**.

**Example: Antihistamines**

**Cell damage** causes the release of **histamine**. Histamine binds to receptors on the surface of other cells and causes **inflammation**. **Antihistamines** work by **blocking histamine receptors** on cell surfaces. This **prevents** histamine from binding to the cell and **stops inflammation**.

## The Permeability of the Cell Membrane can be Investigated in the Lab

The permeability of cell membranes is affected by **different conditions**, e.g. **temperature**, **solvent type** and **solvent concentration**. You can investigate how these things affect permeability by doing an experiment using **beetroot**. Beetroot cells contain a **coloured pigment** that **leaks out** — the **higher** the **permeability** of the membrane, the **more pigment** leaks out of the cell.

Here's how you could investigate how **temperature** affects **beetroot membrane permeability**:
1) Cut five **equal sized** pieces of beetroot and **rinse** them to remove any pigment released during cutting.
2) Place the five pieces in five different **test tubes**, each with **5 cm³ of water**.
3) Place each test tube in a **water bath** at a **different temperature**, e.g. 10 °C, 20 °C, 30 °C, 40 °C, 50 °C, for the **same length of time**.
4) **Remove** the pieces of beetroot from the tubes, leaving just the **coloured liquid**.
5) Now you need to use a **colorimeter** — a machine that passes **light** through the liquid and measures how much of that light is **absorbed** (see p. 31). The **higher** the **permeability** of the membrane, the **more pigment** is **released**, so the **higher** the absorbance of the liquid.

# Cell Membranes

## Increasing the Temperature Increases Membrane Permeability

**Experiments** like the one on the previous page have shown that membrane permeability **changes** with temperature:

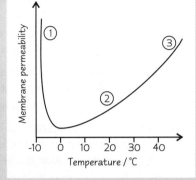

**(1) Temperatures below 0 °C**
The phospholipids don't have much energy, so they can't move very much. They're **packed closely together** and the membrane is **rigid**. But **channel proteins** and **carrier proteins** in the membrane **deform**, increasing the **permeability** of the membrane. **Ice crystals** may form and **pierce** the membrane making it **highly permeable** when it thaws.

**(2) Temperatures between 0 and 45 °C**
The phospholipids can **move** around and **aren't** packed as tightly together — the membrane is **partially permeable**. As the temperature increases the phospholipids **move more** because they have more energy — this increases the **permeability** of the membrane.

**(3) Temperatures above 45 °C**
The phospholipid bilayer starts to **melt** (break down) and the membrane becomes more **permeable**. **Water** inside the cell **expands**, putting pressure on the membrane. **Channel proteins** and **carrier proteins** **deform** so they can't control what enters or leaves the cell — this increases the **permeability** of the membrane.

## Changing the Solvent Affects Membrane Permeability

**Different solvents** and their **concentration** can affect the **permeability** of cell membranes.

1) Surrounding cells in a **solvent** (such as ethanol) **increases** the **permeability** of their cell membranes.

2) This is because solvents **dissolve** the **lipids** in a cell membrane, so the membrane **loses** its **structure**.

3) Some solvents **increase** cell **permeability** more than others, e.g. **ethanol** increases cell permeability more than **methanol**.

4) You could **investigate** the effects of different solvents by doing an experiment using **beetroot** like the one on the previous page.

5) **Increasing** the **concentration** of the solvent will also **increase** membrane **permeability**. For example, this graph shows the effect of alcohol concentration on membrane permeability.

## Practice Questions

Q1 Describe, using an example, how cells communicate with one another.

Q2 Describe how the permeability of a cell membrane changes as the temperature increases.

**Exam Question**

Q1 The table on the right shows the results of an investigation into the effect of alcohol concentration on the permeability of beetroot cell membranes.

| Alcohol concentration / % | Absorbance |
|---|---|
| 0 | 0.14 |
| 25 | 0.22 |
| 50 | 0.49 |
| 75 | 1.03 |
| 100 | 1.28 |

a) Suggest a suitable method that could have been used to obtain these results. [4 marks]

b) What conclusion can be drawn from the results? [2 marks]

c) Suggest an explanation for the results. [1 mark]

## Perm-eability — it's definitely decreased since the 80s...

*Messenger molecules are released by different cells in your body. They travel round and bind to receptors on other cells, causing some kind of response. This signalling fine-tunes all the body's processes and keeps us working properly.*

# Transport Across Cell Membranes

*The beauty of cell membranes is that they're partially permeable — they'll only let certain substances enter and leave. Some substances move across cell membranes by passive transport, which means no energy is involved in the process. Passive transport processes include diffusion, facilitated diffusion (see p. 56) and osmosis (see p. 58).*

## *Diffusion is the **Passive Movement** of Particles*

1) Diffusion is the **net movement** of particles (molecules or ions) from an area of **higher concentration** to an area of **lower concentration**.

2) Molecules will diffuse **both ways**, but the **net movement** will be to the area of **lower concentration**. This continues until particles are **evenly distributed** throughout the liquid or gas.

3) The **concentration gradient** is the path from an area of higher concentration to an area of lower concentration. Particles diffuse **down** a concentration gradient.

4) Diffusion is a **passive process** — **no energy** is needed for it to happen.

*Diffusion — not good in a swimming pool.*

## **Small, Non-Polar** Molecules **Diffuse** Through **Cell Membranes**

- **Small**, **non-polar** molecules such as **oxygen** and **carbon dioxide** are able to **diffuse** easily through spaces between **phospholipids**.

- **Water** is also **small** enough to fit between phospholipids, so it's able to **diffuse** across **plasma membranes** even though it's **polar**. The diffusion of water molecules like this is called **osmosis** (see p. 58).

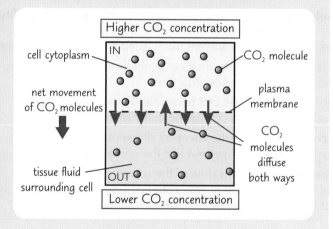

## The **Rate of Diffusion** Depends on **Several Factors**

1) The **concentration gradient** — the **higher** it is, the **faster** the rate of diffusion.

2) The **thickness** of the **exchange surface** — the **thinner** the exchange surface (i.e. the **shorter** the **distance** the particles have to travel), the **faster** the rate of diffusion.

3) The **surface area** — the **larger** the surface area (e.g. of a cell membrane), the **faster** the rate of diffusion.

4) The **temperature** — the **warmer** it is, the **faster** the rate of diffusion because the particles have **more kinetic energy** so they move faster.

# Transport Across Cell Membranes

## You Can *Investigate Diffusion* in *Model Cells*

**Phenolphthalein** is a **pH indicator** — it's **pink** in alkaline solutions and **colourless** in acidic solutions. You can use it to investigate **diffusion** in **agar jelly**:

1) First, make up some agar jelly with **phenolphthalein** and dilute **sodium hydroxide**. This will make the jelly a lovely shade of **pink**.

2) Then fill a **beaker** with some dilute **hydrochloric acid**. Using a **scalpel**, cut out a few **cubes** from the jelly and put them in the beaker of acid.

3) If you **leave** the cubes for a while they'll eventually turn **colourless** as the **acid diffuses into** the agar jelly and **neutralises** the sodium hydroxide.

*In this experiment the agar jelly cubes are used to represent the cells.*

Dilute acid

Pink agar cube          Colourless agar cube

Using this experiment you can **investigate factors** that affect the **rate of diffusion**. For example:

**SURFACE AREA** — Cut the agar jelly into **different sized** cubes and work out their **surface area to volume ratio** (see p. 68). Time how long it takes each cube to go **colourless** when placed in the **same concentration** of hydrochloric acid. You would expect the cubes with the **largest surface area to volume ratio** to go colourless **fastest**.

**CONCENTRATION GRADIENT** — Prepare test tubes containing **different concentrations** of hydrochloric acid. Put an equal-sized cube of the agar jelly in each test tube and time how long it takes each one to turn **colourless**. You would expect the cubes in the **highest concentration** of hydrochloric acid to go colourless **fastest**.

**TEMPERATURE** — Prepare several boiling tubes containing the same concentration of hydrochloric acid and put the tubes into water baths of **varying temperatures**. Put an equal-sized cube of the agar jelly into each boiling tube and time how long it takes each cube to go **colourless**. You would expect the cubes in the **highest temperature** to go colourless **fastest**.

*Don't increase the temperature above 65 °C or the agar jelly will start to melt.*

## Practice Questions

Q1 Diffusion is a passive transport process. What does this mean?

Q2 Other than concentration gradient, give three factors that affect the rate of diffusion.

Q3 Describe an experiment you could use to investigate the effect of concentration gradient on the rate of diffusion.

### Exam Question

Q1 A student carried out an experiment with gelatine blocks containing cresol red, a pH indicator that changes from red to yellow when it comes into contact with acid. She cut cubes into three different sizes and placed each cube into a hydrochloric acid solution. She observed when each cube turned yellow and recorded the time taken. She repeated the experiment four times for each size of cube. Her results are shown in the table.

| Size of cube (mm) | Surface area to volume ratio | Time taken for cube to become yellow (s) | | | |
|---|---|---|---|---|---|
| | | Trial 1 | Trial 2 | Trial 3 | Trial 4 |
| 5 × 5 × 5 | 1.2:1 | 174 | 167 | 177 | 182 |
| 7 × 7 × 7 | 0.9:1 | 274 | 290 | 284 | 292 |
| 10 ×10 × 10 | 0.6:1 | 835 | 825 | 842 | 838 |

a) Give two variables that should have been controlled during the experiment. [2 marks]

b) What conclusion about the rate of diffusion can be drawn from the results of the experiment? [1 mark]

c) Suggest one reason why the results of the experiment might not be very precise. [1 mark]

## *All these molecules moving about — you'd think they'd get tired...*

*Diffusion is simple really — it's just particles spreading themselves out evenly. Make sure you learn the different factors that can affect the rate of diffusion and know how you can investigate the rate of diffusion in the lab.*

# Transport Across Cell Membranes

*Facilitated diffusion is another passive transport process, but there's also an active transport process involving energy, which is imaginatively named 'active transport'. Facilitated diffusion and active transport are actually quite similar though — they both involve proteins.*

## Facilitated Diffusion uses Carrier Proteins and Channel Proteins

1) Some **larger molecules** (e.g. amino acids, glucose), **ions** and **polar molecules don't diffuse directly through** the phospholipid bilayer of the cell membrane.

2) Instead they diffuse through **carrier proteins** or **channel proteins** in the cell membrane — this is called **facilitated diffusion**.

3) Like diffusion, facilitated diffusion moves particles **down** a **concentration gradient**, from a higher to a lower concentration.

4) It's also a passive process — it **doesn't** use **energy**.

*Andy needed all his concentration for this particular gradient...*

**Carrier proteins** move **large molecules** into or out of the cell, down their concentration gradient. **Different carrier proteins** facilitate the diffusion of **different molecules**.

1) First, a large molecule **attaches** to a carrier protein in the membrane.

2) Then, the protein **changes shape**.

3) This **releases** the molecule on the **opposite side** of the membrane.

**Channel proteins** form **pores** in the membrane for **charged particles** to diffuse through (down their concentration gradient). **Different channel proteins** facilitate the diffusion of **different charged particles**.

## Active Transport Moves Substances Against a Concentration Gradient

Active transport uses **energy** to move **molecules** and **ions** across plasma membranes, **against** a **concentration gradient**. This process involves **carrier proteins**.

1) The process is pretty similar to facilitated diffusion — a molecule **attaches** to the carrier protein, the protein **changes shape** and this moves the molecule **across** the membrane, **releasing it** on the other side.

2) The only difference is that **energy** is used (from **ATP** — a common source of energy used in the cell), to move the solute against its concentration gradient.

3) The diagram on the right shows the active transport of **calcium ions** ($Ca^{2+}$).

# Transport Across Cell Membranes

## Cells can **Take in** Substances by **Endocytosis**

1) Some molecules are way too **large** to be taken into a cell by carrier proteins, e.g. proteins, lipids and some carbohydrates.

2) Instead a cell can **surround** a substance with a **section** of its **plasma membrane**.

3) The membrane then **pinches off** to form a **vesicle** inside the cell containing the **ingested substance** — this is **endocytosis**.

4) Some cells also take in much **larger objects** by endocytosis — for example, some **white blood cells** (mainly phagocytes, see p. 98) use endocytosis to take in things like **microorganisms** and **dead cells** so that they can destroy them.

5) Like active transport, (see previous page), this process also uses **ATP** for **energy**.

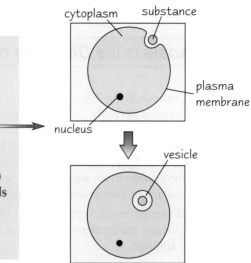

## Cells can **Secrete** Substances by **Exocytosis**

1) Some substances **produced** by the cell (e.g. **digestive enzymes, hormones, lipids**) need to be **released** from the cell — this is done by **exocytosis**.

2) **Vesicles** containing these substances **pinch off** from the sacs of the **Golgi apparatus** (see p. 12) and **move towards** the plasma membrane.

3) The vesicles **fuse** with the **plasma membrane** and **release** their contents **outside** the cell.

4) Some substances (like membrane proteins) **aren't** released outside the cell — instead they are **inserted** straight into the plasma membrane.

5) Exocytosis uses **ATP** as an **energy source**.

Vesicle buds off from Golgi apparatus.

Vesicle moves to plasma membrane.

Vesicle fuses with plasma membrane.

Contents of vesicle released outside the cell.

## Practice Questions

Q1 When would facilitated diffusion take place rather than simple diffusion?

Q2 What is active transport?

Q3 Which molecule provides the energy for active transport?

### Exam Questions

Q1 Describe the role of membrane proteins in facilitated diffusion. [3 marks]

Q2 Explain the difference between endocytosis and exocytosis. [4 marks]

## Revision — like working against a concentration gradient...

*Wouldn't it be great if you could revise by endocytosis — you could just stick this book on your head and your brain would slowly surround it and take it in... actually when I put it like that it sounds a bit gross. Maybe just stick to the good old 'closing the book and scribbling down the diagrams till you know them off by heart' method.*

# Transport Across Cell Membranes

*Here is the last bit on molecules crossing cell membranes. These pages are entirely about the movement of water molecules. Don't worry though — if you've mastered diffusion (see p. 54) you'll nail this in no time.*

## Osmosis is the Diffusion of Water Molecules

1) Osmosis is the **diffusion** of **water molecules** across a **partially permeable membrane** down a **water potential gradient**. This means water molecules move from an area of **higher water potential** (i.e. higher concentration of water molecules) to an area of **lower water potential** (i.e. lower concentration of water molecules).

2) **Water potential** is the potential (likelihood) of water molecules to diffuse out of or into a solution.

3) **Pure water** has the **highest water potential**. All solutions have a **lower** water potential than pure water.

## Cells are Affected by the Water Potential of the Surrounding Solution

**Water** moves **in** or **out** of a cell by osmosis. **How much** moves in or out depends on the **water potential** of the **surrounding solution**. Animal and plant cells behave differently in different solutions.

**ANIMAL CELL**

Solution with a <u>higher water potential</u> than the cell (hypotonic solution).

plasma membrane
nucleus
cytoplasm

Net movement of water molecules is <u>into</u> the cell. Cell <u>bursts</u>.

Solution with the <u>same water potential</u> as the cell (isotonic solution).

Water molecules pass into and out of the cell in <u>equal amounts</u>. The cell <u>stays the same</u>.

Solution with a <u>lower water potential</u> than the cell (hypertonic solution).

Net movement of water molecules is <u>out</u> of the cell. The cell <u>shrinks</u>.

**PLANT CELL**

<u>Hypotonic</u> solution

cytoplasm
vacuole
plasma membrane
nucleus
cell wall

Net movement of water is <u>into</u> cell. The <u>vacuole swells</u>. The vacuole and cytoplasm push against the cell wall. The cell becomes <u>turgid</u> (swollen).

<u>Isotonic</u> solution

Water molecules move into and out of the cell in <u>equal amounts</u>. The cell <u>stays the same</u>.

<u>Hypertonic</u> solution

Net movement of water is out of the cell. The cell becomes <u>flaccid</u> (limp). The <u>cytoplasm</u> and the membrane pull away from the cell wall. This is called <u>plasmolysis</u>.

# Transport Across Cell Membranes

## You can do **Experiments** to Investigate **Water Potential**

You can do a simple **experiment**, using potato cylinders, to find out the **water potential** of **plant tissue**. This experiment involves putting potato cylinders into **different concentrations** of sucrose solution — remember, the **higher** the sucrose **concentration**, the **lower** the water **potential**.

1) Prepare **sucrose solutions** of the following concentrations: 0.0 M, 0.2 M, 0.4 M, 0.6 M, 0.8 M, 1.0 M.

2) Use a cork borer or chip maker to cut **potatoes** into **the same sized** pieces. (They need to be about 1 cm in diameter.)

*You might also see M written as mol dm$^{-3}$.*

0.0 M   0.2 M   0.4 M   0.6 M   0.8 M   1.0 M

3) Divide the chips into **groups of three** and use a **mass balance** to measure the **mass** of each **group**.

4) Place **one group** in each solution.

5) **Leave** the chips in the solution for **as long as possible** (making sure that they all get the **same amount of time**). Try to leave them for at least 20 minutes.

6) **Remove** the chips and pat dry **gently** with a paper towel.

7) **Weigh** each **group** again and record your results.

8) Calculate the % **change in mass** for each group.

9) Plot your results on a **graph** like this:

*This point is where the water potential of the sucrose solution is the same as the water potential of the potato cells.*

*If you could see the potato cells under a microscope, you'd see them becoming turgid as the chip gains mass and plasmolysed as the chip loses mass (see previous page).*

## You can do a **Similar Experiment** with **Eggs**

You can carry out a **similar experiment** using chickens' eggs that have had their **shells dissolved**. The remaining **membrane** is **partially permeable**, so it's a good **model** for showing the effects of **osmosis** in **animal tissue**.

## Practice Questions

Q1 Define osmosis.

Q2 What happens to an animal cell if it is placed in a solution with the same water potential as the cell?

Q3 What happens to a plant cell if it is placed in a solution with a higher water potential than the cell?

### Exam Question

Q1 Pieces of potato of equal mass were put into different concentrations of sucrose solution for 24 hours. The difference in mass for each is recorded in the table.

| Concentration of sucrose / % | 1 | 2 | 3 | 4 |
|---|---|---|---|---|
| Mass difference / g | 0.4 | 0.2 | 0 | − 0.2 |

a) Explain why the pieces of potato in 1% and 2% sucrose solutions gained mass. [3 marks]

b) Suggest a reason why the mass of the piece of potato in 3% sucrose solution stayed the same. [1 mark]

c) What would you expect the mass difference for a potato in a 5% solution to be? Explain your answer. [2 marks]

## *I always knew that glass of water had potential...*

*Osmosis is just a fancy name for the diffusion of water molecules. But whether water moves in or out of a cell depends on the water potential of the surrounding solution. Water potential can be pretty confusing — if you can't make head nor tail of an exam question about it try replacing the word 'potential' with 'concentration' and it'll become clearer.*

# The Cell Cycle and Mitosis

*Ever wondered how you grow from one tiny cell to a complete whole person?*
*No, oh... well it's because your cells replicate and you need to learn the processes involved.*

## The Cell Cycle is the Process of Cell Growth and Division

The **cell cycle** is the process that all body cells in **multicellular organisms** use to **grow** and **divide**.

G2 Checkpoint
The cell checks whether all the DNA has been replicated without any damage. If it has, the cell can enter mitosis.

M PHASE
(mitosis and cytokinesis)

Metaphase Checkpoint
(see below)

GAP PHASE 1
cell grows and new organelles and proteins are made

GAP PHASE 2
cell keeps growing and proteins needed for cell division are made

INTERPHASE

G1 checkpoint
The cell checks that the chemicals needed for replication are present and for any damage to the DNA before entering S-phase.

SYNTHESIS
cell replicates its DNA, ready to divide by mitosis

1) The cell cycle **starts** when a cell has been produced by cell division and **ends** with the cell dividing to produce two identical cells.

2) The cell cycle consists of a period of **cell growth** and **DNA replication**, called **interphase**, and a period of **cell division**, called **M phase**. M phase involves **mitosis** (nuclear division) and **cytokinesis** (cytoplasmic division).

3) **Interphase** (cell growth) is subdivided into three separate growth stages. These are called $G_1$, **S** and $G_2$.

4) The cell cycle is regulated by **checkpoints**. Checkpoints occur at key points during the cycle to make sure it's **OK** for the **process** to **continue**.

## Mitosis has Four Division Stages

1) Mitosis is needed for the **growth** of multicellular organisms (like us) and for **repairing damaged tissues**. It is also a method of **asexual reproduction** for some plants, animals and fungi.

2) Mitosis is really one **continuous process**, but it's described as a series of **division stages** — prophase, metaphase, anaphase and telophase.

3) **Interphase** comes **before** mitosis in the cell cycle. It's when cells grow and replicate their DNA ready for division.

**Interphase** — The cell carries out normal functions, but also prepares to divide. The cell's **DNA** is unravelled and **replicated**, to double its genetic content. The **organelles** are also **replicated** so it has spare ones, and its ATP content is increased (ATP provides the energy needed for cell division).

Homologous pair    Interphase
Cell
Chromosome
Cytoplasm
Nucleus
Centriole
Unravelled DNA containing two copies of each chromosome

1) **Prophase** — The **chromosomes condense**, getting shorter and fatter. Tiny bundles of protein called **centrioles** start moving to opposite ends of the cell, forming a network of protein fibres across it called the **spindle**. The **nuclear envelope** (the membrane around the nucleus) **breaks down** and chromosomes lie free in the cytoplasm.

Nuclear envelope starts to break down
Centrioles move to opposite ends of the cell
Centromere

As mitosis begins, the chromosomes are made of two strands joined in the middle by a centromere. The separate strands are called chromatids.

One chromatid — Centromere
Sister chromatids

There are two strands because each chromosome has already made an identical copy of itself during interphase. When mitosis is over, the chromatids end up as one-strand chromosomes in the new daughter cells.

2) **Metaphase** — The chromosomes (each with two chromatids) **line up** along the middle of the cell and become **attached** to the spindle by their **centromere**. At the **metaphase checkpoint**, the cell **checks** that all the **chromosomes** are **attached** to the **spindle** before **mitosis** can continue.

Spindle fibres
Centromeres on spindle equator

# The Cell Cycle and Mitosis

3) <u>Anaphase</u> — The centromeres divide, **separating** each pair of sister **chromatids**. The spindles contract, pulling chromatids to opposite ends of the cell, centromere first.

Sister chromatids moving to opposite ends of the cell

4) <u>Telophase</u> — The chromatids reach the **opposite poles** on the spindle. They uncoil and become long and thin again. They're now called **chromosomes** again. A **nuclear envelope** forms around each group of chromosomes, so there are now **two nuclei**.

Centriole

Nuclear envelopes form

**Cytokinesis** — The **cytoplasm divides**. In animal cells, a **cleavage furrow** forms to **divide** the **cell membrane**. There are now **two daughter cells** that are **genetically identical** to the original cell and to each other. **Cytokinesis** usually begins in **anaphase** and ends in **telophase**. It's a **separate** process to **mitosis**.

Centriole

Cleavage furrow

## You can **Observe** the **Cell Cycle** and **Mitosis** by **Staining Chromosomes**

You can **stain chromosomes** so you can see them under a **microscope**. This means you can watch what happens to them **during mitosis** — and it makes high-adrenaline viewing, I can tell you. These are some **plant root cells** shown under a **light microscope** at different stages of the **cell cycle** and **mitosis**. You need to be able to **recognise**, **draw** and **label** each stage.

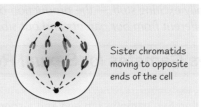

Prophase

Anaphase

Telophase

Metaphase

Interphase

HERVE CONGE, ISM/SCIENCE PHOTO LIBRARY

These plant roots cells are being viewed on a 'squash' microscope slide. In other words, they've been deliberately squashed beneath the cover slip. This makes it easier to see the chromosomes.

You can recognise cells in interphase because the chromosomes will be spread out and not condensed.

### Practice Questions

Q1 What happens during interphase?

Q2 List in order the four stages of mitosis.

Q3 At what stage in mitosis does the nuclear envelope break down?

**Exam Question**

Q1 The diagrams show cells at different stages of mitosis.

a) Which of the cells, A, B or C, is undergoing anaphase? Give a reason for your answer. [2 marks]

b) Name the structures labelled X, Y and Z in cell B. [3 marks]

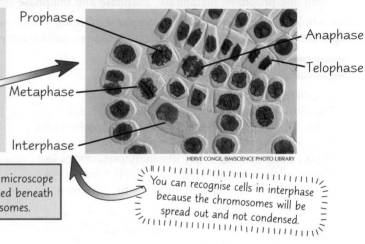

Cell A    X    Cell B    Cell C

Z

Y

---

## *Doctor, Doctor, I'm getting short and fat — don't worry, it's just a phase...*

*Quite a lot to learn in this topic — but it's all dead important stuff, so no slacking. Most body cells undergo mitosis — it's needed for cells to multiply so organisms like us can grow and develop. Remember that chromosomes during mitosis are made up of two sister chromatids joined by a centromere. Nice to know family values are important to genetic material too.*

# Sexual Reproduction and Meiosis

*Ahh, now on to some really exciting stuff — the production of gametes (sex cells to you and me).*
*This is how we end up different from our parents and our siblings — and yet, in some ways, strangely alike...*

## Meiosis Produces Gametes for Sexual Reproduction

1) In sexual reproduction two **gametes** (an egg and a sperm) join together at **fertilisation** to form a **zygote**. The zygote then divides and develops into a **new organism**.

2) **Meiosis** is a type of **cell division** that happens in the reproductive organs to **produce gametes**.

3) Meiosis involves a **reduction division**. Cells that divide by meiosis have the **full number** of chromosomes to start with, but the cells that are formed from meiosis have **half the number**. Cells with half the normal number of chromosomes are called **haploid cells**.

4) Cells formed by meiosis are all **genetically different** because each new cell ends up with a **different combination** of chromosomes.

*Without meiosis, you'd get double the number of chromosomes when the gametes fused. Not good.*

## Meiosis Involves Two Divisions

1) **Meiosis** involves two divisions: **meiosis I** and **meiosis II**. **Meiosis I** is the **reduction division** (it halves the chromosome number).

2) Like **mitosis** (see previous two pages) meiosis I and meiosis II are each split into **prophase**, **metaphase**, **anaphase** and **telophase** stages.

The whole of meiosis begins with **interphase**. During interphase, the DNA **unravels** and **replicates** to produce double-armed chromosomes called **sister chromatids** (see page 60).

*You need to learn what homologous chromosomes are.*

### Meiosis I (first division)

**Prophase I**
The **chromosomes condense**, getting shorter and fatter. The chromosomes then arrange themselves into **homologous pairs** (see yellow box) and **crossing-over** occurs (see next page). Just like in mitosis, **centrioles** start moving to opposite ends of the cell, forming the **spindle fibres**. The **nuclear envelope breaks down**.

A Note About Homologous Pairs:
Humans have 46 chromosomes in total — 23 pairs. One chromosome in each pair came from mum and one from dad, e.g. there are two number 1's (one from mum and one from dad), two number 2's etc. The chromosomes that make up each pair are the same size and have the same genes, although they could have different versions of those genes (called alleles). These pairs of chromosomes are called homologous pairs.

**Metaphase I**
The **homologous pairs line up** across the **centre** of the cell and **attach** to the **spindle fibres** by their **centromeres**.

**Anaphase I**
The **spindles contract**, separating the **homologous pairs** — one chromosome goes to **each end** of the cell.

**Telophase I**
A **nuclear envelope** forms around each group of chromosomes.

**Cytokinesis** (division of the cytoplasm) occurs and **two haploid daughter cells** are produced.

Homologous pair, Nuclear envelope, Nucleus, Cytoplasm, Cell, Prophase I, Centrioles, Metaphase I, Spindle fibres, Anaphase I, Telophase I, Chromosome number is halved

### Meiosis II (second division)

The two daughter cells undergo **prophase II, metaphase II, anaphase II, telophase II** and **cytokinesis** — which are a lot like the stages in **mitosis**.

In **anaphase II**, the pairs of **sister chromatids** are **separated** — each **new** daughter cell inherits **one chromatid** from each chromosome. **Four** (genetically different) **haploid** daughter cells are produced — these are the **gametes**.

End of meiosis I = two haploid daughter cells

STAGES OF MEIOSIS II

End of meiosis II = four haploid daughter cells

# Sexual Reproduction and Meiosis

## Chromatids **Cross Over** in **Prophase I**

During prophase I of meiosis I, **homologous pairs** of chromosomes come together and pair up. The chromatids twist around each other and bits of **chromatids** swap over. The chromatids still contain the **same genes** but now have a different combination of **alleles**.

Chromatids of one chromosome

Crossing over occurs between chromatids

Chromatids now have a new combination of alleles

## **Meiosis** Produces Cells that are **Genetically Different**

There are two main events during meiosis that lead to **genetic variation**:

### 1 Crossing over of chromatids

The **crossing over** of chromatids in meiosis I means that each of the **four daughter cells** formed from meiosis contains chromatids with **different alleles**:

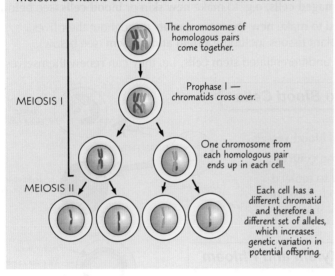

The chromosomes of homologous pairs come together.

MEIOSIS I

Prophase I — chromatids cross over.

One chromosome from each homologous pair ends up in each cell.

MEIOSIS II

Each cell has a different chromatid and therefore a different set of alleles, which increases genetic variation in potential offspring.

### 2 Independent assortment of chromosomes

1) Each **homologous pair** of chromosomes in your cells is made up of **one chromosome** from your mum (**maternal**) and **one chromosome** from your dad (**paternal**).

2) When the homologous pairs **line up** in **metaphase I** and are **separated** in **anaphase I**, it's completely **random** which chromosome from each pair ends up in which daughter cell.

3) So the **four daughter cells** produced by meiosis have completely **different combinations** of those **maternal and paternal chromosomes**.

4) This is called **independent assortment** (separation) of the chromosomes.

5) This 'shuffling' of chromosomes leads to **genetic variation** in any **potential** offspring.

MEIOSIS I

Paternal — Maternal

OR

Possible combinations in daughter cells

## Practice Questions

Q1 Explain what is meant by the term haploid.

Q2 What happens to homologous pairs of chromosomes during meiosis I?

Q3 How many cells does meiosis produce?

**Exam Question**

Q1 *Drosophila* (fruit flies) only have four chromosomes.
The diagram on the right summarises one of the meiotic divisions in *Drosophila*.

a) Does the diagram show meiosis I or meiosis II? Give a reason for your answer. [1 mark]

b) Crossing over does not occur very frequently in male *Drosophila*.
Explain what crossing over is and how it leads to genetic variation. [4 marks]

c) Explain how independent assortment leads to genetic variation. [2 marks]

## *Reproduction isn't as exciting as some people would have you believe...*

*These pages are quite tricky, so use the diagrams to help you understand — they might look evil, but they really do help. The key thing to understand is that meiosis produces four genetically different haploid daughter cells. And that the genetic variation in the daughter cells occurs because of two processes — crossing over and independent assortment.*

# Stem Cells and Differentiation

*If I had to choose a favourite type of cell, I'd choose a stem cell and here's why...*

## Stem Cells are Unspecialised Cells

1) **Multicellular organisms** are made up from many **different** cell types that are **specialised** for their function, e.g. liver cells, muscle cells, white blood cells.

2) **All** these specialised cell types originally came from **stem cells**.

3) Stem cells are **unspecialised** cells — they can develop into **different types** of cell.

4) **All** multicellular organisms have some form of **stem cell**.

5) In **humans**, stem cells are found in **early embryos** and in a few places in **adults**. Stem cells in **early embryos** can develop into **any type** of human cell. Stem cells in **adults** can only develop into a **limited range** of cells.

*Tina, Joe and Bex knew their cells were specialised — specialised to look good.*

## Stem Cells Differentiate into Specialised Cells

1) Stem cells **divide** to become **new cells**, which then become **specialised**.

2) The process by which a cell becomes specialised for its job is called **differentiation**.

3) In animals, adult stem cells are used to replace **damaged cells**, e.g. to make **new skin** or **blood cells** (see below).

4) **Plants** are always growing, so stem cells are needed to make **new shoots** and **roots** throughout their lives. Stem cells in plants can **differentiate** into various plant tissues including **xylem and phloem** (see below).

5) Stem cells are also able to **divide** to produce **more** undifferentiated **stem cells**, i.e. they can **renew** themselves.

### Cells in the Bone Marrow Differentiate into Blood Cells

1) **Bones** are living organs, containing nerves and **blood vessels**.

2) The main bones of the body have **marrow** in the **centres**.

3) Here, **adult stem cells** divide and **differentiate** to replace worn out blood cells — **erythrocytes** (red blood cells) and **neutrophils** (white blood cells that help to fight infection).

### Cells in the Meristems Differentiate into Xylem and Phloem

1) In plants, **stem cells** are found in the **meristems** (parts of the plant where growth can take place).

2) In the root and stem, stem cells of the **vascular cambium** divide and **differentiate** to become **xylem vessels** and **phloem sieve tubes**.

There's more about the function of xylem and phloem on p. 86.

## It's Hoped That Stem Cells Might Cure Diseases Like Parkinson's

1) **Stem cells** can develop into **different specialised cell types**, so scientists think they could be used to **replace damaged tissues** in a **range** of **diseases**. For example, it might be possible to use **stem cells** to treat **neurological disorders** like **Alzheimer's** and **Parkinson's**:

With **Alzheimer's**, **nerve cells** in the brain **die** in increasing numbers. This results in severe **memory loss**. Researchers are hoping to use stem cells to **regrow healthy nerve cells** in people with Alzheimer's.

Patients with **Parkinson's** suffer from **tremors** that they can't control. The disease causes the loss of a particular type of **nerve cell** found in the **brain**. These cells release a **chemical** called **dopamine**, which is needed to **control movement**. **Transplanted stem cells** may help to **regenerate** the dopamine-producing cells.

2) Stem cells are also used by scientists researching **developmental biology**, i.e. how organisms **grow** and **develop**. Studying stem cells can help us to understand more about things like **developmental disorders** and **cancer**.

# Stem Cells and Differentiation

## Cells are *Specialised* for their Particular Function

Once cells **differentiate**, they have a **specific function**. Their **structure** is **adapted** to perform that function.
You need to **know** how the following cell types are specialised for their functions:

**Animal cells**

1) **Neutrophils** (a type of white blood cell) defend the body against disease. Their **flexible shape** allows them to **engulf** foreign particles or pathogens (see p. 98). The many **lysosomes** in their cytoplasm contain **digestive enzymes** to **break down** the engulfed particles.

2) **Erythrocytes** (red blood cells) carry oxygen in the blood. The **biconcave** disc shape provides a **large surface area** for gas exchange. They have **no nucleus** so there's more room for **haemoglobin** (see p. 84), the protein that carries oxygen.

3) **Epithelial cells** cover the surfaces of organs. The cells are **joined** by **interlinking** cell membranes and a membrane at their base. **Ciliated** epithelia (e.g. in the **airways**) have **cilia** that beat to move particles away. **Squamous** epithelia (e.g. in the **lungs**) are very thin to allow **efficient diffusion** of **gases**.

4) **Sperm cells** (male sex cells) have a **flagellum** (tail) so they can **swim** to the egg (female sex cell). They also have lots of **mitochondria** to provide the **energy** to swim. The **acrosome** contains **digestive enzymes** to enable the sperm to **penetrate** the surface of the egg.

Neutrophil — Flexible shape, Lots of lysosomes, Nucleus

Erythrocyte — Large surface area, Biconcave (concave on both sides), No nucleus, Cross-section

Ciliated epithelial cell — Cilia, Cell membrane interlink, Nucleus, Membrane

Sperm cell — Flagellum (tail), Acrosome

**Plant cells**

Palisade cell — Nucleus, Vacuole, Cell wall, Lots of chloroplasts, Cytoplasm

Guard cells — Cells turgid, stoma opens; Cells flaccid, stoma closes

1) **Palisade mesophyll cells** in leaves do most of the **photosynthesis**. They contain **many chloroplasts**, so they can absorb a lot of sunlight. The walls are **thin**, so carbon dioxide can **easily diffuse** into the cell.

2) **Root hair cells** absorb water and mineral ions from the soil. They have a **large surface area** for absorption and a **thin**, permeable cell wall, for entry of water and ions. The cytoplasm contains **extra mitochondria** to provide the **energy** needed for **active transport** (see p. 56).

Root hair cell — Nucleus, Thin cell wall

3) **Guard cells** are found in pairs, with a gap between them to form a **stoma**. This is one of the tiny **pores** in the surface of the leaf used for **gas exchange**. In the **light**, guard cells **take up water** and become **turgid**. Their **thin outer walls** and **thickened inner walls** force them to bend outwards, **opening** the stomata. This allows the leaf to exchange gases for photosynthesis.

## Practice Questions

Q1 What are stem cells?

Q2 Stem cells in bone marrow can differentiate into other cell types. Name two of these cell types.

Q3 Describe how stem cells might be used to treat Parkinson's.

### Exam Questions

Q1 Describe how a palisade cell is adapted for its role in photosynthesis. [2 marks]

Q2 Describe, with an example, the role of stem cells in adult mammals. [3 marks]

## *And you thought differentiation was just boring maths stuff...*

*Stem cells are pretty amazing when you think about it — they can differentiate to become any cell in the whole body. Scientists are excited about them because they could be used to repair damaged cells, like nerve cells in the brain.*

# Tissues, Organs and Systems

*Multicellular organisms are made up of lots of different cell types, which are organised to work together
— cells that carry out the same job are organised into tissues (e.g. epithelium), different tissues are organised
into organs (e.g. the lungs) and organs work together as organ systems (e.g. the respiratory system).*

## Similar Cells are Organised into Tissues

A **tissue** is a group of cells (plus any **extracellular material** secreted by them) that are specialised to **work
together** to carry out a **particular function**. A tissue can contain **more than one** cell type.

Here are some examples you need to know:

### Animal Tissues

1) **Squamous epithelium** is a **single layer** of
**flat cells** lining a surface. It's found in many
places, including the alveoli in the lungs.

Nucleus

Basement membrane

2) **Ciliated epithelium** is a layer of cells covered in
cilia (see page 13). It's found on surfaces where
things need to be **moved** — in the trachea for
instance, where the cilia waft mucus along.

Cilia

Nucleus

3) **Muscle tissue** is made up of bundles of
elongated cells called **muscle fibres**. There
are three **different** types of muscle tissue:
smooth (e.g. found lining the **stomach wall**),
**cardiac** (found in the **heart**) and **skeletal**
(which you use to **move**). They're all slightly
different in structure. Here's what **skeletal
muscle tissue** looks like:

bundles of muscle fibres

one muscle fibre (cell)

muscle

4) **Cartilage** is a type of **connective tissue** found in
the **joints**. It also **shapes** and **supports** the **ears**,
**nose** and **windpipe**. It's formed when cells
called chondroblasts **secrete**
an extracellular **matrix**
(a jelly-like substance
containing protein **fibres**),
which they become
**trapped inside**.

two cells
trapped
together

fibre-filled matrix

### Plant Tissues

1) **Xylem tissue** is a plant tissue with two jobs
— it **transports water** around the plant,
and it **supports** the plant. It contains
hollow **xylem vessel cells**, which are dead,
and living **parenchyma cells**.

Xylem vessel cell
with thickened wall
perforated by pits

Xylem parenchyma
cell (fills in gaps
between vessels)

2) **Phloem tissue** transports sugars around the plant.
It's arranged in **tubes** and is made up of **sieve cells**,
**companion cells**, and some **ordinary** plant cells.
Each sieve cell has end walls with **holes** in them,
so that sap can move easily through them.
These end walls are called **sieve plates**.

Perforated
cell wall
(sieve plate)

Ordinary
plant cells

Sieve cell

Companion cell
assists sieve
cells with living
functions

Sieve tube

*There's more on xylem
and phloem tissue on
pages 86-87.*

# Tissues, Organs and Systems

## Different Tissues Make up an Organ

An **organ** is a group of different tissues that **work together** to perform a particular function.  Examples include:

- The **lungs** — they contain **squamous epithelial tissue** (in the alveoli) and **ciliated epithelial tissue** (in the bronchi, etc.).  They also have **elastic connective tissue** and **vascular tissue** (in the blood vessels).
- **Leaves** — they contain **palisade tissue** for photosynthesis, as well as **epidermal** tissue (to prevent water loss from the leaf), and **xylem** and **phloem** tissues in the veins.

## Different Organs Make up an Organ System

Organs work together to form **organ systems** — each system has a **particular function**.
Yup, you've guessed it, more examples:

1) The **respiratory system** is made up of all the organs, tissues and cells involved in **breathing**.
   The lungs, trachea, larynx, nose, mouth and diaphragm are all part of the respiratory system.

John and Fido —
working together as part
of an organ system.

2) The **circulatory system** is made up of the organs involved in **blood supply**.
   The heart, arteries, veins and capillaries are all parts of this system.

## Practice Questions

Q1 Define what is meant by a tissue.

Q2 Briefly describe squamous epithelium.

Q3 What is the difference between the functions of xylem and phloem tissues?

Q4 Name one organ found in plants and one organ found in animals.

**Exam Questions**

Q1 The liver is made of hepatocyte cells that form the main tissue, blood vessels to
provide nutrients and oxygen, and connective tissue that holds the liver together.
Is the liver best described as a tissue, organ or an organ system?  Explain your answer.     [2 marks]

Q2 Phloem tissue is found in plants.  Which of the following statements correctly describe phloem tissue?

Statement 1:  Phloem tissue is arranged in tubes.
Statement 2:  Phloem tissue contains sieve cells.
Statement 3:  Phloem tissue contains squamous epithelial cells.

Answer:     A    Statement 1 to 3          C    Statements 2 and 3 only
            B    Statement 1 and 2 only    D    Statement 1 only              [1 mark]

---

## *Soft and quilted — the best kind of tissues...*

*So, similar cells group together to form tissues.  Then, because they love being so helpful, tissues work together in an organ to perform a particular function.  But even organs are better together — along comes the organ system.  Lovely.*

# Specialised Exchange Surfaces

*Exchanging things with the environment is pretty easy if you're a single-celled organism, but if you're multicellular it all gets a bit more complicated... and it's all down to this 'surface area to volume ratio' malarkey.*

## Organisms Need to **Exchange Substances** with their **Environment**

Every organism, whatever its size, needs to exchange things with its environment.

1) Cells need to take in things like **oxygen** and **glucose** for aerobic respiration and other **metabolic reactions**.

2) They also need to excrete **waste products** from these reactions — like **carbon dioxide** and **urea**.

Raj was glad he'd exchanged his canoe for a bigger boat.

How easy the exchange of substances is depends on the organism's **surface area to volume ratio** (SA:V).

## Smaller Animals have Higher **Surface Area : Volume Ratios**

A mouse has a bigger surface area **relative to its volume** than a hippo. This can be hard to imagine, but you can prove it mathematically. Imagine these animals as cubes:

The hippo could be represented by a block measuring 2 cm × 4 cm × 4 cm.

Its **volume** is 2 × 4 × 4 = **32 cm³**

Its **surface area** is 2 × 4 × 4 = 32 cm² (top and bottom surfaces of cube)
               + 4 × 2 × 4 = 32 cm² (four sides of the cube)

Total surface area = **64 cm²**

So the hippo has a **surface area : volume ratio** of 64 : 32 or **2:1**.

"cube hippo"

Compare this to a mouse cube measuring 1 cm × 1 cm × 1 cm

Its **volume** is 1 x 1 x 1 = **1 cm³**

Its **surface area** is 6 x 1 x 1 = **6 cm²**

"cube mouse" So the mouse has a **surface area : volume ratio** of **6:1**.

The cube mouse's surface area is six times its volume, but the cube hippo's surface area is only twice its volume. Smaller animals have a bigger surface area compared to their volume.

To calculate the surface area to volume ratio you just **divide** the **surface area** by the **volume**. Easy.

It helps to know how to calculate the area and volume of different shapes for the exam. E.g. to calculate the volume of a sphere, you need to formula $\frac{4}{3}\pi r^3$.

## Multicellular Organisms Need **Exchange Surfaces**

An organism needs to supply **every one of its cells** with substances like **glucose** and **oxygen** (for respiration). It also needs to **remove waste products** from every cell to avoid damaging itself.

1) In **single-celled** organisms, these substances can **diffuse directly** into (or out of) the cell across the cell surface membrane. The diffusion rate is quick because of the small distances the substances have to travel (see p. 54).

2) In **multicellular** animals, diffusion across the outer membrane is **too slow**, for several reasons:

- Some cells are deep **within the body** — there's a big distance between them and the **outside environment**.

- Larger animals have a **low surface area to volume ratio** — it's difficult to exchange **enough** substances to supply a **large volume of animal** through a relatively **small outer surface**.

- Multicellular organisms have a **higher metabolic rate** than single-celled organisms, so they use up oxygen and glucose faster.

So rather than using straightforward diffusion to absorb and excrete substances, multicellular animals need specialised **exchange surfaces** — like the **alveoli** in the **lungs**...

# Specialised Exchange Surfaces

## Exchange Surfaces Have *Special Features* to *Improve* their *Efficiency*

### Most Exchange Surfaces Have A *Large Surface Area*...

A root hair cell

#### Example — ROOT HAIR CELLS

1) The cells on plant roots grow into long '**hairs**' which stick out into the soil. Each branch of a root will be covered in **millions** of these microscopic hairs.

2) This gives the roots a **large surface area**, which helps to **increase** the **rate** of **absorption** of **water** (by osmosis) and **mineral ions** (by active transport) from the soil.

### ...They're also *Thin*...

An alveolus

capillary endothelium

alveolar space

$O_2$

$CO_2$

alveolar epithelium

blood capillary

#### Example — the ALVEOLI

1) The **alveoli** are the **gas exchange surface** in the **lungs**.

2) Each alveolus is made from a **single layer** of **thin, flat cells** called the **alveolar epithelium**.

3) $O_2$ **diffuses out** of the alveolar space into the blood. $CO_2$ diffuses in the **opposite direction**.

4) The thin alveolar epithelium helps to **decrease the distance** over which $O_2$ and $CO_2$ diffusion takes place, which **increases** the **rate** of diffusion (see p. 54).

### ...And They Have a *Good Blood Supply* and/or *Ventilation*

#### Example 1 — ALVEOLI

1) The alveoli are surrounded by a **large capillary network**, giving **each alveolus** its **own blood supply**. The blood constantly **takes oxygen away** from the alveoli, and brings **more carbon dioxide**.

2) The **lungs** are also **ventilated** (you breathe in and out — see page 72) so the **air** in each alveolus is **constantly replaced**.

3) These features help to **maintain concentration gradients** of $O_2$ and $CO_2$.

> There's more on how a concentration gradient is maintained in fish gills on page 74.

#### Example 2 — FISH GILLS

1) The **gills** are the **gas exchange surface** in fish. In the gills, $O_2$ and $CO_2$ are exchanged between the fish's **blood** and the surrounding **water**.

2) Fish gills contain a **large network of capillaries** — this keeps them **well-supplied** with **blood**. They're also **well-ventilated** — **fresh water** constantly **passes over** them. These features help to maintain a **concentration gradient** of $O_2$ — **increasing** the **rate** at which $O_2$ diffuses into the blood.

### Practice Questions

Q1 Name four substances an organism needs to exchange with its environment.

Q2 How do the surface area to volume ratios of large and small organisms differ?

**Exam Questions**

Q1 Give two ways in which the alveoli are adapted for efficient gas exchange. [2 marks]

Q2 Nutrients such as amino acids are absorbed into the bloodstream in the small intestine. Cells in the wall of the small intestine are covered in microvilli. Microvilli are tiny extensions of the plasma membrane. Suggest how microvilli increase the efficiency of nutrient absorption in the small intestine. [2 marks]

## *Cube hippos... very Picasso...*

*I know you've just got to the end of a page, but it would be a pretty smart idea to have another look at diffusion on page 54. It'll help these pages make much more sense — all I can think about at the moment is cube hippos.*

# The Gaseous Exchange System in Mammals

*The gaseous exchange system in mammals consists of the lungs, plus a few related tubes, muscles, etc., all enclosed in a protective ribcage. You need to know how it all works...*

## In Mammals the Lungs are Exchange Organs

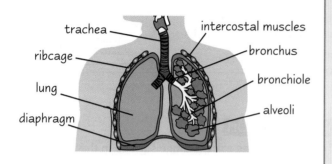

- trachea
- ribcage
- lung
- diaphragm
- intercostal muscles
- bronchus
- bronchiole
- alveoli

1) As you breathe in, air enters the trachea (windpipe).
2) The trachea splits into two bronchi — one bronchus leading to each lung.
3) Each bronchus then branches off into smaller tubes called bronchioles.
4) The bronchioles end in small 'air sacs' called alveoli (see previous page) where gases are exchanged.
5) The ribcage, intercostal muscles and diaphragm all work together to move air in and out (see page 72).

*There are actually three layers of intercostal muscles. You need to know about two of them (the internal and external intercostal muscles — see p. 72) for your exam. We've only shown one layer here for simplicity.*

## Structures in the Gaseous Exchange System Have Different Functions

The gaseous exchange system is made up of different **cells** and **tissues**. These help it to exchange gases **efficiently**.

1) **Goblet cells** (lining the airways) secrete **mucus**. The mucus **traps** microorganisms and dust particles in the inhaled air, stopping them from reaching the alveoli.

goblet cell    cilia

2) **Cilia** (on the surface of cells lining the airways) **beat** the **mucus**. This **moves** the mucus (plus the trapped microorganisms and dust) upward away from the alveoli towards the throat, where it's swallowed. This helps **prevent lung infections**.

3) **Elastic fibres** in the walls of the trachea, bronchi, bronchioles and alveoli help the process of **breathing out** (see p. 72). On breathing in, the lungs inflate and the elastic fibres are **stretched**. Then, the fibres **recoil** to help push the air out when exhaling.

*Derek was quickly mastering efficient gaseous exchange.*

4) **Smooth muscle** in the walls of the trachea, bronchi and bronchioles allows their **diameter to be controlled**. During exercise the smooth muscle **relaxes**, making the tubes **wider**. This means there's **less resistance** to airflow and air can move in and out of the lungs more easily.

5) **Rings of cartilage** in the walls of the trachea and bronchi **provide support**. It's strong but flexible — it stops the trachea and bronchi **collapsing** when you breathe in and the pressure drops (see p. 72).

- trachea
- rings of cartilage

# The Gaseous Exchange System in Mammals

## The Different **Parts** are Found in **Different Places** in the System

| Part of the lung | Cross section | Cartilage | Smooth muscle | Elastic fibres | Goblet cells | Epithelium |
|---|---|---|---|---|---|---|
| trachea | smooth muscle / elastic fibres / c-shaped cartilage / ciliated epithelium | large C-shaped pieces | ✓ | ✓ | ✓ | ciliated |
| bronchi | smooth muscle / small cartilage pieces / elastic fibres / ciliated epithelium | smaller pieces | ✓ | ✓ | ✓ | ciliated |
| larger bronchiole | smooth muscle and elastic fibres | none | ✓ | ✓ | ✓ | ciliated |
| smaller bronchiole | | none | ✓ | ✓ | ✗ | ciliated |
| smallest bronchiole | ciliated epithelium | none | ✗ | ✓ | ✗ | no cilia |
| alveoli | blood capillary / elastic fibres / alveolar epithelium | none | ✗ | ✓ | ✗ | no cilia |

## Practice Questions

Q1 What is the function of goblet cells in the mammalian gas exchange system?

Q2 Describe the distribution of smooth muscle in the mammalian gas exchange system.

Q3 Describe the distribution of ciliated epithelium in the mammalian gas exchange system.

### Exam Questions

Q1  A student is observing a dissection of a pig's lungs.

a)  The student is given the pig's trachea, a bronchus and a larger bronchiole. Apart from the differences in size, explain how the student will be able to tell the trachea, bronchus and bronchiole apart. [3 marks]

b)  The student is given two tissue samples. One was taken from one of the smallest bronchioles and one was taken from a larger bronchiole. The student looks at each sample under the microscope. Suggest one way in which the student will be able to tell the two samples apart. [1 mark]

Q2 a)  Smoking destroys the elastic fibres in the walls of the alveoli. Suggest and explain what effect this will have on the process of breathing out. [2 marks]

b)  Smoking also destroys cilia in the gaseous exchange system. Suggest two problems this could cause. [2 marks]

---

## Rings of cartilage — I prefer mine in gold... with diamonds...

*There's a fair bit to learn on these two pages. Copying out my beautiful blue table will help — and then you can write out what the function of each part is. You won't be coughing and spluttering in the exam once you know this lot.*

# Ventilation in Mammals

*If you're in need of inspiration then there's plenty on this page... sadly I'm only talking about the kind of inspiration that gets air into your lungs — if you want the other sort head over to the Grand Canyon.*

## Ventilation in Mammals is Breathing In and Out

Ventilation can also mean 'changing air' in general. Fish gills are ventilated, but fish don't breathe in and out like we do.

**Ventilation** consists of **inspiration** (breathing in) and **expiration** (breathing out).
It's controlled by the movements of the **diaphragm**, **internal** and **external intercostal muscles** and **ribcage**.

### Inspiration

1) The **external intercostal** and **diaphragm muscles contract**.

2) This causes the **ribcage** to move **upwards and outwards** and the **diaphragm** to **flatten, increasing the volume** of the thorax (the space where the lungs are).

3) As the volume of the thorax increases the **lung pressure decreases** (to below atmospheric pressure).

4) This causes air to flow **into the lungs**.

5) Inspiration is an **active process** — it requires **energy**.

air flows in

volume increases, air pressure decreases

external intercostal muscles contract, causing ribs to move outwards and upwards

diaphragm muscles contract, causing diaphragm to move downwards and flatten

### Expiration

air is forced out

volume reduces, air pressure increases

external intercostal muscles relax, causing ribs to move inwards and downwards

diaphragm muscles relax, causing diaphragm to become curved again

1) The **external intercostal** and **diaphragm muscles relax**.

2) The **ribcage** moves **downwards and inwards** and the **diaphragm** becomes **curved** again.

3) The thorax volume **decreases**, causing the **air pressure** to **increase** (to above atmospheric pressure).

4) Air is forced **out of the lungs**.

5) Normal expiration is a **passive process** — it **doesn't** require energy.

6) Expiration can be **forced** though (e.g. if you want to blow out the candles on your birthday cake). During forced expiration, the **internal intercostal muscles contract**, to **pull the ribcage down** and **in**.

## Tidal Volume is the Volume of Air in a Normal Breath

Here are some terms that you need to know about breathing:

1) **Tidal volume (TV)** — the volume of air in **each breath** — usually about **0.4 dm³**.

2) **Vital capacity** — the **maximum** volume of air that can be breathed **in** or **out**.

3) **Breathing rate** — **how many** breaths are taken — usually in a minute.

4) **Oxygen consumption** or **oxygen uptake** — the rate at which an organism **uses up** oxygen (e.g. the number of dm³ used per minute).

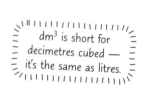

dm³ is short for decimetres cubed — it's the same as litres.

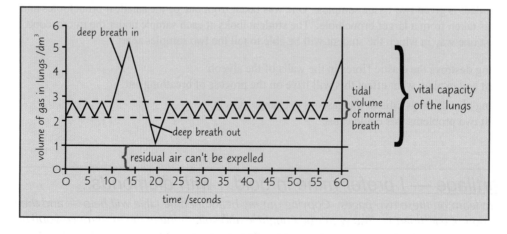

# Ventilation in Mammals

## Spirometers Can be Used to Investigate Breathing

A spirometer is a machine that can give readings of **tidal volume**, **vital capacity**, **breathing rate** and **oxygen uptake**.

1) A spirometer has an **oxygen-filled** chamber with a **movable lid**.

2) The person breathes through a **tube** connected to the oxygen chamber.

3) As the person breathes in and out, the lid of the chamber moves **up and down**.

4) These movements can be recorded by a **pen** attached to the lid of the chamber — this writes on a **rotating drum**, creating a **spirometer trace**. Or the spirometer can be hooked up to a **motion sensor** — this will use the movements to produce **electronic signals**, which are picked up by a **data logger**.

5) The **soda lime** in the tube the subject breathes into absorbs **carbon dioxide**.

The **total volume of gas** in the chamber **decreases** over time. This is because the air that's breathed out is a **mixture** of oxygen and carbon dioxide. The carbon dioxide is absorbed by the **soda lime** — so there's **only oxygen** in the chamber which the subject inhales from. As this oxygen gets **used up** by respiration, the **total volume decreases**.

## You Need to be Able to Analyse Data from a Spirometer

*This graph looks different to the one on the previous page because it shows the volume of air in the spirometer, not in the lungs.*

In the exam, you might have to work out **breathing rate**, **tidal volume**, **vital capacity** and **oxygen consumption** from a spirometer trace. For example:

1) In this trace, the **breathing rate** in the first minute is **10 breaths per minute** (there are 10 'peaks' in the first minute).

2) The **tidal volume** may change from time to time, but in this trace it's about **0.5 dm³**.

3) The graph shows a **vital capacity** of **2.65 dm³**.

4) **Oxygen consumption** is the **decrease** in the **volume of gas** in the **spirometer chamber**. It can be read from the graph by taking the **average slope** of the trace. In this case, it drops by 0.7 dm³ in the first minute — so, oxygen consumption is **0.7 dm³/min**.

## Practice Questions

Q1 What is meant by tidal volume and vital capacity?

Q2 Describe how a spirometer can be used to measure oxygen uptake.

**Exam Question**

Q1 Describe the changes that take place in the human thorax during inspiration. [5 marks]

## Investigate someone's breathing — make sure they've had a mint first...

*I thought spirometers were those circular plastic things you draw crazy patterns with... apparently not. I know the graphs don't look that approachable, but it's important you understand what the squiggly lines show, and the four terms used when investigating breathing — I'd bet my right lung there'll be a question on spirometer graphs in the exam.*

# Ventilation in Fish and Insects

*If you're squeamish, you might want to brace yourself for this topic. You do need to know it all though...*

## Fish Use a Counter-Current System for Gas Exchange

There's a **lower concentration** of oxygen in water than in air. So **fish** have special **adaptations** to get enough of it.

1) Water, containing oxygen, enters the fish through its **mouth** and passes out through the **gills** (see below).

2) Each gill is made of lots of **thin branches** called **gill filaments** or **primary lamellae**, which give a **big surface area** for **exchange of gases**. The gill filaments are covered in lots of tiny structures called **gill plates** or **secondary lamellae**, which **increase the surface area** even more. Each gill is supported by a **gill arch**.

3) The gill plates have lots of **blood capillaries** and a **thin surface layer of cells** to speed up diffusion.

vessels (oxygenated blood from the gill)
gill plate / secondary lamella (plural = lamellae)
artery (deoxygenated blood to gill)
gill arch
gill filaments / primary lamellae

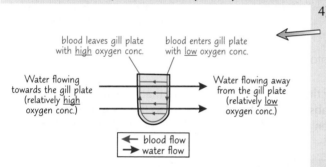

blood leaves gill plate with <u>high</u> oxygen conc.
blood enters gill plate with <u>low</u> oxygen conc.

Water flowing towards the gill plate (relatively <u>high</u> oxygen conc.)
Water flowing away from the gill plate (relatively <u>low</u> oxygen conc.)

← blood flow
→ water flow

4) **Blood** flows through the gill plates in one direction and **water** flows over in the opposite direction. This is called a **counter-current system**. It maintains a **large concentration gradient** between the water and the blood. The **concentration of oxygen** in the **water** is always **higher** than that in the **blood**, so as much oxygen as possible diffuses from the water into the blood.

oxygen concentration
water
blood
distance along gill plate

## You Need to Know How Fish Gills are Ventilated

Here's how the gills are usually ventilated in **bony fish**:

1) The fish **opens** its **mouth**, which **lowers** the **floor** of the **buccal cavity** (the space inside the mouth). The **volume** of the buccal cavity **increases**, **decreasing** the **pressure** inside the cavity. **Water** is then **sucked in** to the cavity.

2) When the fish **closes** its **mouth**, the **floor** of the **buccal cavity** is **raised again**. The **volume** inside the cavity **decreases**, the **pressure increases**, and **water** is **forced out** of the cavity **across the gill filaments**.

3) Each gill is covered by a **bony flap** called the **operculum** (which protects the gill). The **increase** in **pressure** forces the operculum on each side of the head to **open**, allowing **water** to **leave the gills**.

*Bony fish include salmon and cod. Unsurprisingly, they have a skeleton made of bone — not all fish do.*

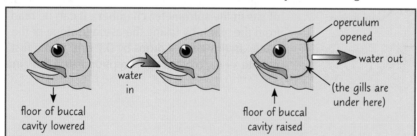

water in
floor of buccal cavity lowered

water in
floor of buccal cavity raised

operculum opened
water out
(the gills are under here)

*In some bony fish, the operculum bulges out (increasing the volume of the cavity behind the operculum) just after the floor of the buccal cavity lowers. This contributes to the decrease in pressure that causes water to enter the fish's mouth.*

## You Need to Know How to Dissect Fish Gills

1) First up, fish dissection is **messy** so make sure you're wearing an **apron** or **lab coat**, and **gloves**.

2) Place your chosen fish (something like a perch or salmon works well) in a **dissection tray** or on a **cutting board**.

3) **Push back** the **operculum** and use **scissors** to carefully **remove the gills**. Cut each **gill arch** through the bone at the **top** and **bottom**. They should look a bit like this:

4) If you look closely, you should be able to see the **gill filaments**.

5) Finish off by **drawing** the gill and **labelling** it.

A single gill arch

gill filaments

HERVE CONGE, ISM/SCIENCE PHOTO LIBRARY

# Ventilation in Fish and Insects

## Insects use *Tracheae* to *Exchange Gases*

1) Insects have microscopic air-filled pipes called **tracheae** which they use for gas exchange.

   *'Tracheae' is the plural of 'trachea'.*

2) Air moves into the tracheae through pores on the insect's surface called **spiracles**.

3) **Oxygen** travels down the **concentration gradient** towards the **cells**. **Carbon dioxide** from the cells moves down its own concentration gradient towards the **spiracles** to be **released** into the atmosphere.

4) The tracheae branch off into smaller **tracheoles** which have **thin, permeable walls** and go to individual cells. The tracheoles also contain **fluid**, which oxygen **dissolves** in.

5) When the insect is **active**, it **respires more** and the **concentration** of solutes in its **cells increases**. The **fluid** in the **tracheoles** is then **drawn into** the respiring cells by **osmosis** — leaving the tracheoles filled with $O_2$ gas. The oxygen then **diffuses directly** into the respiring cells — the insect's circulatory system doesn't transport $O_2$.

6) Insects use **rhythmic abdominal movements** to **change** the **volume** of their bodies and **move air in** and **out** of the spiracles. When larger insects are **flying**, they use their **wing movements** to **pump** their **thoraxes** too.

*tracheae and tracheoles give large surface area*

*spiracle*

*thorax*  *abdomen*  *trachea*

*tracheole lined with single layer of cells to minimise diffusion distance*

*$CO_2$ diffuses into tracheoles*

*$O_2$ diffuses into respiring cells*

## You Can *Dissect* the *Gaseous Exchange System* in *Insects* too

**Big insects** like **grasshoppers** or **cockroaches** are usually **best** for dissecting because they're easier to handle. For dissection, you'll need to use an insect that's been **humanely killed** fairly recently.

1) First fix the insect to a **dissecting board**. You can put **dissecting pins** through its legs to hold it in place.

2) To examine the **tracheae**, you'll need to carefully **cut** and **remove** a piece of **exoskeleton** (the insect's hard outer shell) from along the length of the insect's **abdomen**.

3) Use a syringe to fill the abdomen with **saline solution**. You should be able to see a network of **very thin, silvery-grey tubes** — these are the **tracheae**. They look silver because they're **filled** with **air**.

4) You can examine the tracheae under a **light microscope** using a **wet mount slide** (see page 18). Again, the tracheae will appear silver or grey. You should also be able to see **rings** of **chitin** in the walls of the **tracheae** — these are there for **support** (like the rings of cartilage in a human trachea).

*Some live insects, e.g. grasshoppers, can cause allergic reactions in some people. They need to be handled carefully.*

## Practice Questions

Q1 What is the function of the gill filaments and gill plates in fish gills?

Q2 What is the advantage to fish of having a counter-current exchange system in their gills?

Q3 Name the structures on an insect's surface that allow air to enter the tracheae.

Q4 Describe the structure of an insect's tracheoles.

### Exam Questions

Q1 A student is examining grasshopper tracheae under the microscope.

a) The tracheae were taken from a preserved grasshopper specimen. The grasshopper was killed some time ago and kept in a liquid preservative. The tracheae do not appear silver under the microscope, instead they are a dark grey. Suggest why this is the case. [1 mark]

b) The tracheae are surrounded by rings of chitin. What is their function? [1 mark]

Q2 Salmon are bony fish. Explain how water is drawn into the salmon's mouth during ventilation. [4 marks]

## *Keep revising and you'll be on the right trachea...*

*Ventilation in fish is actually a lot like ventilation in mammals. In fish, when the volume of the buccal cavity is increased, the pressure drops and water rushes in. In mammals, it's the volume of the lungs that's increased, and they fill with air instead of water, but the principle is the same. Lucky for you really because it should make all this easier to learn.*

# Circulatory Systems

*Right then, this section's all about blood and hearts and veins and things, so if that's not up your street, then prepare to feel queasy. Unfortunately for you, it's all really important for the exams. And besides, without a circulatory system you'd probably have some issues when it comes to things like... ooh I dunno... living.*

## Multicellular Organisms need Transport Systems

1) As you saw on page 68, **single-celled** organisms can get substances that they need by **diffusion** across their outer membrane.

2) If you're **multicellular** though, it's a bit **harder** to supply all your cells with everything they need — multicellular organisms are relatively **big**, they have a **low surface area to volume ratio** and a **higher metabolic rate** (the speed at which chemical reactions take place in the body).

3) A lot of multicellular organisms (e.g. mammals) are also **very active**. This means that a **large number of cells** are all **respiring very quickly**, so they need a constant, rapid supply of glucose and oxygen.

4) To make sure that every cell has a good enough supply, multicellular organisms need a **transport system**.

5) In mammals, this is the **circulatory system**, which uses **blood** to carry glucose and oxygen around the body. It also carries hormones, antibodies (to fight disease) and waste (like $CO_2$).

## Fish and Mammals have Different Circulatory Systems

Not all organisms have the same type of circulatory system — **fish** have a **single circulatory system** and **mammals** have a **double circulatory system**.

1) In a **single** circulatory system, blood only passes through the heart **once** for each complete circuit of the body.

2) In a **double** circulatory system, the blood passes through the heart **twice** for each complete circuit of the body.

| Fish |
| --- |

In **fish**, the **heart** pumps blood to the **gills** (to pick up oxygen) and then on through the **rest of the body** (to deliver the oxygen) in a single circuit.

Single you say? How interesting. Now pass us the tartare sauce...

| Mammals |
| --- |

In **mammals**, the heart is **divided** down the middle, so it's really like **two** hearts joined together.

1) The **right side** of the heart pumps blood to the **lungs** (to pick up oxygen).

2) From the lungs it travels to the **left side** of the heart, which pumps it to the rest of the **body**.

3) When blood **returns** to the heart, it enters the right side again.

So, our circulatory system is really two linked loops. One sends blood to the lungs — this is called the **pulmonary** system, and the other sends blood to the rest of the body — this is called the **systemic** system.

The right and left sides of the heart are reversed in the diagram because it's the right and left of the person the heart belongs to.

An **advantage** of the mammalian double circulatory system is that the heart can give the blood an **extra push** between the lungs and the rest of the body. This makes the blood travel **faster**, so oxygen is delivered to the tissues **more quickly**.

# Circulatory Systems

## Circulatory Systems can be Open or Closed

All vertebrates (e.g. fish and mammals) have **closed circulatory systems** — the blood is **enclosed** inside **blood vessels**.

1) The heart pumps blood into **arteries**. These **branch out** into millions of **capillaries** (see p. 78).
2) Substances like oxygen and glucose **diffuse** from the blood in the capillaries into the body cells, but the blood **stays inside** the blood vessels as it circulates.
3) **Veins** take the blood back to the heart.

Some invertebrates (e.g. insects) have an **open circulatory system** — blood **isn't enclosed** in blood vessels all the time. Instead, it flows freely through the **body cavity**.

1) The heart is **segmented**. It **contracts** in a **wave**, starting from the back, pumping the blood into a **single main artery**.
2) That artery **opens up** into the body cavity.
3) The blood flows around the insect's **organs**, gradually making its way back into the heart segments through a series of **valves**.

The circulatory system supplies the insect's cells with nutrients, and transports things like hormones around the body. It **doesn't supply** the insect's cells with **oxygen** though — this is done by a system of tubes called the **tracheal system** (see p. 75 for more).

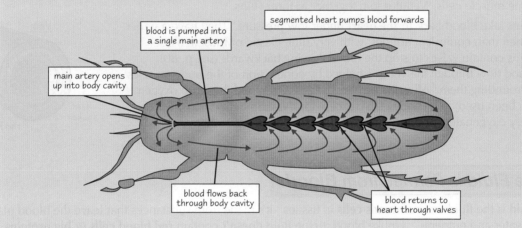

blood is pumped into a single main artery

segmented heart pumps blood forwards

main artery opens up into body cavity

blood flows back through body cavity

blood returns to heart through valves

## Practice Questions

Q1 Give three reasons why multicellular organisms usually need a transport system, but unicellular organisms don't.

Q2 Explain why the mammalian circulatory system is described as a double circulatory system.

Q3 What is an open circulatory system?

**Exam Questions**

Q1 Explain why the circulatory system of a trout is described as being closed. [1 mark]

Q2 Briefly describe the circulatory system of a beetle. [2 marks]

Q3 The Atlantic salmon (*Salmo salar)* and the red fox *(Vulpes vulpes)* have circulatory systems. Describe one way in which the circulatory system of the Atlantic salmon is:

a) similar to that of the red fox. [1 mark]

b) different from that of the red fox. [1 mark]

## OK, open circulatory systems are officially grim. Body cavities?! Bleurgh...

*After reading this page, we can all finally put to rest the idea that the Earth will eventually be overrun by giant insects. Their circulatory system just isn't up to it you see... All the nutrients and stuff in their blood have to diffuse through the whole body cavity, so if they were giant they wouldn't be able to supply all their organs and bits and pieces properly...*

# Blood Vessels

*Watch out — now you need to learn about all the bits and bobs that make up that useful circulatory system of yours...*

## Blood Vessels Transport Substances Round the Body

The five types of blood vessel that you need to know about are **arteries**, **arterioles**, **capillaries**, **venules** and **veins**:

1) **Arteries** carry blood **from** the heart **to** the rest of the body. Their walls are thick and **muscular** and have elastic tissue to **stretch** and **recoil** as the heart beats, which helps maintain the **high pressure**. The inner lining (**endothelium**) is **folded**, allowing the artery to **expand** — this also helps it to maintain the high pressure. All arteries carry oxygenated blood except for the **pulmonary arteries**, which take deoxygenated blood to the lungs.

2) Arteries branch into **arterioles**, which are **much smaller** than arteries. Like arteries, arterioles have a layer of **smooth muscle**, but they have less elastic tissue. The **smooth muscle** allows them to **expand** or **contract**, thus controlling the amount of blood flowing to tissues.

3) Arterioles branch into **capillaries**, which are the **smallest** of the blood vessels. Substances like glucose and oxygen are exchanged between cells and capillaries, so they're adapted for **efficient diffusion**, e.g. their walls are only **one cell thick**.

4) Capillaries connect to **venules**, which have very **thin walls** that can contain some muscle cells. Venules join together to form veins.

5) **Veins** take blood **back to the heart** under low pressure. They have a **wider lumen** than equivalent arteries, with very little elastic or muscle tissue. Veins contain **valves** to stop the blood flowing backwards (see p. 80). Blood flow through the veins is helped by contraction of the **body muscles** surrounding them. All veins carry **deoxygenated** blood (because oxygen has been used up by body cells), except for the **pulmonary veins**, which carry oxygenated blood to the heart from the lungs.

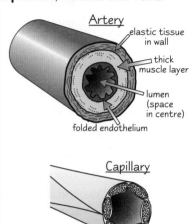

Artery
elastic tissue in wall
thick muscle layer
lumen (space in centre)
folded endothelium

Capillary
endothelium (one cell thick)

Vein
large lumen
endothelium
thin muscle wall

## Tissue Fluid is Formed from Blood

**Tissue fluid** is the fluid that **surrounds cells** in tissues. It's made from substances that leave the blood plasma, e.g. oxygen, water and nutrients. (Unlike blood, tissue fluid **doesn't** contain **red blood cells** or **big proteins**, because they're **too large** to be pushed out through the capillary walls.) Cells take in oxygen and nutrients from the tissue fluid, and release metabolic waste into it. In a **capillary bed** (the network of capillaries in an area of tissue), substances move out of the capillaries, into the tissue fluid, by **pressure filtration**:

1) At the start of the capillary bed, nearest the arteries, the **hydrostatic (liquid) pressure** inside the capillaries is **greater** than the hydrostatic pressure in the tissue fluid. This difference in hydrostatic pressure **forces fluid out** of the **capillaries** and into the **spaces** around the cells, forming tissue fluid.

2) As fluid leaves, the hydrostatic pressure reduces in the capillaries — so the hydrostatic pressure is much **lower** at the **end** of the capillary bed that's nearest to the venules.

3) There is another form of pressure at work here called **oncotic pressure** — this is generated by **plasma proteins** present in the capillaries which lower the water potential. At the venule end of the capillary bed, the water potential in the capillaries is **lower** than the water potential in the tissue fluid due to the **fluid loss** from the capillaries and the **high oncotic pressure**. This means some **water re-enters** the capillaries from the tissue fluid at the venule end by **osmosis**.

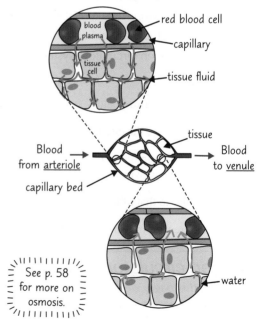

red blood cell
capillary
blood plasma
tissue cell
tissue fluid

tissue
Blood from arteriole
capillary bed
Blood to venule

water

*See p. 58 for more on osmosis.*

# Blood Vessels

## Excess Tissue Fluid Drains into the Lymph Vessels

Not all of the tissue fluid **re-enters** the capillaries at the venule end of the capillary bed — some **excess tissue fluid** is left over. This extra fluid eventually gets returned to the blood through the **lymphatic system** — a kind of **drainage** system, made up of **lymph vessels**.

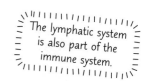
The lymphatic system is also part of the immune system.

1) The smallest lymph vessels are the **lymph capillaries**.

2) Excess tissue fluid passes into lymph vessels. Once inside, it's called **lymph**.

3) **Valves** in the lymph vessels stop the lymph going **backwards**.

4) Lymph gradually moves towards the main lymph vessels in the **thorax** (chest cavity). Here, it's returned to the **blood**, near the **heart**.

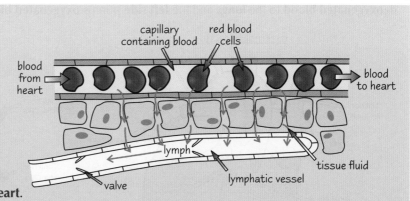

## You Need to Know the Differences Between Blood, Tissue Fluid and Lymph

Blood, tissue fluid and lymph are all quite **similar** — **tissue fluid** is formed from **blood**, and **lymph** is formed from **tissue fluid**. The main differences are shown in the table.

|  | blood | tissue fluid | lymph | comment |
|---|---|---|---|---|
| **red blood cells** | ✓ | ✗ | ✗ | Red blood cells are too big to get through capillary walls into tissue fluid. |
| **white blood cells** | ✓ | very few | ✓ | Most white blood cells are in the lymph system. They only enter tissue fluid when there's an infection. |
| **platelets** | ✓ | ✗ | ✗ | Only present in tissue fluid if the capillaries are damaged. |
| **proteins** | ✓ | very few | only antibodies | Most plasma proteins are too big to get through capillary walls. |
| **water** | ✓ | ✓ | ✓ | Tissue fluid and lymph have a higher water potential than blood. |
| **dissolved solutes** | ✓ | ✓ | ✓ | Solutes (e.g. salt) can move freely between blood, tissue fluid and lymph. |

## Practice Questions

Q1 Is the blood pressure highest in veins or arteries?

Q2 Explain the differences between blood, tissue fluid and lymph.

**Exam Questions**

Q1 The diameter of different types of blood vessel are shown on the right. Select the row that shows the most appropriate diameter for each type of blood vessel.

| Type of blood vessel and its diameter | | | |
|---|---|---|---|
| | Artery | Arteriole | Capillary | Vein |
| A | 13 mm | 8 μm | 2 cm | 200 μm |
| B | 8 μm | 2 cm | 200 μm | 13 mm |
| C | 200 μm | 13 mm | 2 cm | 8 μm |
| D | 2 cm | 200 μm | 8 μm | 13 mm |

[1 mark]

Q2 At the arteriole end of a capillary bed the hydrostatic pressure is 5.1 kPa in a capillary and 0.13 kPa in the space around the cells. Explain the effect this has on the movement of fluid between the capillary and cell space. [2 marks]

## Tissue fluid... Imagine draining the fluid out of a used tissue. Urrrgh.

*That table looks a bit terrifying, but a lot of it's pretty obvious when you think about it — there can't be any red blood cells floating around loose in your tissues, otherwise you'd be bright red. And platelets are the bits that cause blood clots, so they're going to be in your blood... In fact, proteins and white blood cells are the only tricky bits.*

# The Heart

*You saw on page 76 that mammals have a double circulatory system — well that means that our hearts have to be a bit more complicated than just a big old pump.*

## The **Heart** Consists of **Two Muscular Pumps**

The diagrams below show the **internal** and **external structure** of the heart. The **right side** of the heart pumps **deoxygenated blood** to the **lungs** and the **left side** pumps **oxygenated blood** to the **rest of the body**.

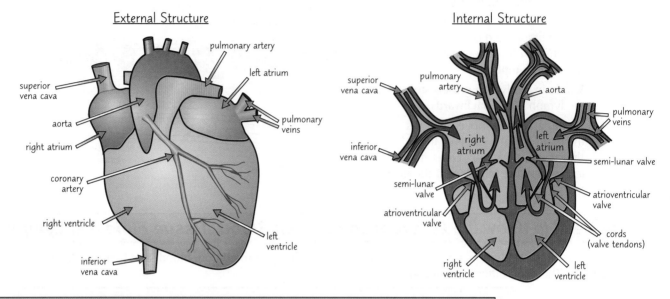

External Structure

Internal Structure

## *Valves* in the Heart **Prevent** Blood Flowing the **Wrong Way**

The **atrioventricular valves** link the atria to the ventricles, and the **semi-lunar** valves link the ventricles to the pulmonary artery and aorta — they all stop blood flowing the **wrong way**. Here's how they work:

1) The **valves** only open one way — whether they're open or closed depends on the **relative pressure** of the heart chambers.

2) If there's higher pressure **behind** a valve, it's **forced open**.

3) If pressure is higher **in front** of the valve, it's **forced shut**.

lower pressure

higher pressure

valve open

higher pressure

lower pressure

valve closed

## You Need to be Able to Carry Out a **Heart Dissection**

**Equipment:** You'll need a **pig or cow's heart**, a **dissecting tray**, a **scalpel**, an **apron** and **lab gloves**.

**External examination:** Look at the outside of the heart and try to identify the **four main vessels** attached to it. **Feel inside** the vessels to help you — remember arteries are thick and rubbery, whereas veins are much thinner.

Identify the right and left **atria**, the right and left **ventricles** and the **coronary arteries**. Draw a **sketch** of the outside of the heart with labels.

**Internal examination:** **Cut** along the lines shown on the diagram to **look inside** each ventricle. **Measure** and **record** the **thickness** of the ventricle walls and note any **differences** between them.

**Cut** open the **atria** and **look inside** them too. Note whether the **atria walls** are thicker or thinner than the ventricle walls.

Find the **atrioventricular valves**, followed by the **semi-lunar valves**. Look at the **structure** of the valves.

Draw a **sketch** to show the valves and the inside of the ventricles and atria.

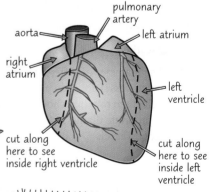

The left ventricle wall is thicker and more muscular than the right, to push blood all the way round the body. Also, the ventricles have thicker walls than the atria because they have to push blood out of the heart.

# The Heart

## The **Cardiac Cycle** Pumps Blood Round the Body

The cardiac cycle is an ongoing sequence of **contraction** and **relaxation** of the atria and ventricles that keeps blood **continuously circulating** round the body. The **volumes** of the atria and ventricles **change** as they contract and relax, altering the **pressure** in each chamber. This causes **valves** to open and close, which directs the **blood flow** through the heart. The cardiac cycle can be simplified into three stages:

**1** Ventricles relax, atria contract

The **ventricles are relaxed**. The **atria contract**, which decreases their volume and **increases** their **pressure**. This **pushes** the blood into the ventricles through the **atrioventricular valves**. There's a slight **increase** in **ventricular pressure** and **volume** as the **ventricles receive the ejected blood** from the contracting atria.

**2** Ventricles contract, atria relax

The **atria relax**. The **ventricles contract** (decreasing their volume), **increasing** their **pressure**. The pressure becomes **higher** in the ventricles than the atria, which forces the **atrioventricular valves shut** to prevent back-flow. The high pressure in the ventricles **opens** the semi-lunar valves — blood is forced out into the **pulmonary artery** and **aorta**.

**3** Ventricles relax, atria relax

The **ventricles and the atria both relax**. The higher pressure in the pulmonary artery and aorta causes the semi-lunar valves to **close**, preventing back-flow. The **atria fill** with blood (**increasing** their **pressure**) due to the higher pressure in the vena cava and pulmonary vein. As the ventricles continue to **relax**, their **pressure falls below the pressure in the atria**. This causes the **atrioventricular valves** to **open** and blood flows **passively** (without being pushed by atrial contraction) into the ventricles from the atria. The atria contract, and the whole process begins again.

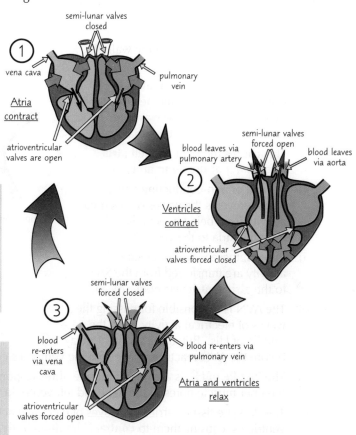

If you listen to a human heartbeat you can hear a 'lub-dub' sound. The first '**lub**' sound is caused by the **atrioventricular valves closing** (stage 2). The second '**dub**' sound is caused by the **semi-lunar valves closing** (stage 3).

## Practice Questions

Q1 Which chamber of the heart receives blood from the lungs?

Q2 What causes the second 'dub' sound of the heart?

**Exam Question**

Q1 The graph shows the pressure changes in the left side of the heart during one heartbeat.

a) At which labelled point (A-H) on the graph does:

  i) the semi-lunar valve open? [1 mark]

  ii) the atrioventricular valve close? [1 mark]

b) On the diagram, sketch the graph that you would expect for the right ventricle. [2 marks]

---

## *Apparently an adult heart is the size of two fists. Two whole fists! Huge!*

*Thank goodness for heart valves I say — they stop everything shooting backwards and they mean that the heart makes a cool sound every time it beats. Make sure you know everything on these two pages off by heart...*

# Heart Activity

*You don't have to think about making your heart beat — your body does it for you.*
*So you couldn't stop it beating even if for some strange reason you wanted to.  Which is nice to know.*

## Cardiac Muscle Controls the Regular Beating of the Heart

Cardiac (heart) muscle is '**myogenic**' — it can contract and relax without receiving signals from nerves.
This pattern of contractions controls the **regular heartbeat**.

1) The process starts in the **sino-atrial node (SAN)**, which is in the wall of the **right atrium**.

2) The SAN is like a pacemaker — it sets the **rhythm** of the heartbeat by sending out regular **waves of electrical activity** to the atrial walls.

3) This causes the right and left **atria** to **contract at the same time**.

4) A band of non-conducting **collagen tissue** prevents the waves of electrical activity from being passed directly from the atria to the ventricles.

5) Instead, these waves of electrical activity are transferred from the SAN to the **atrioventricular node (AVN)**.

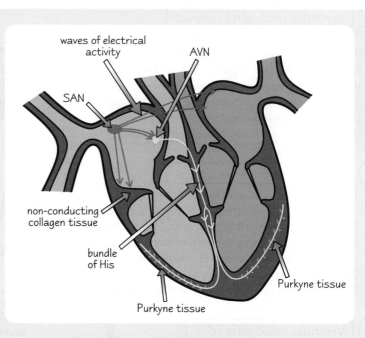

6) The AVN is responsible for passing the waves of electrical activity on to the bundle of His.  But, there's a **slight delay** before the AVN reacts, to make sure the ventricles contract **after** the atria have emptied.

7) The **bundle of His** is a group of muscle fibres responsible for conducting the waves of electrical activity to the finer muscle fibres in the right and left ventricle walls, called the **Purkyne tissue**.

8) The Purkyne tissue carries the waves of electrical activity into the muscular walls of the right and left ventricles, causing them to **contract simultaneously**, from the bottom up.

## An Electrocardiograph Records the Electrical Activity of the Heart

A doctor can check someone's **heart function** using an **electrocardiograph** — a machine that **records the electrical activity** of the heart.  The heart muscle **depolarises** (loses electrical charge) when it **contracts**, and **repolarises** (regains charge) when it **relaxes**. An electrocardiograph records these changes in electrical charge using **electrodes** placed on the chest.

The trace produced by an electrocardiograph is called an **electrocardiogram**, or **ECG**.  A **normal** ECG looks like this:

When Ed did that special thing to her beak, Polly's heart activity increased 10-fold.

1) The **P wave** is caused by **contraction** (depolarisation) of the **atria**.

2) The main peak of the heartbeat, together with the dips at either side, is called the **QRS complex** — it's caused by **contraction** (depolarisation) of the **ventricles**.

3) The **T wave** is due to **relaxation** (repolarisation) of the **ventricles**.

4) The **height** of the wave indicates how much electrical charge is passing through the heart — a **bigger wave** means more electrical charge, so (for the P and R waves) a bigger wave means a **stronger contraction**.

# Heart Activity

## *Doctors use ECGs to Diagnose Heart Problems*

Doctors **compare** their patients' ECGs with a **normal trace**. This helps them to diagnose any heart problems.

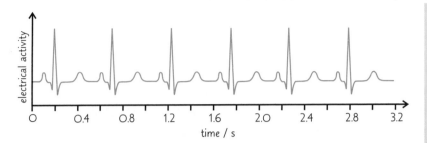

This heartbeat is **too fast** — around 120 beats per minute. It's called **tachycardia**. That might be OK during **exercise**, but at **rest** it shows that the heart **isn't pumping blood efficiently**. A heartbeat can also be **too slow** — below 60 beats per minute at rest. This is called **bradycardia**.

The 5th heartbeat on this ECG is an **ectopic heartbeat** — an 'extra' heartbeat. Here it's caused by an **earlier contraction of the atria** than in the previous heartbeats (you can see that the P wave is different and that it comes earlier than it should). However, it can be caused by **early contraction of the ventricles** too. Occasional ectopic heartbeats in a healthy person don't cause a problem.

early contraction of atria

This is **fibrillation** — a really **irregular heartbeat**. The atria or ventricles completely **lose their rhythm** and **stop contracting properly**. It can result in anything from chest pain and fainting to lack of pulse and death.

## *Practice Questions*

Q1  What prevents impulses from the atria travelling straight into the ventricles?

Q2  What is the name of the structure that picks up impulses from the atria and passes them on to the ventricles?

Q3  What causes the QRS part of an ECG trace?

**Exam Questions**

Q1  Describe the function of:

    a)  the sino-atrial node. [1 mark]

    b)  the Purkyne tissue. [1 mark]

Q2  Suggest the cause of an ECG which has a QRS complex that is not as high as normal. [2 marks]

---

## *The cardiac cycle — a bewilderingly complicated pump-action bicycle...*

*It's pretty incredible that your heart manages to go through all those stages in the right order, at exactly the right time, without getting it even slightly wrong. It does it perfectly, about 70 times every minute. That's about 100 800 times a day. If only my brain was that efficient. I'd have all this revision done in five minutes, then I could go and watch TV...*

# Haemoglobin

*Aaagh, complicated topic alert. Don't worry though, because your poor, over-worked brain cells will recover from the brain-strain of these pages thanks to haemoglobin. So the least you can do is learn how it works.*

## Oxygen is Carried Round the Body as Oxyhaemoglobin

1) **Red blood cells** contain **haemoglobin** (Hb).

2) Haemoglobin is a large **protein** with a **quaternary** structure (see pages 27 and 28 for more) — it's made up of **more than one** polypeptide chain (**four** of them in fact).

*'Affinity' for oxygen means tendency to combine with oxygen.*

3) Each chain has a **haem group** which contains **iron** and gives haemoglobin its **red** colour.

4) Haemoglobin has a **high affinity for oxygen** — each molecule can carry **four oxygen molecules**.

5) In the lungs, oxygen **joins** to the **iron** in haemoglobin to form **oxyhaemoglobin**.

6) This is a **reversible reaction** — when oxygen leaves oxyhaemoglobin (**dissociates** from it) near the body cells, it turns back to haemoglobin.

$$Hb + 4O_2 \rightleftharpoons HbO_8$$

haemoglobin + oxygen $\rightleftharpoons$ oxyhaemoglobin

## Haemoglobin Saturation Depends on the Partial Pressure of Oxygen

1) The **partial pressure** of **oxygen** ($pO_2$) is a measure of **oxygen concentration**. The **greater** the concentration of dissolved oxygen in cells, the **higher** the partial pressure.

2) Similarly, the **partial pressure** of **carbon dioxide** ($pCO_2$) is a measure of the concentration of $CO_2$ in a cell.

3) Haemoglobin's **affinity** for oxygen **varies** depending on the **partial pressure** of **oxygen**:

> Oxygen **loads onto** haemoglobin to form oxyhaemoglobin where there's a **high** $pO_2$.
> Oxyhaemoglobin **unloads** its oxygen where there's a **lower** $pO_2$.

4) Oxygen enters blood capillaries at the **alveoli** in the **lungs**. Alveoli have a **high** $pO_2$ so oxygen **loads onto** haemoglobin to form oxyhaemoglobin.

5) When **cells respire**, they use up oxygen — this **lowers** the $pO_2$. Red blood cells deliver oxyhaemoglobin to respiring tissues, where it unloads its oxygen.

6) The haemoglobin then returns to the lungs to pick up more oxygen.

There was no use pretending — the partial pressure of $CH_4$ had just increased, and Keith knew who was to blame.

## Dissociation Curves Show How Affinity for Oxygen Varies

An oxygen **dissociation curve** shows how **saturated** the haemoglobin is with oxygen at any given partial pressure.

*100% saturation means every haemoglobin molecule is carrying the maximum of 4 molecules of oxygen.*

Dissociation Curve for Adult Human Haemoglobin

% saturation of haemoglobin with oxygen

partial pressure of $O_2$ / kPa

*0% saturation means none of the haemoglobin molecules are carrying any oxygen.*

Where $pO_2$ is high (e.g. in the lungs), haemoglobin has a **high affinity** for oxygen (i.e. it will **readily combine** with oxygen), so it has a **high saturation** of oxygen.

Where $pO_2$ is low (e.g. in respiring tissues), haemoglobin has a **low affinity** for oxygen, which means it **releases oxygen** rather than combines with it. That's why it has a **low saturation** of oxygen.

1) The graph is 'S-shaped' because when haemoglobin (Hb) combines with the **first $O_2$ molecule**, its **shape alters** in a way that makes it **easier** for other molecules to join too.

2) But as the Hb starts to become saturated, it gets **harder** for more oxygen molecules to join.

3) As a result, the curve has a **steep** bit in the middle where it's really easy for oxygen molecules to join, and **shallow** bits at each end where it's harder. When the curve is steep, a **small change in** $pO_2$ causes a **big change** in the **amount of oxygen** carried by the Hb.

# Haemoglobin

## Fetal Haemoglobin has a Higher Affinity for Oxygen than Adult Haemoglobin

Adult haemoglobin and fetal haemoglobin have different affinities for oxygen. Fetal haemoglobin
has a **higher affinity** for oxygen (the fetus's blood is **better at absorbing** oxygen than its mother's blood)
at the **same partial pressure** of oxygen. This is really important:

1) The fetus gets oxygen from its **mother's blood** across the placenta.
2) By the time the mother's blood reaches the placenta, its oxygen saturation has **decreased** (because some has been used up by the mother's body).
3) For the fetus to get **enough oxygen** to survive its haemoglobin has to have a **higher affinity** for oxygen (so it takes up enough).
4) If its haemoglobin had the **same** affinity for oxygen as adult haemoglobin its blood **wouldn't** be **saturated enough**.

## Carbon Dioxide Concentration Affects Oxygen Unloading

To complicate matters, haemoglobin gives up its oxygen **more readily** at **higher partial pressures of carbon dioxide**
($pCO_2$). It's a cunning way of getting more oxygen to cells during activity. When cells respire they produce carbon
dioxide, which raises the $pCO_2$, increasing the rate of oxygen unloading. The reason for this is linked to how $CO_2$
affects blood pH.

1) Most of the $CO_2$ from respiring tissues diffuses into red blood cells. Here it reacts with **water** to form **carbonic acid**, catalysed by the enzyme **carbonic anhydrase**. (The rest of the $CO_2$, around 10%, binds directly to haemoglobin and is carried to the lungs.)
2) The carbonic acid **dissociates** (splits up) to give **hydrogen ($H^+$) ions** and **hydrogencarbonate ($HCO_3^-$) ions**.
3) This increase in $H^+$ ions causes oxyhaemoglobin to **unload** its oxygen so that haemoglobin can take up the $H^+$ ions. This forms a compound called **haemoglobinic acid**. (This process also stops the hydrogen ions from increasing the cell's acidity.)
4) The $HCO_3^-$ ions diffuse out of the red blood cells and are **transported in the blood plasma**. To compensate for the loss of $HCO_3^-$ ions from the red blood cells, **chloride ($Cl^-$) ions** diffuse into the red blood cells. This is called the **chloride shift** and it prevents any change in pH that could affect the cells.
5) When the blood reaches the **lungs** the low $pCO_2$ causes some of the $HCO_3^-$ and $H^+$ ions to **recombine into $CO_2$** (and water).
6) The $CO_2$ then diffuses into the **alveoli** and is breathed out.

When carbon dioxide levels increase, the
dissociation curve 'shifts' right, showing
that more oxygen is released from the
blood (because the lower the saturation
of haemoglobin with $O_2$, the more $O_2$ is
released). This is called the Bohr effect.

## Practice Questions

Q1 How many oxygen molecules can each haemoglobin molecule carry?

Q2 What is carbon dioxide converted to in red blood cells?

**Exam Question**

Q1 Which statement correctly describes the Bohr effect?

 A When $pCO_2$ increases, less $O_2$ is released from the blood and the $O_2$ dissociation curve shifts right.
 B When $pCO_2$ increases, more $O_2$ is released from the blood and the $O_2$ dissociation curve shifts right.
 C When $pCO_2$ increases, less $O_2$ is released from the blood and the $O_2$ dissociation curve shifts left.
 D When $pCO_2$ increases, more $O_2$ is released from the blood and the $O_2$ dissociation curve shifts left. [1 mark]

## The Bore effect — it's happening right now...

*Dissociation graphs can be a bit confusing — but basically, when tissues contain lots of oxygen (i.e. $pO_2$ is high),
haemoglobin readily combines with the oxygen, so the blood has a high saturation of oxygen (and vice versa when $pO_2$
is low). Simple. Also, make sure you get the lingo right, like 'partial pressure' and 'affinity' — hey, I'm hip, I'm groovy.*

# Xylem and Phloem

*A whole section on transport in plants... just what I always dreamed of...*

## Multicellular Plants Need Transport Systems

*Plants also need carbon dioxide, but this enters at the leaves (where it's needed).*

1) Plants need substances like **water**, **minerals** and **sugars** to live. They also need to **get rid of waste substances**.

2) Like animals, plants are **multicellular** — so they have a **small surface area : volume ratio** (SA:V, see page 68). They're also relatively **big** with a relatively **high metabolic rate**.

3) Exchanging substances by **direct diffusion** (from the outer surface to the cells) would be **too slow** to meet their metabolic needs.

4) So plants **need transport systems** to move substances to and from individual cells **quickly**.

## Two Types of Tissue are Involved in Transport in Plants

1) **Xylem tissue** transports **water** and **mineral ions** in solution. These substances move **up** the plant from the roots to the leaves. **Phloem tissue** mainly transports **sugars** (also in solution) both **up and down** the plant.

2) Xylem and phloem make up a plant's **vascular system**. They are found **throughout** a plant and **transport materials** to all parts. **Where** they're found in each part is connected to the **xylem's** other function — **support**:

- In a **root**, the xylem is in the **centre** surrounded by phloem to **provide support** for the root as it **pushes** through the soil.
- In the **stems**, the xylem and phloem are **near the outside** to provide a sort of 'scaffolding' that reduces bending.
- In a **leaf**, xylem and phloem make up a **network of veins** which support the thin leaves.

Root cross-section — root hair, xylem, phloem

*These diagrams all show the xylem and phloem in 'herbaceous dicotyledonous plants' — basically just flowering plants without a woody stem.*

Leaf cross-section — xylem, vein, phloem

Stem cross-section — phloem, xylem

3) The position of the xylem and phloem in the root, leaf and stem are shown in these **transverse cross-sections**. Transverse means the sections cut through each structure at a **right angle** to its **length**.

4) You can also get **longitudinal** cross-sections. These are taken **along the length** of a structure. For example, this cross-section shows where the **xylem** and **phloem** are located in a **typical stem**.

phloem, xylem (on inside)

## Xylem Vessels are Adapted for Transporting Water and Mineral Ions

Xylem is a **tissue** made from several **different cell types** (see page 66). You need to learn about **xylem vessels** — the part of xylem tissue that actually transports the water and ions. Xylem vessels are adapted for their **function**:

1) Xylem vessels are very **long, tube-like** structures formed from cells (**vessel elements**) joined end to end.

2) There are **no end walls** on these cells, making an **uninterrupted tube** that allows water to pass up through the middle easily.

3) The cells are **dead**, so they contain **no cytoplasm**.

4) Their walls are **thickened** with a **woody substance** called **lignin**, which helps to **support** the xylem vessels and stops them **collapsing inwards**. Lignin can be deposited in xylem walls in different ways, e.g. in a **spiral** or as **distinct rings**.

5) The amount of lignin **increases** as the cell gets **older**.

6) **Water** and **ions** move **into** and **out of** the vessels through **small pits** in the walls where there's **no lignin**.

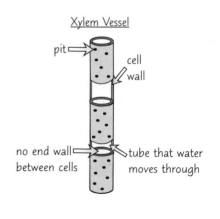

Xylem Vessel — pit, cell wall, no end wall between cells, tube that water moves through

# Xylem and Phloem

## Phloem Tissue is Adapted for Transporting Solutes

1) Phloem tissue transports **solutes** (dissolved substances), mainly sugars like sucrose, round plants.
2) Like xylem, phloem is formed from cells arranged in **tubes**.
   But, unlike xylem, it's purely a **transport tissue** — it **isn't** used for support as well.
3) Phloem tissue contains **phloem fibres**, **phloem parenchyma**, **sieve tube elements** and **companion cells**.
4) **Sieve tube elements** and **companion cells** are the most important cell types in phloem for **transport**:

Phloem tissue — longitudinal cross-section

Transverse view

| **1** | Sieve tube elements |
|---|---|

1) These are **living cells** that form the tube for **transporting solutes** through the plant.
2) They are joined **end to end** to form **sieve tubes**.
3) The 'sieve' parts are the **end walls**, which have lots of **holes** in them to allow **solutes** to pass through.
4) Unusually for living cells, sieve tube elements have **no nucleus**, a **very thin** layer of **cytoplasm** and **few organelles**.
5) The cytoplasm of adjacent cells is **connected** through the holes in the sieve plates.

| **2** | Companion cells |
|---|---|

1) The **lack** of a **nucleus** and **other organelles** in sieve tube elements means that they **can't survive** on their own. So there's a **companion cell** for **every** sieve tube element.
2) Companion cells carry out the living functions for **both** themselves and their sieve cells. For example, they provide the **energy** for the **active transport** of solutes.

*The active transport of solutes requires energy (see p. 56).*

## You Need to be Able to Dissect Plant Stems

You can **look at plant tissue** (e.g. part of a plant stem) under a **microscope**, and then **draw** it. But first you need to **dissect** the plant and **prepare** a section of the tissue. You can do this using the following method:

1) Use a **scalpel** (or razor blade) to cut a **cross-section** of the stem (transverse or longitudinal). Cut the sections as **thinly** as possible — thin sections are better for viewing under a microscope.
2) Use **tweezers** to gently place the cut sections in **water** until you come to use them. This stops them from **drying out**.
3) Transfer each section to a dish containing a **stain**, e.g. **toluidine blue O (TBO)**, and leave for one minute. TBO stains the **lignin** in the walls of the xylem vessels **blue-green**. This will let you see the **position** of the xylem vessels and examine their **structure**.
4) **Rinse off** the sections in water and **mount** each one onto a slide (see page 18).

*You can use different stains to highlight different parts of the cells.*

## Practice Questions

Q1 Why do multicellular plants need transport systems?
Q2 What is the name of the substance that thickens the walls of xylem vessels?
Q3 What is the function of companion cells?

**Exam Question**

Q1 Explain two ways in which the structure of the xylem vessels makes them well-adapted to their function. [4 marks]

---

## *Sieve tube — WLTM like-minded cell for long-term companionship...*

*Sieve tube elements sound a bit feeble to me — not being able to survive on their own, and all that. Anyway, some of the structures and functions of the cell types covered here are quite similar, so it's important you learn them properly. You don't want to mix up your sieve tube elements with your vessel elements in the exam — you'd never forgive yourself...*

# Water Transport

*Water enters a plant through its roots and eventually, if it's not used, exits via the leaves. "Ah-ha", I hear you say, "but how does it flow upwards, against gravity?" Well that, my friends, is a mystery that's about to be explained...*

## *Water* Enters a Plant through its *Root Hair Cells*

1) Water has to get from the **soil**, through the **root** and into the **xylem** to be transported around the plant.

2) Water enters through **root hair cells** and then passes through **the root cortex**, including the **endodermis**, to reach the xylem (see below).

3) Water is drawn into the roots via **osmosis**. This means it travels down a **water potential gradient**:

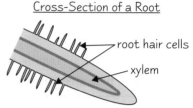

<u>Cross-Section of a Root</u>

root hair cells

xylem

- Water always moves from areas of **higher water potential** to areas of **lower water potential** — it goes down a **water potential gradient**.

- The **soil** around roots generally has a **high water potential** (i.e. there's lots of water there) and **leaves** have a **lower water potential** (because water constantly **evaporates** from them).

- This creates a water potential gradient that keeps water moving through the plant in the right direction, **from roots (high) to leaves (low)**.

Remember: osmosis is the diffusion of water molecules across a partially permeable membrane, from an area of higher water potential to an area of lower water potential — see p. 58.

## Water *Moves* Through the *Root* into the *Xylem*...

Water travels through the **roots** (via the **root cortex**) into the **xylem** by **two** different paths:

1) The **symplast pathway** — goes through the **living** parts of cells — the **cytoplasm**. The cytoplasms of neighbouring cells connect through **plasmodesmata** (small channels in the cell walls). Water moves through the symplast pathway via **osmosis**.

2) The **apoplast pathway** — goes through the **non-living** parts of the cells — the **cell walls**. The walls are very absorbent and water can simply **diffuse** through them, as well as pass through the spaces between them. The water can carry **solutes** and move from areas of **high hydrostatic pressure** to areas of **low hydrostatic pressure** (i.e. along a pressure gradient). This is an example of **mass flow** (see page 92).

The prison had been strangely quiet ever since plasmodesmata were installed.

- When water in the **apoplast pathway** gets to the **endodermis** cells in the root, its path is blocked by a **waxy strip** in the cell walls, called the **Casparian strip**. Now the water has to take the **symplast pathway**.

- This is useful, because it means the water has to go through a **cell membrane**. Cell membranes are **partially permeable** and are able to **control** whether or not substances in the water get through (see p. 50).

- Once past this barrier, the water moves into the **xylem**.

3) Both pathways are used, but the main one is the **apoplast pathway** because it provides the **least resistance**.

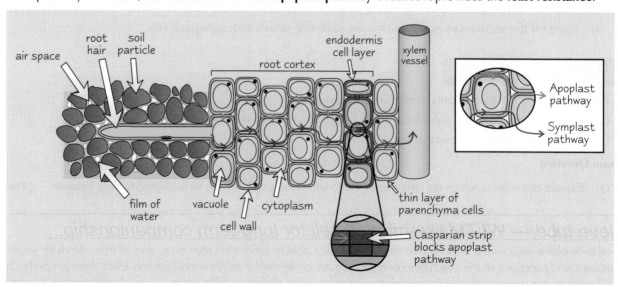

air space

root hair

soil particle

root cortex

endodermis cell layer

xylem vessel

Apoplast pathway

Symplast pathway

film of water

vacuole

cytoplasm

cell wall

thin layer of parenchyma cells

Casparian strip blocks apoplast pathway

# Water Transport

## ...then *Up* the *Xylem* and *Out* at the *Leaves*

1) **Xylem vessels** transport the water **all around** the plant.

2) At the **leaves**, water leaves the xylem and moves into the cells mainly by the **apoplast pathway**.

3) Water **evaporates** from the cell walls into the **spaces** between cells in the leaf.

4) When the **stomata** (tiny pores in the surface of the leaf) open, the water **diffuses** out of the leaf (down the **water potential gradient**) into the **surrounding air**.

5) The loss of water from a plant's surface is called **transpiration** (see next page).

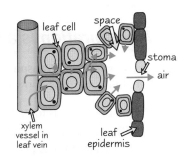

## *Water Moves* **Up** *a Plant* **Against** *the Force of* **Gravity**

The movement of water from **roots to leaves** is called the **transpiration stream**. The **mechanisms** that **move** the water include **cohesion, tension** and **adhesion**.

**Cohesion** and **tension** help water move up plants, from roots to leaves, **against** the force of gravity.

1) Water **evaporates** from the **leaves** at the 'top' of the xylem (**transpiration**).

2) This creates a **tension** (**suction**), which pulls more water into the leaf.

3) Water molecules are **cohesive** (they **stick together**) so when some are pulled into the leaf others follow. This means the whole **column** of water in the **xylem**, from the leaves down to the roots, **moves upwards**.

4) **Water** enters the stem through the **root cortex cells**.

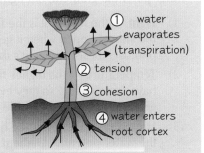

① water evaporates (transpiration)
② tension
③ cohesion
④ water enters root cortex

**Adhesion** is also partly responsible for the **movement of water**.

1) As well as being attracted to each other, water molecules are **attracted to the walls** of the xylem vessels.

2) This helps water to **rise up** through the xylem vessels.

*Cohesion and tension allow the mass flow of water over long distances up the stem.*

## Practice Questions

Q1 In terms of water potential, why does water move into the roots from the soil?

Q2 Describe how water moves through a plant root via the symplast pathway.

Q3 What is the Casparian strip?

Q4 How does adhesion help to move water through a plant?

**Exam Questions**

Q1 Explain the role of cohesion and tension in the loss of water from the leaves of plants. [4 marks]

Q2 Plants that are infected by a pathogen are able to block their plasmodesmata. This is thought to be an attempt to reduce the spread of the pathogen. Suggest how this would affect the way that water travels through a plant. [2 marks]

## *So many routes through the roots...*

*As you've probably noticed, there are lots of impressive biological words on these pages that you can amaze your friends with. Go over the pages again, and whenever you see a word like plasmodesmata, stop and check you know exactly what it means. (Personally I think they should just call them cell wall channels, but nobody ever listens to me.)*

# Transpiration

*Plants can't sing, juggle or tap dance (as you will hopefully be aware). But they can exchange gases — how exciting. What makes it all the more thrilling though is that they lose water vapour as they do it. Gripping stuff.*

## Transpiration is a Consequence of Gas Exchange

So you know that **transpiration** is the evaporation of **water** from a plant's surface, especially the **leaves**. But I bet you didn't know it happens as a result of **gas exchange**. Read on...

1)  A plant needs to **open** its **stomata** to let in **carbon dioxide** so that it can produce **glucose** (by **photosynthesis**).

2)  But this **also lets water out** — there's a **higher concentration** of water **inside** the leaf than in the air **outside**, so water moves **out** of the leaf down the **water potential gradient** when the stomata open.

3)  So transpiration's really a **side effect** of the gas exchange needed for photosynthesis.

## Four Main Factors Affect Transpiration Rate

Temperature, humidity and wind all alter the **water potential gradient**, but **light** is a bit different:

*Water moves from areas of higher water potential to areas of lower water potential — it moves down the water potential gradient.*

1)  <u>Light</u> — the **lighter** it is the **faster** the **transpiration rate**. This is because the **stomata open** when it gets **light**, so $CO_2$ can diffuse into the leaf for photosynthesis. When it's **dark** the stomata are usually **closed**, so there's little transpiration.

2)  <u>Temperature</u> — the **higher the temperature** the **faster** the **transpiration rate**. Warmer water molecules have more energy so they **evaporate** from the cells inside the leaf **faster**. This **increases** the **water potential gradient** between the inside and outside of the leaf, making water **diffuse** out of the leaf **faster**.

3)  <u>Humidity</u> — the <u>lower</u> the **humidity**, the **faster** the **transpiration rate**. If the air around the plant is **dry**, the **water potential gradient** between the leaf and the air is **increased**, which increases transpiration.

4)  <u>Wind</u> — the **windier** it is, the **faster** the **transpiration rate**. Lots of air movement **blows away** water molecules from around the stomata. This **increases** the water potential gradient, which increases the rate of transpiration.

## A Potometer can be Used to Estimate Transpiration Rate

A **potometer** is a special piece of apparatus used to **estimate transpiration rates**. It actually measures **water uptake** by a plant, but it's **assumed** that water uptake by the plant is **directly related** to **water loss** by the **leaves**. You can use it to estimate how different factors **affect** the transpiration rate.

A potometer

Reservoir of water used to return bubble to start for repeats.

As the plant takes up water, the air bubble moves along the scale.

water moves this way

Tap is shut off during experiment.

capillary tube with a scale

bubble moves this way

beaker of water

*The air bubble is sometimes called the air-water meniscus.*

Here's what you'd do:

1)  **Cut** a **shoot underwater** to prevent air from entering the xylem. Cut it at a **slant** to increase the surface area available for water uptake.

2)  Assemble the potometer **in water** and insert the shoot **underwater**, so no air can enter.

3)  Remove the apparatus from the water but keep the **end of the capillary tube submerged** in a beaker of water.

4)  Check that the apparatus is **watertight** and **airtight**.

5)  **Dry** the leaves, allow time for the shoot to **acclimatise**, and then **shut the tap**.

6)  Remove the end of the capillary tube from the beaker of water until **one air bubble** has formed, then put the end of the tube back into the water.

7)  Record the **starting position** of the **air bubble**.

8)  Start a **stopwatch** and record the **distance** moved by the bubble **per unit time**, e.g. per hour. The **rate of air bubble movement** is an estimate of the **transpiration rate**.

9)  Remember, only change **one variable** (e.g. temperature) at a time. All other **conditions** (e.g. light, humidity) must be kept **constant**.

# Transpiration

## Xerophytic Plants are Adapted to Reduce Water Loss

**Xerophytes** are plants like **cacti** and **marram grass** (which grows on sand dunes). They're **adapted** to live in **dry climates**. Their adaptations prevent them **losing too much water** by **transpiration**...

1) Marram grass has **stomata** that are sunk in **pits**, so they're **sheltered from the wind**. This helps to slow transpiration down.

2) It also has a layer of **'hairs'** on the epidermis — this **traps moist air** round the stomata, which **reduces** the water potential gradient between the leaf and the air, **slowing** transpiration down.

3) In hot or windy conditions **marram grass** plants roll their leaves — again this **traps moist air**, slowing down transpiration. It also reduces the **exposed surface area** for losing water and protects the stomata from wind.

4) Both marram grass and cacti have a **thick, waxy layer** on the epidermis — this **reduces** water loss by evaporation because the layer is **waterproof** (water can't move through it).

5) Cacti have **spines** instead of leaves — this reduces the **surface area** for water loss.

6) Cacti also **close** their **stomata** at the hottest times of the day when transpiration rates are the **highest**.

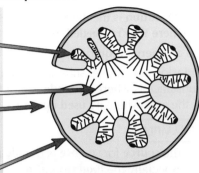

Cross-section through a marram grass leaf.

Cacti spines          Marram grass

## Hydrophilic Plants are Adapted to Survive in Water

**Hydrophytes** are plants like **water lilies**, which live in **aquatic habitats**. As they **grow in water**, they **don't need** adaptations **to reduce water loss** (like xerophytes), but they do need adaptations to help them cope with a **low oxygen level**. Here are some adaptations of hydrophytes...

1) **Air spaces** in the tissues help the plants to **float** and can act as a **store of oxygen** for use in respiration. For example, **water lilies** have **large air spaces** in their **leaves**. This allows the leaves to **float on the surface** of the water, **increasing** the amount of **light** they receive. Air spaces in the **roots** and **stems** allow **oxygen** to move from the floating leaves down to parts of the plant that are **underwater**.

2) **Stomata** are usually only present on the **upper surface** of **floating leaves**. This helps **maximise gas exchange**.

3) Hydrophytes often have **flexible leaves and stems** — these plants are **supported** by the **water** around them, so they don't need rigid stems for support. Flexibility helps to **prevent damage** by water currents.

## Practice Questions

Q1 Explain why transpiration is a consequence of gaseous exchange.

Q2 Name a piece of apparatus used to measure transpiration.

Q3 What is a hydrophyte?

**Exam Question**

Q1 The diagram shows a section of a leaf of a xerophytic plant. Describe and explain two ways, visible in the picture, in which this leaf is adapted to reduce water loss.     [4 marks]

Inside leaf     Stoma

Outside leaf

## *Xerophytes — an exciting word for a boring subject...*

*Actually, that's unfair. It's taken millions of years for plants to evolve those adaptations, and here I am slagging them off. When I've managed to develop a thick waxy cuticle on my leaves and stems, then I can comment, and not before.*

# Translocation

*Translocation is the movement of dissolved solutes through a plant. Annoyingly, translocation sounds a lot like transpiration. Or is that just me? Make sure you don't get them confused.*

## Translocation is the Movement of Dissolved Substances

1) **Translocation** is the **movement** of dissolved substances (e.g. sugars like sucrose, and amino acids) to **where they're needed** in a plant. Dissolved substances are sometimes called **assimilates**.

2) It's an **energy-requiring** process that happens in the **phloem** (see p.87 for more on the phloem).

3) Translocation moves substances from '**sources**' to '**sinks**'. The **source** of a substance is **where it's made** (so it's at a **high concentration** there). The **sink** is the area where it's **used up** (so it's at a **lower concentration** there).

> Sugars are transported as sucrose because sucrose is both soluble and metabolically inactive — so it doesn't get used up during transport.

> **EXAMPLE**
>
> The **source** for **sucrose** is usually the **leaves** (where it's made), and the **sinks** are the **other parts** of the plant, especially the **food storage organs** and the **meristems** (areas of growth) in the roots, stems and leaves.

4) Some parts of a plant can be both a **sink** and a **source**.

> **EXAMPLE**
>
> Sucrose can be **stored** in the **roots**. During the **growing season**, sucrose is transported from the roots to the **leaves** to provide the leaves with **energy** for **growth**. In this case, the **roots** are the **source** and the **leaves** are a **sink**.

Howard liked a bit of translocation in his spare time.

5) **Enzymes** maintain a **concentration gradient** from the source to the sink by **changing** the dissolved substances at the **sink** (e.g. by breaking them down or making them into something else). This makes sure there's always a **lower concentration** at the sink than at the source.

> **EXAMPLES**
>
> In **potatoes**, **sucrose** is converted to **starch** in the **sink** areas, so there's always a **lower concentration** of sucrose **at the sink** than inside the phloem. This makes sure a **constant supply** of new sucrose reaches the sink from the phloem. In other sinks, enzymes such as invertase **break down sucrose** into **glucose** (and fructose) for use by the plant — again this makes sure there's a **lower concentration** of sucrose **at the sink**.

## The Mass Flow Hypothesis Best Explains Phloem Transport

Scientists still aren't certain **exactly how** the dissolved substances (solutes) are transported from source to sink by **translocation**. The best supported theory is the **mass flow hypothesis**:

**(1)**
1) Active transport is used to **actively load** the **solutes** (e.g. sucrose from photosynthesis) into the **sieve tubes** of the phloem at the **source** (e.g. the **leaves**). There's more on this on the next page.

2) This **lowers** the **water potential** inside the **sieve tubes**, so **water** enters the tubes by **osmosis** from the **xylem** and **companion cells**.

3) This creates a **high pressure** inside the sieve tubes at the **source end** of the phloem.

**(2)**
1) At the **sink** end, **solutes** are removed from the phloem to be used up.

2) This **increases** the **water potential** inside the sieve tubes, so water also leaves the tubes by **osmosis**.

3) This **lowers the pressure** inside the sieve tubes.

**(3)**
1) The result is a **pressure gradient** from the **source** end to the **sink** end.

2) This gradient pushes solutes along the sieve tubes to where they're needed.

**① SOURCE**
low water potential, high pressure

Water enters from xylem

water flow

solute flow

sieve plate

plasmodesma

Water flows to xylem

companion cell

HIGH

Pressure gradient forces sap down.

③

LOW

solute (e.g. sucrose)

**② SINK**
high water potential, low pressure

# Translocation

## Substances Enter the Phloem at the Source by Active Loading

1) Active loading is used to move substances into the **companion cells** from **surrounding tissues**, and from the companion cells into the **sieve tubes**, **against** a **concentration gradient**.

2) The **concentration** of **sucrose** is usually **higher** in the **companion cells** than the **surrounding tissue cells**, and **higher** in the **sieve tube cells** than the companion cells.

3) So sucrose is moved to where it needs to go using **active transport** and **co-transporter proteins**. Here's how it works:

> Active transport uses energy to move substances against their concentration gradient — see p. 56.

- In the **companion cell**, ATP is used to **actively transport hydrogen ions (H⁺) out of** the cell and into surrounding tissue cells.

- This sets up a **concentration gradient** — there are **more H⁺ ions** in the **surrounding tissue** than in the **companion cell**.

- An **H⁺** ion binds to a **co-transport protein** in the companion cell membrane and **re-enters the cell** (down the concentration gradient).

- A **sucrose molecule** binds to the co-transport protein **at the same time**. The movement of the H⁺ ion is used to move the sucrose molecule **into the cell**, against its concentration gradient.

- Sucrose molecules are then transported out of the companion cells and into the **sieve tubes** by the same process.

sucrose

companion cell

movement of H⁺

movement of sucrose

ATP is one of the products of **respiration**. The **breakdown** of **ATP** supplies the initial **energy** needed for the **active transport** of the H⁺ ions.

## Practice Questions

Q1 Explain the terms source and sink in connection with translocation.

Q2 Explain how the process of active loading increases the concentration of sucrose in companion cells.

**Exam Question**

Q1 A student has set up an experimental model of mass flow as shown in the diagram.

top tube

SOURCE
concentrated sugar solution

flow of solution

SINK
weak sugar solution

selectively permeable membranes

A

B

Water in          bottom tube          Water out

a) Explain how the concentrated sugar solution is forced to flow along the top tube. [3 marks]

b) i) What part of a plant does the top tube represent? [1 mark]

   ii) The bottom tube only transports water. What part of the plant does this tube represent? [1 mark]

## Human mass flow — running out of the hall at the end of an exam...

*The mass flow hypothesis is just the best theory that scientists have come up with so far. If other evidence came along, a different theory could be developed based on the new findings (see p. 2). However, that doesn't mean that there's no point in learning about it — it could be in your exam. Don't look so sad — what else would you do with your time...*

# Pathogens and Communicable Diseases

*Coughs and sneezes spread diseases, as they say. Well now it's time to find out why...*

## Pathogens Can Cause Communicable Diseases

1) **Disease** is a **condition** that **impairs** the **normal functioning** of an **organism**.
   Both **plants** and **animals** can get diseases.

2) A **pathogen** is an organism that causes **disease**. Types of pathogen include **bacteria**, **viruses**, **fungi** and **protoctista** (a type of single-celled eukaryotic organism).

3) A **communicable disease** is a disease that can **spread between organisms**.

> You might have heard communicable diseases referred to as infectious diseases.

4) You need to **learn all** the **communicable diseases** in the table below, as well as the **pathogens** that cause them:

| Disease: | Affects: | Pathogen Responsible: Bacterium | Virus | Fungus | Protoctist |
|---|---|:---:|:---:|:---:|:---:|
| Tuberculosis (TB) | Animals, typically humans and cattle | ✔ | | | |
| Bacterial meningitis | Humans | ✔ | | | |
| Ring rot | Potatoes, tomatoes | ✔ | | | |
| HIV/AIDS | Humans | | ✔ | | |
| Influenza | Animals, including humans | | ✔ | | |
| Tobacco mosaic virus | Plants | | ✔ | | |
| Black sigatoka | Banana plants | | | ✔ | |
| Ringworm | Cattle | | | ✔ | |
| Athlete's foot | Humans | | | ✔ | |
| Potato/tomato late blight | Potatoes/tomatoes | | | | ✔ |
| Malaria | Animals, including humans | | | | ✔ |

## Communicable Diseases Can be Transmitted Directly or Indirectly

1) **Direct transmission** is when a disease is transmitted **directly** from one organism to another.
   Direct transmission can happen in several ways, including: **droplet infection** (**coughing** or **sneezing** tiny droplets of mucus or saliva directly onto someone), **sexual intercourse**, or **touching** an infected organism.

   **Examples:**
   - **HIV** can be transmitted directly between humans via **sexual intercourse**.
   - **Athlete's foot** can be spread via **touch**.

2) **Indirect transmission** is when a disease is transmitted from one organism to another **via an intermediate**.
   Intermediates include **air**, **water**, **food** or **another organism** (known as a **vector**).

   > Spores are the cells that some organisms use to reproduce asexually, including some protoctista and all fungi.

   **Examples:**
   - **Potato/tomato late blight** is spread when **spores** are carried between plants — first in the **air**, then in **water**.
   - **Malaria** is spread between humans (and other animals) via **mosquitoes** — insects that feed on blood. The mosquitoes act as **vectors** — they don't cause malaria themselves, they just spread the protoctista that cause it.

# Pathogens and Communicable Diseases

## Living Conditions, Climate and Social Factors Affect Disease Transmission

1) **Overcrowded** living conditions **increase** the **transmission** of many communicable diseases.

> **Example:**
>
> **TB** is spread **directly** via **droplet infection** (see previous page). It's also spread **indirectly** because the bacteria can **remain** in the **air** for **long periods** of time and infect new people. The risk of TB infection is **increased** when **lots of people** live **crowded together** in a small space.

2) **Climate** can also affect the spread of communicable diseases.

> **Examples:**
>
> • **Potato/tomato late blight** is especially common during **wet summers** because the **spores** need **water** to **spread** (see previous page).
> • **Malaria** is most common in **tropical countries**, which are **humid** and **hot**. This is because these are the **ideal conditions** for **mosquitoes** (the malaria **vectors**) to **breed**.

3) In **humans**, **social factors** can increase the transmission of communicable diseases.

> **Example:**
>
> The risk of **HIV** infection is high in places where there's **limited access** to:
> • **good healthcare** — people are **less likely** to be **diagnosed** and **treated** for HIV, and the **most effective anti-HIV drugs** are **less likely** to be **available**, so the virus is **more likely** to be **passed on** to others.
> • **good health education** — to **inform people** about how HIV is **transmitted** and how it can be **avoided**, e.g. through **safe-sex practices** like using condoms.

## Practice Questions

Q1 What is a communicable disease?
Q2 Name a virus that affects plants.
Q3 What type of pathogen causes malaria?
Q4 Give one way in which a disease can be transferred directly.
Q5 Give one example of how climate can affect the spread of a disease.

### Exam Questions

Q1 Which of the following pathogens is responsible for causing black sigatoka?
    A bacterium      B virus      C fungus      D protoctista      [1 mark]

Q2 The most common way for the tobacco mosaic virus to be transferred between garden plants is via gardeners' hands and tools.
  a) Is this an example of direct or indirect disease transmission? Explain your answer.    [1 mark]
  b) Suggest one thing that gardeners could do to try to prevent transmission of the tobacco mosaic virus between plants.    [1 mark]

Q3 There are more deaths from tuberculosis in low-income countries than in high-income countries.
  a) What type of pathogen causes tuberculosis?    [1 mark]
  b) Suggest two reasons why more deaths from tuberculosis occur in low-income countries compared to wealthier countries.    [2 marks]

## My computer has a virus — I knew I shouldn't have sneezed on it...

You need to learn all the communicable diseases in the big table, as well as the type of pathogen that causes each one. You also need to learn how diseases can be transmitted, as well as the factors that affect disease transmission. Phew.

# Defence Against Pathogens

*Well, all that stuff about disease is making me feel a bit on edge. Luckily both animals and plants have a few tricks up their sleeves to defend themselves against pathogen invasion...*

## Animals Have Several Barriers to Prevent Infection

1) **Pathogens** need to **enter** an **organism** in order to **cause disease**.

2) So most **animals**, including **humans**, have a range of **primary**, **non-specific defences** to help **prevent** this from happening. These include:

> Non-specific means they work in the same way for all pathogens. There's more on non-specific and specific responses on page 98.

Skin — this acts as a **physical barrier**, **blocking pathogens** from **entering** the body. It also acts as a **chemical barrier** by producing **chemicals** that are **antimicrobial** and can **lower pH**, **inhibiting** the **growth** of pathogens.

Mucous membranes — these **protect body openings** that are **exposed** to the **environment** (such as the mouth, nostrils, ears, genitals and anus). Some membranes **secrete mucus** — a sticky substance that **traps pathogens** and contains **antimicrobial enzymes**.

Blood clotting — a blood clot is a mesh of **protein (fibrin) fibres**. Blood clots **plug wounds** to **prevent pathogen entry** and **blood loss**. They're formed by a series of **chemical reactions** that take place when **platelets** (fragments of cells in the blood) are exposed to **damaged blood vessels**.

Inflammation — the signs of inflammation include **swelling**, **pain**, **heat** and **redness**. It can be triggered by **tissue damage** — the damaged tissue releases **molecules**, which **increase** the **permeability** of the **blood vessels**, so they start to **leak fluid** into the surrounding area. This causes **swelling** and helps to **isolate any pathogens** that may have entered the damaged tissue. The molecules also cause **vasodilation** (widening of the blood vessels), which **increases blood flow** to the affected area. This makes the area **hot** and brings **white blood cells** to the area to fight off any pathogens that may be present.

Wound repair — the **skin** is able to repair itself in the event of **injury** and **re-form** a barrier against pathogen entry. The surface is repaired by the **outer layer of skin cells dividing** and **migrating** to the edges of the wound. The **tissue below the wound** then **contracts** to bring the edges of the wound closer together. It is repaired using **collagen fibres** — too many collagen fibres and you'll end up with a **scar**.

Expulsive reflexes — e.g. **coughing** and **sneezing**. A **sneeze** happens when the **mucous membranes** in the **nostrils** are **irritated** by things such as **dust** or **dirt**. A **cough** stems from **irritation** in the **respiratory tract**. Both coughing and sneezing are an attempt to **expel foreign objects**, including **pathogens**, from the body. They happen **automatically**.

*It was all going so beautifully 'til Josie felt an expulsive reflex coming on.*

If pathogens make it past these defences, they'll have the animal's **immune system** to deal with — see pages 98-101.

# Defence Against Pathogens

## Plants Have Physical Defences Against Pathogens...

Like animals, **plants** have **physical defences** against infection by **pathogens**.

1) Most plant leaves and stems have a **waxy cuticle**, which provides a **physical barrier** against pathogen entry. It may also **stop water** collecting on the leaf, which could reduce the risk of infection by pathogens that are transferred between plants in water.

2) Plant cells themselves are surrounded by **cell walls**. These form a **physical barrier** against pathogens that make it past the waxy cuticle.

3) Plants produce a **polysaccharide** called **callose**. Callose gets **deposited** between **plant cell walls** and **plasma membranes** during times of **stress**, e.g. **pathogen invasion**. Callose deposition may make it **harder** for **pathogens** to **enter cells**. Callose deposition at the **plasmodesmata** (small channels in the cell walls) may **limit the spread** of **viruses** between cells.

## ...as Well as Chemical Ones

1) Plants don't just rely on physical defences. They also produce **antimicrobial chemicals** (including **antibiotics**, see page 104) which **kill pathogens** or **inhibit** their **growth**.

> **Examples:**
> - Some plants produce chemicals called **saponins**. These are thought to **destroy** the **cell membranes** of **fungi** and other pathogens.
> - Plants also produce chemicals called **phytoalexins**, which **inhibit** the **growth** of **fungi** and other pathogens.

2) Other chemicals secreted by plants are **toxic** to **insects** — this reduces the amount of **insect-feeding** on plants and therefore reduces the risk of infection by **plant viruses** carried by **insect vectors**.

## Practice Questions

Q1 Give two ways in which skin helps defend animals against infection by pathogens.

Q2 What is the function of the mucous membranes?

Q3 What are expulsive reflexes?

Q4 Give one example of a plant chemical defence against pathogens.

**Exam Question**

Q1 The tobacco mosaic virus is a virus that affects plants.

a) The virus usually infects plants that have been damaged by feeding insects.
Suggest why damaged plant cells are more susceptible to infection by the virus than normal cells. [2 marks]

b) Suggest one way a plant may respond to limit the spread
of infection once the tobacco mosaic virus enters a plant. [1 mark]

---

## Hiding under the duvet — a student's primary defence against revision...

*Plant defences against pathogens are the "absolute bomb", or so says a colleague of mine. He's very excited by them. You don't need to be excited by them (although it's fine if you are), but you do need to learn them. And all those animal primary defences too. You've got your immune system to learn next. What an absolute treat...*

# The Immune System

*If a pathogen enters the body, the immune system will respond.  Bad luck pathogens...*

## Foreign Antigens *Trigger an* Immune Response

1) **Antigens** are **molecules** (usually proteins or polysaccharides) found on the **surface** of **cells**.

2) When a pathogen (like a bacterium) **invades** the body, the antigens on its cell surface are **identified as foreign**, which **activates cells** in the **immune system**.

3) The immune response involves **specific** and **non-specific** stages.  The **non-specific** response happens in the **same way** for **all microorganisms** — whatever foreign antigens they have.  The **specific** response is **antigen-specific** — it is aimed at **specific pathogens**.  It involves **white blood cells** called **T** and **B lymphocytes**.

## There are *Four Main Stages* in the *Immune Response*

### 1) Phagocytes Engulf Pathogens

A **phagocyte** is a type of **white blood cell** that carries out **phagocytosis** (engulfment of pathogens).
They're found in the **blood** and in **tissues** and carry out a **non-specific** immune response.  Here's how they work:

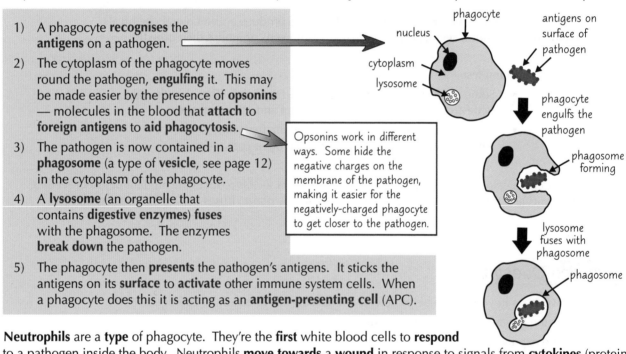

1) A phagocyte **recognises** the **antigens** on a pathogen.

2) The cytoplasm of the phagocyte moves round the pathogen, **engulfing** it.  This may be made easier by the presence of **opsonins** — molecules in the blood that **attach** to **foreign antigens** to **aid phagocytosis**.

3) The pathogen is now contained in a **phagosome** (a type of **vesicle**, see page 12) in the cytoplasm of the phagocyte.

4) A **lysosome** (an organelle that contains **digestive enzymes**) **fuses** with the phagosome.  The enzymes **break down** the pathogen.

Opsonins work in different ways.  Some hide the negative charges on the membrane of the pathogen, making it easier for the negatively-charged phagocyte to get closer to the pathogen.

5) The phagocyte then **presents** the pathogen's antigens.  It sticks the antigens on its **surface** to **activate** other immune system cells.  When a phagocyte does this it is acting as an **antigen-presenting cell** (APC).

**Neutrophils** are a **type** of phagocyte.  They're the **first** white blood cells to **respond** to a pathogen inside the body.  Neutrophils **move towards** a **wound** in response to signals from **cytokines** (proteins that act as messenger molecules — see page 52).  The cytokines are released by cells at the site of the wound.

### 2) Phagocytes Activate T lymphocytes

1) A **T lymphocyte** is another type of **white blood cell**.

2) Their surface is covered with **receptors**.

3) The receptors **bind to antigens** presented by APCs.

4) Each T lymphocyte has a **different receptor** on its surface.

5) When the receptor on the surface of a T lymphocyte meets a **complementary antigen**, it binds to it — so each T lymphocyte will bind to a **different antigen**.

6) This **activates** the T lymphocyte — the process is called **clonal selection**.

7) The T lymphocyte then undergoes **clonal expansion** — it **divides** to produce **clones**, which then **differentiate** into **different types** of T lymphocytes that carry out **different functions** — see next page.

# The Immune System

Once activated, T lymphocytes can become:

1) **T helper cells** — these **release substances** to **activate B lymphocytes** (see below).

2) **T killer cells** — these **attach** to antigens on a pathogen and **kill** the cell.

3) **T regulatory cells** — these **suppress** the **immune response** from **other white blood cells**. This helps to stop immune system cells from mistakenly attacking the host's body cells.

4) **Memory cells** (see next page).

## 3) T lymphocytes *Activate B lymphocytes*, Which Divide Into *Plasma Cells*

1) **B lymphocytes** are another type of **white blood cell**.

2) They're covered with proteins called **antibodies**.

3) Antibodies **bind to antigens** to form an **antigen-antibody complex**.

4) Each B lymphocyte has a **different shaped antibody** on its surface.

5) When the antibody on the surface of a B lymphocyte meets a **complementary shaped antigen**, it binds to it — so each B lymphocyte will bind to a **different antigen**.

6) This, together with substances **released** from T helper cells, **activates** the B lymphocyte. This process is another example of **clonal selection**.

7) The activated B lymphocyte **divides**, by mitosis, into **plasma cells** and **memory cells** (see next page). This is another example of **clonal expansion**.

B lymphocyte

plasma membrane — nucleus — cytoplasm — antibody

See p. 52 for more on cell signalling.

### Cell Signalling

1) Cell signalling is basically how **cells communicate**.

2) A cell may **release** (or present) a **substance** that **binds to the receptors** on **another cell** — this causes a **response** of some kind in the other cell.

3) Cell signalling is really important in the **immune response** because it helps to **activate** all the **different types** of **white blood cells** that are needed.

4) For example, **T helper cells** release **interleukins** (a type of **cytokine**) that bind to receptors on **B lymphocytes**. This **activates** the B lymphocytes — the T helper cells are signalling to the B lymphocytes that there's a pathogen in the body.

## 4) Plasma Cells Make More *Antibodies* to a Specific *Antigen*

1) Plasma cells are **clones** of the B lymphocyte (they're **identical** to the B lymphocyte).

2) They secrete **loads** of the **antibody**, specific to the antigen, into the blood.

3) These antibodies will bind to the antigens on the surface of the pathogen to form **lots** of **antigen-antibody complexes**.

4) You need to **learn** the **structure** of antibodies:

- The **variable regions** of the antibody form the **antigen binding sites**. The **shape** of the variable region is **complementary** to a particular antigen. The variable regions **differ** between antibodies.

- The **hinge region** allows **flexibility** when the antibody binds to the antigen.

- The **constant regions** allow binding to **receptors** on **immune system cells**, e.g. phagocytes. The constant region is the **same** (i.e. it has the same sequence of amino acids) **in all** antibodies.

- **Disulfide bridges** (a type of bond) hold the polypeptide chains of the protein together.

An Antigen-Antibody Complex

antigen — variable regions (orange) — light chain — hinge protein — disulfide bridge — heavy chain — constant regions (blue)

*MODULE 4: SECTION 1 — DISEASE AND THE IMMUNE SYSTEM*

# The Immune System

Antibodies **help** to **clear** an **infection** by:

1) <u>Agglutinating pathogens</u> — each antibody has **two binding sites**, so an antibody can **bind** to **two pathogens** at the **same time** — the pathogens become **clumped together**. Phagocytes then bind to the antibodies and phagocytose a lot of pathogens **all at once**. Antibodies that behave in this way are known as **agglutinins**.

2) <u>Neutralising toxins</u> — like antigens, toxins have **different shapes**. Antibodies called **anti-toxins** can **bind** to the **toxins** produced by pathogens. This **prevents** the toxins from **affecting human cells**, so the toxins are **neutralised** (inactivated). The toxin-antibody complexes are also phagocytosed.

3) <u>Preventing the pathogen binding to human cells</u> — when antibodies bind to the antigens on pathogens, they may **block** the cell surface **receptors** that the pathogens need to **bind to the host cells**. This means the pathogen **can't attach to** or **infect** the host cells.

Agglutination

antibody

pathogen

antigen

## The **Primary Response** is **Slow...**

1) When a **pathogen** enters the body for the **first time**, the **antigens** on its surface **activate** the **immune system**. This is called the **primary response**.

2) The primary response is **slow** because there **aren't many B lymphocytes** that can make the antibody needed to bind to it.

3) Eventually the body will produce **enough** of the right antibody to overcome the infection. Meanwhile the infected person will show **symptoms** of the disease.

4) After being exposed to an antigen, both T and B lymphocytes produce **memory cells**. These memory cells **remain in the body** for a **long** time.

5) **Memory T lymphocytes** remember the **specific antigen** and will recognise it a second time round. **Memory B lymphocytes** record the specific **antibodies** needed to bind to the antigen.

6) The person is now **immune** — their immune system has the **ability** to respond **quickly** to a second infection.

*Don't get the primary response mixed up with primary defences (see p. 96).*

Neil's primary response — to his parents.

## ...the **Secondary Response** is **Faster**

1) If the **same pathogen** enters the body again, the immune system will produce a **quicker, stronger** immune response — the **secondary response**.

2) **Clonal selection** happens faster. **Memory B lymphocytes** are activated and divide into **plasma cells** that produce the right antibody to the antigen. **Memory T lymphocytes** are activated and divide into the **correct type** of **T lymphocytes** to kill the cell carrying the antigen.

3) The secondary response often gets rid of the pathogen **before** you begin to show any **symptoms**.

The **similarities** and **differences** between the primary and secondary are summarised in the table:

| | | Primary response | Secondary response |
|---|---|---|---|
| | Pathogen | Enters for 1st time | Enters for 2nd time |
| | Speed of response | Slow | Fast |
| | Cells activated | B and T lymphocytes | Memory cells |
| | Symptoms | Yes | No |

*MODULE 4: SECTION 1 — DISEASE AND THE IMMUNE SYSTEM*

# The Immune System

## You Need to be Able to **Examine** and **Draw Blood Smears**

1) As the name suggests, a **blood smear** is a sample of blood smeared over a **microscope slide**.

2) **Stains** are added to the sample to make the **different cells** easy to see (see page 18 for more on staining microscope images).

3) When looking at a blood smear you're likely to see **red blood cells**, **white blood cells** and **platelets** (tiny fragments of cells involved in blood clotting). Some types of white blood cells have **granules** in their cytoplasm (so they look **grainy**) and other types don't.

4) Here's an **example** of what a blood smear looks like:

Most of the cells are red blood cells (see page 65). They're easy to spot because they don't have a nucleus.

This is a neutrophil. Its nucleus looks like three interconnected blobs — the posh way of saying this is that the nucleus is 'multi-lobed'. The cytoplasm of a neutrophil is grainy.

This is a lymphocyte. It's much smaller than the neutrophil. The nucleus takes up most of the cell and there's very little cytoplasm to be seen (it's not grainy either). You can't tell whether this is a T lymphocyte or a B lymphocyte under a light microscope.

BIOPHOTO ASSOCIATES/SCIENCE PHOTO LIBRARY

This is a monocyte. It's the biggest white blood cell and a type of phagocyte. It has a kidney-bean shaped nucleus and a non-grainy cytoplasm.

## Practice Questions

Q1 What are antigens?

Q2 What structures are found on the surface of T lymphocytes?

Q3 Draw and label the structure of a B lymphocyte.

Q4 Draw and label the structure of an antibody.

Q5 Give two differences between the primary and secondary response.

**Exam Questions**

Q1 Three types of white blood cell are shown in the table.
Select the row in the table that correctly describes the function of each type of cell.
[1 mark]

|   | Neutrophil | T helper cell | B lymphocyte |
|---|---|---|---|
| A | Releases interleukins to activate other cells | Divides to form plasma cells | Engulfs pathogens |
| B | Engulfs pathogens | Divides to form plasma cells | Releases interleukins to activate other cells |
| C | Releases interleukins to activate other cells | Engulfs pathogens | Divides to form plasma cells |
| D | Engulfs pathogens | Releases interleukins to activate other cells | Divides to form plasma cells |

Q2 IgG is a type of antibody, as well as an agglutinin and opsonin. Suggest how IgG works. [2 marks]

Q3 A scientist is looking at a blood smear under the microscope.
Explain how she will be able to tell the difference between a neutrophil and a B lymphocyte. [3 marks]

Q4 A person had chickenpox as a child. She was exposed to the virus that causes it again as a teenager, but did not experience any symptoms. Explain why. [5 marks]

---

## *The student-revision complex — only present the night before an exam...*

*Memory cells are still B and T lymphocytes, but they're the ones that stick around for a long time. So if a pathogen is stupid enough to invade the body again, these cells can immediately divide into more of themselves, and release antibodies specifically against the pathogen or bind to the pathogen and destroy it. Ha ha (evil laugh).*

# Immunity and Vaccinations

*Immunity is the ability to respond quickly to an infection — because your immune system recognises the foreign antigens. There are different types of immunity though and different ways of developing it. And sometimes your immune system gets a bit mixed up, leading to autoimmunity...*

## Immunity can be Active or Passive

### ACTIVE IMMUNITY

This is the type of immunity you get when **your immune system makes its own antibodies** after being **stimulated** by an **antigen**. There are **two** different types of active immunity:

1) **Natural** — this is when you become immune after **catching a disease**. E.g. if you have measles as a child, you shouldn't be able to catch it again in later life.

2) **Artificial** — this is when you become immune after you've been given a **vaccination** containing a harmless dose of antigen (see next page).

### PASSIVE IMMUNITY

This is the type of immunity you get from being **given antibodies made by a different organism** — your immune system **doesn't** produce any antibodies of its own. Again, there are **two** types:

1) **Natural** — this is when a **baby** becomes immune due to the antibodies it receives from its **mother**, through the **placenta** and in **breast milk**.

2) **Artificial** — this is when you become immune after being **injected** with **antibodies** from **someone else**. E.g. If you contract tetanus you can be injected with antibodies against the tetanus toxin, collected from blood donations.

*Claire was grateful for her mum's antibodies. She was less grateful for the dress.*

## Learn the Similarities and Differences Between Active and Passive Immunity

This handy summary table should help:

| Active immunity | Passive immunity |
|---|---|
| Requires exposure to antigen | No exposure to antigen |
| It takes a while for protection to develop | Protection is immediate |
| Protection is long-term | Protection is short-term |
| Memory cells are produced | Memory cells aren't produced |

## Autoimmune Diseases Involve an Abnormal Immune Response

1) Sometimes, an organism's immune system **isn't able** to **recognise self-antigens** — the antigens present on the organism's **own cells**.

2) When this happens, the immune system treats the self-antigens as **foreign antigens** and launches an **immune response** against the organism's **own tissues**.

3) A disease resulting from this abnormal immune response is known as an **autoimmune disease**.

**Examples of autoimmune diseases:**

- **Lupus** — caused by the immune system attacking cells in the **connective tissues**. This **damages** the tissues and causes painful **inflammation** (see page 96). Lupus can affect the **skin** and **joints**, as well as **organs** such as the **heart** and **lungs**.

- **Rheumatoid arthritis** — caused by the immune system attacking cells in the **joints**. Again this causes **pain** and **inflammation**.

4) Autoimmune diseases are usually **chronic** (long-term). They can often be **treated**, but **not cured**.

# Immunity and Vaccinations

## Vaccines Help to Control Disease and Prevent Epidemics

1) While your B lymphocytes are busy **dividing** to build up their numbers to deal with a pathogen (i.e. the **primary response** — see p. 100), you **suffer** from the disease. **Vaccination** can help avoid this.

2) Vaccines **contain antigens** that cause your body to **produce memory cells** against a particular pathogen, **without** the pathogen **causing disease**. This means you become **immune** without getting any **symptoms**.

3) If most people in a **community** are **vaccinated**, the disease becomes extremely **rare**. This means that even people who haven't been vaccinated are **unlikely** to get the disease, because there's no one to catch it from. This is called **herd immunity**. It helps to **prevent epidemics** — **mass outbreaks** of **disease**.

4) Vaccines always contain antigens — these may be **free** or attached to a **dead** or **attenuated** (weakened) **pathogen**.

5) Sometimes **booster** vaccines are given later on (e.g. after several years) to **make sure** memory cells are produced.

6) **Vaccination** is **not the same** as **immunisation**. Vaccination is the **injection of antigens** (in a vaccine) into the body. **Immunisation** is the **process** by which you **develop immunity**. Vaccination **causes** immunisation.

*Not all vaccines are actually injected — some are taken orally or in an aerosol.*

**Routine vaccines** are offered to everybody. They include:

- the **MMR** — protects against **measles**, **mumps** and **rubella**. The MMR is usually given to **children** as an **injection** at around a year old, and again before they start school. It contains **attenuated measles**, **mumps** and **rubella viruses**.

- the **Meningitis C vaccine** — protects against the **bacteria** that cause **Meningitis C**. It is first given as an **injection** to babies at **3 months**. **Boosters** are then given to **1-year-olds** and **teenagers**.

## Vaccines and Vaccination Programmes Change — EXAMPLE: the Influenza Vaccine

1) The **influenza (flu) vaccine** changes every year. That's because the **antigens** on the surface of the influenza virus **change regularly**, forming **new strains** of the virus.

2) **Memory cells** produced from **vaccination** with **one strain** of the flu will **not recognise** other strains with **different antigens**. The strains are **immunologically distinct**.

3) Every year there are **different strains** of the influenza virus **circulating** in the **population**, so a **different vaccine** has to be made.

4) **Laboratories** collect **samples** of these different strains, and organisations, such as the **WHO** (World Health Organisation) and **CDC** (Centre for Disease Control), **test** the **effectiveness** of different influenza **vaccines** against them.

5) **New vaccines** are **developed** and one is chosen **every year** that is the **most effective** against the **recently** circulating influenza viruses.

6) Governments and health authorities then implement a **programme** of **vaccination** using the most **suitable** vaccine. Sometimes people are given a vaccine that protects them from a strain causing an epidemic in **another country** — this helps to stop the strain spreading **globally**.

## Practice Questions

Q1 What is the difference between active and passive immunity?

Q2 What are autoimmune diseases? Give an example.

Q3 Explain how vaccines help prevent epidemics.

**Exam Question**

Q1 Influenza is caused by a virus that constantly changes its antigens. Explain why a new influenza vaccine is made every year. [2 marks]

## An injection of dead bugs — roll on my next vaccine...

*The influenza virus is so clever that it would almost make you think it had a mind of its own. I mean, as soon as we catch up with it and develop a vaccine, off it goes and changes its surface antigens again. Influenza virus 1: humans 0.*

# Antibiotics and Other Medicines

*Our immune systems aren't always enough to fight off an infection by pathogens.*
*Sometimes we need a bit of extra help from medicines like antibiotics.*

## Antibiotics are Extremely Useful

1) **Antibiotics** are **chemicals** that **kill** or **inhibit** the **growth** of **bacteria**.

2) They're **used** by humans as **drugs** to **treat bacterial infections**. They're useful because they can usually **target** bacterial cells **without damaging** human body cells.

3) **Penicillin** was the **first antibiotic** to be **isolated** (by Alexander Fleming, in 1928).

4) Antibiotic use became **widespread** from the **mid-twentieth century** — partly thanks to the successful treatment of soldiers with penicillin in the Second World War.

5) For the **past few decades**, we've been able to deal with bacterial infections **pretty easily** using **antibiotics**. As a result of this, the **death rate** from **infectious bacterial disease** has **fallen dramatically**.

6) Despite their usefulness, there are **risks** to using antibiotics. For example, they can cause **side effects** and even **severe allergic reactions** in some people. Perhaps the **biggest risk** though, is from **antibiotic resistance**...

*Antibiotics are used to treat bacterial infections in animals too.*

## Antibiotic Resistance is a Big Problem

1) There is **genetic variation** in a population of bacteria. Genetic **mutations** make some bacteria **naturally resistant** to an **antibiotic**.

2) For the bacterium, this ability to **resist an antibiotic** is a big **advantage**. It's better able to **survive**, even in a host who's being treated with antibiotics to get rid of the infection, and so it lives for longer and **reproduces** many more times.

3) This leads to the **allele** for **antibiotic resistance** being **passed on** to lots of **offspring**. It's an example of **natural selection** — see page 123. This is how antibiotic resistance **spreads** and becomes **more common** in a population of bacteria over time.

*An allele is a version of a gene — see page 119.*

4) This is a **problem** for people who become **infected** with these bacteria, because you **can't easily get rid of them** with antibiotics.

5) **Increased use** of antibiotics means that **antibiotic resistance** is **increasing**. **'Superbugs'** that are resistant to **most known antibiotics** are becoming **more common**. This means we are **less able to treat** some **potentially life-threatening** bacterial **infections**.

### Learn These Examples of Antibiotic-Resistant Bacteria:

- **MRSA** (meticillin-resistant *Staphylococcus aureus*) causes **serious wound infections** and is **resistant** to **several antibiotics**, including **meticillin** (which used to be called methicillin).

- *Clostridium difficile* infects the **digestive system**, usually causing problems in people who have **already been treated** with **antibiotics**. It is thought that the **harmless bacteria** that are **normally present** in the digestive system are **killed** by the antibiotics, which *C. difficile* is **resistant** to. This allows *C. difficile* to **flourish**. *C. difficile* produces a **toxin**, which causes severe **diarrhoea**, **fever** and **cramps**.

*MRSA and Clostridium difficile infections are most common in hospitals, where many antibiotics are used and patients who are already ill have weakened immune systems.*

**Developing new antibiotics** and **modifying** existing ones are two ways of **overcoming** the current problem of antibiotic resistance. This isn't easy though.

To reduce the likelihood of antibiotic resistance developing in the first place, **doctors** are being encouraged to **reduce** their **use of antibiotics**, e.g. **not** to prescribe them for **minor infections** and **not** to prescribe them to **prevent infections** (except in patients with already weak immune systems, e.g. the elderly or people with HIV). **Patients** are advised to take **all** of the antibiotics they're **prescribed** to make sure the infection is fully cleared and all the bacteria have been killed (which reduces the likelihood of a population of antibiotic-resistant bacteria developing).

# Antibiotics and Other Medicines

## Possible **Sources** of **Medicines** Need to be **Protected**

1) Many **medicinal drugs** are manufactured **using natural compounds** found in **plants, animals** or **microorganisms**. E.g. **penicillin** is obtained from a **fungus**, some **cancer drugs** are made using **soil bacteria**, and **daffodils** are now grown to produce a drug used to treat **Alzheimer's disease**.

2) Only a **small proportion** of organisms have been **investigated** so far, so it's possible that plants or microorganisms **exist** that contain compounds that could be used to treat **currently incurable** diseases, such as AIDS. Others may produce **new antibiotics**.

3) Possible **sources of drugs** need to be **protected** by **maintaining** the **biodiversity** (the variety of different species) on Earth. If we **don't** protect them, some species could **die** out before we get a **chance** to study them.

4) Even organisms that have **already** been studied could still prove to be **useful** sources of medicines as **new techniques** are developed for identifying, purifying and testing compounds.

## The **Future** of **Medicine** Looks Pretty **High-Tech**

### Personalised Medicines

1) Your **genes** determine how your body **responds** to certain **drugs**. **Different people** respond to the **same drug** in **different ways** — which makes certain drugs **more effective** for **some people** than others. This is where **personalised medicines** come in.

2) Personalised medicines are medicines that are **tailored** to an **individual's DNA**. The theory is that if doctors have your **genetic information**, they can use it to **predict** how you will respond to different drugs and only prescribe the ones that will be **most effective** for you.

3) Scientists hope that by studying the **relationship** between someone's genetic make-up and their responsiveness to drugs, **more effective drugs** can be produced in the future.

### Synthetic biology

1) Synthetic biology involves using **technology** to **design** and **make** things like **artificial proteins**, **cells** and even **microorganisms**.

2) It has applications in lots of different areas, including **medicine**. For example, scientists are looking at engineering **bacteria** to **destroy cancer cells**, while leaving **healthy body cells intact**.

Not an example of
synthetic biology.

## Practice Questions

Q1 What are antibiotics?

Q2 Name two strains of antibiotic-resistant bacteria.

Q3 Why is protecting biodiversity important for the development of new medicines?

**Exam Question**

Q1 MRSA bacteria are resistant to several antibiotics, including meticillin.
Suggest how *Staphylococcus aureus* bacteria developed resistance to the antibiotic meticillin. [4 marks]

## The Market Research Society of Australia — not a deadly bacterium...

*In 2014, the World Health Organisation (WHO) released a report on the worldwide threat posed by antibiotic resistance — and it's not good news. Unless we take action now, relatively minor bacterial infections (that we've been able to treat successfully with antibiotics for decades) will once again become life-threatening illnesses. So we need to work on stopping the spread of antibiotic resistance and developing new antibiotics as soon as possible.*

# Studying Biodiversity

*Bet you've noticed how there are loads of different living things in the world — well that's biodiversity in a nutshell.*

## Biodiversity is the Variety of Organisms

Before you can sink your teeth into the real meat of biodiversity, there are a few definitions you need to know:

1) **Biodiversity** — the **variety** of **living organisms** in an area.

2) **Species** — a group of **similar organisms** able to **reproduce** to give **fertile offspring**.

3) **Habitat** — the **area inhabited** by a species. It includes the **physical** factors, like the soil and temperature range, and the **living** (biotic) factors, like availability of food or the presence of predators.

*Pete wasn't sure that the company's new increased biodiversity policy would be good for productivity.*

Areas with a **high** biodiversity are those with lots of **different species**.

## Biodiversity Can be Considered at Different Levels

1) **Habitat diversity** — the number of **different habitats** in an **area**. For example, a particular area could contain many different habitats — sand dunes, woodland, meadows, streams, etc.

2) **Species diversity** — the number of **different species** (species richness) and the **abundance** of each species (species evenness) in an **area**. For example, a woodland could contain many different species of plants, insects, birds and mammals.

*Alleles are different versions of genes.*

3) **Genetic diversity** — the variation of **alleles** within a species (or a population of a species). For example, the variation of alleles within the dog species gives rise to different breeds, such as a Labrador or poodle.

## Sampling Can be Used to Measure Biodiversity

In most cases it'd be **too time-consuming** to count every individual organism in a habitat. Instead, a **sample** of the population is taken. **Estimates** about the whole habitat are based on the sample. Here's what sampling involves:

1) **Choose** an **area** to **sample** — a small area within the habitat being studied.

2) **Count** the number of individuals of **each species**. How you do this depends on **what** you're counting, for example: →

3) **Repeat** the process — take as many samples as possible. This gives a better indication of the **whole habitat**.

4) Use the results to **estimate** the total number of individuals or the total number of different species in the habitat being studied.

5) When sampling **different habitats** and comparing them, always use the **same sampling technique**.

- For plants you'd use a quadrat (a frame which you place on the ground).
- For flying insects you'd use a sweep net (a net on a pole).
- For ground insects you'd use a pitfall trap (a small pit that insects can't get out of).
- For aquatic animals you'd use a net.

You could **investigate** the **impact** of **mowing** on the **biodiversity** of your school playing field by sampling a mowed and an un-mowed field. Calculate the biodiversity for each field using Simpson's Index (see next page).

## Sampling Can be Random or Non-Random

1) To avoid **bias** in your results, the **sample** should be **random**. For example, if you were looking at plant species in a field, you could pick random sample sites by dividing the field into a **grid** using **measuring tapes** and using a **random number generator** to select **coordinates**.

2) However, sometimes it's **necessary** to take a **non-random sample**. E.g. when there's a lot of variety in the distribution of species in the habitat and you want to make sure all the different areas are sampled.

3) There are **three** types of **non-random** sample:

- **Systematic** — This is when samples are taken at **fixed intervals**, often along a **line**. E.g. **quadrats** could be placed along a line (called a **transect**) from an area of shade in the corner to the middle of the field.

- **Opportunistic** — This is when samples are **chosen** by the **investigator**. It's used because it is **simple** to carry out, but the data will be **biased**.

- **Stratified** — This is when **different areas** in a habitat are **identified** and **sampled** separately in **proportion** to their part of the **habitat** as a **whole**. E.g. a heathland may have patches of gorse in it — the heath and gorse areas would be sampled separately according to how much of each there was in the habitat.

# Studying Biodiversity

## Species Richness and Species Evenness Affect Biodiversity

The **greater** the **species richness** and **species evenness** in an area, the **higher** the biodiversity.

1) **Species richness** is the number of **different species** in an area. The **higher** the number of species, the **greater** the species richness. It's measured by taking random samples of a habitat (see previous page) and counting the number of different species.

2) **Species evenness** is a measure of the **relative abundance** of **each species** in an area. The **more similar** the **population size** of each species, the **greater** the species evenness. It's measured by taking random samples of a habitat, and counting the **number of individuals** of each different species.

**Example** Habitat X and habitat Y both contain **two different species** and **30 individual organisms**.

|  | Habitat X | Habitat Y |
|---|---|---|
| species 1 | 28 | 15 |
| species 2 | 2 | 15 |
| total | 30 | 30 |

- **Species richness** in the two habitats is the **same** — **2**.
- In **habitat Y** the individual organisms are **more evenly distributed** between the different species — it has **greater species evenness**.

## Diversity is Measured using Simpson's Index of Diversity

1) Species present in a habitat in very **small** numbers shouldn't be treated the same as those with **bigger** populations.
2) **Simpson's Index of Diversity** takes into account both **species richness** and **species evenness**.
3) Simpson's Index of Diversity (**D**) can be calculated using this formula.
4) Simpson's Index of Diversity is always a value **between 0 and 1**. The **closer to 1** the index is, the **more diverse** the habitat. The greater the species richness and evenness, the higher the number.

$$D = 1 - \left( \sum \left( \frac{n}{N} \right)^2 \right)$$

n = **Total number** of individuals of **one species**
N = **Total number** of organisms of **all species**
Σ = **'Sum of'** (i.e. added together)

Here's a simple example of the index of diversity in a field:

There are 3 different species of flower in this field — a red species, a white and a blue. There are 11 organisms altogether, so N = 11. There are 3 of the red species, 5 of the white and 3 of the blue. So the index of diversity for this field is:

$$D = 1 - \left( \left( \frac{3}{11} \right)^2 + \left( \frac{5}{11} \right)^2 + \left( \frac{3}{11} \right)^2 \right) = 1 - 0.36 = 0.64$$

*You need to work out the (n/N)² bit for each different species then add them all together.*

The field has an index of diversity of 0.64, which is fairly high.

## Practice Questions

Q1 What is meant by habitat diversity, species diversity and genetic diversity?

Q2 What is stratified sampling?

|  | Field A | Field B |
|---|---|---|
| Species A | 80 | 20 |
| Species B | 110 | 50 |
| Species C | 210 | 330 |
| **Total** | **400** | **400** |

**Exam Question**

Q1 A group of students is investigating the diversity of millipedes (small ground insects) in a habitat. They sampled two fields (A and B) and counted the number of millipedes of different species, as shown in the table above. They want to find out the species richness and species evenness in the area, and work out Simpson's Index of Diversity.

    a) Describe what is meant by species richness and species evenness. [2 marks]

    b) Calculate Simpson's Index of Diversity for each field. Give your answers to two decimal places. [2 marks]

## *Species richness — goldfish and money spiders top the list...*

*Make sure you know the definitions of species richness and species evenness and can describe how you'd measure them. As for Simpson's Index of Diversity — be prepared to use it and to say what the numbers it churns out actually mean.*

# More on Biodiversity

*Advances in genetics mean we can now assess genetic diversity. This helps us to understand the human impacts on global biodiversity (the total number of species on Earth). You'll need to learn all about this for your exam...*

## Genetic Diversity Can be Assessed

1) You know from page 106 that **genetic diversity** is the **variation** of **alleles** within a **species** (or within a population of a species).

2) You can do **calculations** to work out the **genetic diversity** of a **population**.

3) This is important because if a population has **low genetic diversity**, they might **not** be able to **adapt** to a **change in the environment** and the **whole population** could be **wiped out** by a single event (e.g. a disease).

4) Populations in which genetic diversity may be low include **isolated populations** such as those bred in **captivity** (e.g. in zoos, and pedigree animals and rare breeds).

5) **Calculations** can be used to **monitor** the **genetic diversity** of these populations over time and efforts can be made to **increase** the genetic diversity of the population if needed. E.g. **breeding programmes** in **zoos** are very closely **managed** to **maximise** genetic **diversity**.

> A <u>pedigree animal</u> is one that has been bred purely from animals of the same breed. A <u>rare breed</u> is usually a breed of farm animal that's not used in large-scale farming.

## Genetic Polymorphism is Used to Measure Genetic Diversity

1) You know that **alleles** are different versions of a **gene**.

2) **Alleles** of the **same gene** are found at the **same point** (called a **locus**) on a chromosome.

3) **Polymorphism** describes a **locus** that has **two or more alleles**.

4) Working out the **proportion** of **polymorphic gene loci** in an organism (i.e. those points on a chromosome which can have more than one allele) gives you a **measure** of **genetic diversity**.

> Loci is the plural of locus.

> different alleles at the same locus
>
> B   b

5) There's a nifty **formula** you can use:

$$\text{proportion of polymorphic gene loci} = \frac{\text{number of polymorphic gene loci}}{\text{total number of loci}}$$

> If you multiply the proportion of polymorphic gene loci in a sample by 100, you'll get the percentage of genes in the sample that have alleles.

**Example:**
If 40 of the genes sampled in a population are polymorphic out of 100 genes sampled in total, then the proportion of polymorphic gene loci $= \frac{40}{100} = \mathbf{0.4}$.

## Factors Affecting Global Biodiversity Include...

### 1) Human Population Growth

The **human population** of the planet has **grown hugely** in the last couple of centuries and is **continuing to rise**. This is **decreasing global biodiversity** because of the following factors:

1) **Habitat loss** — human development is **destroying habitats**, e.g. there is deforestation in the Amazon to make way for grazing and agriculture. This **decreases habitat diversity**.

2) **Over-exploitation** — a **greater demand** for **resources** (such as food, water and energy) means a lot of resources are being **used up faster** than they can be **replenished**. E.g. industrial fishing can deplete the populations of certain fish species and may even cause extinction (a species to die out). This **decreases genetic diversity** within populations, as well as **decreasing species diversity** (as a result of extinction).

3) **Urbanisation** — sprawling cities and major road Bdevelopments can **isolate species**, meaning populations are unable to **interbreed** and **genetic diversity** is decreased.

4) **Pollution** — high amounts of **pollutants** can **kill species** or **destroy habitats**, e.g. high levels of **fertiliser** flowing into a river can lead to a **decrease** in fish species in that river. This **decreases biodiversity**.

# More on Biodiversity

## 2) Increased Use of Monoculture in Agriculture

In order to **feed** an ever growing number of **people**, **large areas** of land are devoted to **monoculture** — the growing of a **single variety** of a **single crop**. E.g. in Africa, large areas of land are used for palm oil plantations. This leads to a **decline** in **global biodiversity** because of the following factors:

1) **Habitats** are **lost** as **land** is **cleared** to make way for the large fields, **reducing habitat diversity**.
2) **Local** and naturally occurring **plants** and **animals** are seen as **weeds** and **pests**, and so are destroyed with **pesticides** and **herbicides**, **reducing species diversity**.
3) **Heritage** (traditional) **varieties** of crops are **lost** because they **don't make enough money** and so are not **planted** any more, which **reduces species diversity**.

## 3) Climate Change

1) **Climate change** is the **variation** in the Earth's climate, e.g. things like changes in **temperature** and **rainfall patterns**.
2) It occurs **naturally**, but the **scientific consensus** is that the climate change we're **experiencing at the moment** is **caused** by **humans** increasing emissions of **greenhouse gases** (such as **carbon dioxide**).
3) Greenhouse gases cause **global warming** (**increasing global average temperature**), which causes **other types** of climate change, e.g. changing rainfall patterns.
4) Climate change will affect **different areas** of the world in **different ways** — some places will get **warmer**, some **colder**, some **wetter** and others **drier**. All of these are likely to **affect global biodiversity**:

- Most species need a particular **climate** to survive.
- A change in climate may mean that an area that was previously **inhabitable** becomes **uninhabitable** (and **vice versa**).
- This may cause an **increase** or **decrease** in the **range** of some species (the area in which they live). This could increase or decrease biodiversity.
- Some species may be forced to **migrate** to a more suitable area, causing a change in **species distribution**. Migrations usually **decrease** biodiversity in the areas the species migrate from, and **increase** biodiversity in the areas they migrate to.
- If there isn't a suitable habitat to migrate to, the species is a plant and **can't migrate**, or if the change is **too fast**, the species may become **extinct**. This will **decrease** biodiversity.

**Range change example**

The southern **range** limit of the **Sooty Copper Butterfly** has **moved** 60 miles north in recent decades.

**Extinction example**

**Corals** die if water temperature **changes** by just one or two degrees. In 1998 a coral reef near Panama was badly damaged because the water **temperature** had **increased** — at least one species of coral became **extinct** as a result.

## Practice Questions

Q1 What is the formula used to work out the proportion of polymorphic gene loci?

Q2 Give two ways in which climate change affects global biodiversity.

**Exam Questions**

Q1 In a population of Species A, a sample of 80 gene loci were tested for polymorphism.
36 of the genes were found to be polymorphic.
What is the proportion of polymorphic loci in this sample? [1 mark]

Q2* Describe how human population growth and monoculture during
the last 30 years could have decreased global biodiversity. [6 marks]

* You will be assessed on the quality of your written response in this question.

## Extinction — coming soon to a habitat near you...

All of this makes the future look a bit bleak — deforestation, loads of different species dying out and climate change. Now you know why biodiversity's at risk, it's time to take a look at why it's so important and worth saving...

# Importance of Biodiversity

*You're probably wondering what all this fuss about biodiversity is for. Well, it turns out that everything is connected, so if you eliminate even just one species you might just end up with all sorts of problems you'd never even thought of.*

## Maintaining Biodiversity is Important for Ecological Reasons...

The ecological reasons for maintaining biodiversity are all down to the **complex relationships** between **organisms** and their **environments**.

### 1) To Protect Species, Including **Keystone Species**

Organisms in an ecosystem are **interdependent** — they depend on each other to survive. This means that the loss of **just one species** can have pretty **drastic effects** on an ecosystem, such as:

> *An ecosystem is all the organisms living in a particular area and all the non-living conditions, e.g. temperature.*

1) **Disruption** of **food chains**, e.g. some species of bear feed on salmon, which feed on herring. If the number of herring decline it can affect **both** the salmon and the bear populations.

2) **Disruption** of **nutrient cycles**, e.g. decomposers like worms improve the **quality of soil** by recycling nutrients. If worm numbers decline, soil quality will be affected. This will affect the **growth** of plants and the **amount of food** available to animals.

There are some species on which many of the other species in an ecosystem **depend** and without which the ecosystem would **change dramatically** — these are called **keystone species**. Keystone species are often **predators** — keeping the population of prey in check, but can also be **modifiers** — maintaining the environment needed for the ecosystem (e.g. beavers building dams), or **hosts** — plants that provide a particular environment, such as palm trees.

> **Example**: The **wolf** is a **keystone species** in America. **Wolf populations** were **eliminated** in most American states during the 20th century. Without the wolves to hunt them, **elk populations increased**, leading to **overgrazing**. This led to the **loss of plant species**, as well as the loss of species that depend on those plants such as **beavers** and **songbirds**. The situation has since been reversed in some national parks.

### 2) To Maintain **Genetic Resources**

**Genetic resources** refer to any **material** from **plants**, **animals** or **microorganisms**, containing **genes**, that we find **valuable**. Genetic resources could be crops, plants used for medicines, micro-organisms used in industrial processes, or animal breeds. We need to **maintain** genetic resources for the following reasons:

1) Genetic resources provide us with a **variety** of **everyday products**, such as:

- **Food** and **drink** — plants and animals are the source of almost all **food** and some **drinks**.
- **Clothing** — a lot of **fibres** and **fabrics** are made from plants and animals (e.g. cotton from plants and leather from animals).
- **Drugs** — many are made from plant compounds (e.g. the painkiller **morphine** is made from **poppies**).
- **Fuels** — we use a number of organisms to produce **renewable** fuels, including ethanol and biogas. Fossil fuels are **non-renewable** (they'll run out), so other sources are of **major economic importance**.
- **Other industrial materials** — a huge variety of other materials are produced from plant and animal species, including **wood**, **paper**, **dyes**, **adhesives**, **oils**, **rubber** and chemicals such as **pesticides**.

Many genetic resources are important to the **global economy**. Products derived from plant and animal species are traded on a local and global scale.

2) Genetic resources allow us to **adapt** to **changes in the environment**. For example, **climate change** (see page 109) may mean that some crops won't be able to grow in the same areas as they do now, e.g. there might be **droughts** in those areas. However, we may be able to use **genes** from a plant that's **resistant** to droughts to genetically engineer a **drought-resistant crop** — that's if we have such genetic resources to choose from.

# Importance of Biodiversity

## ...Economic Reasons...

### To Reduce Soil Depletion

1) **Monoculture** is growing a **single variety** of a **single crop** (see p. 109).
2) **Continuous monoculture** involves planting the **same crop** in the **same field** without interruption.
3) Continuous monoculture causes **soil depletion** because the **nutrients** required by the crop are gradually **used up**. (In more traditional farming methods crops are rotated with other types of crops, so that the **nutrients** and **organic** matter are **replaced**.)
4) The **economic costs** of soil depletion include **increased spending** on **fertilisers** (to artificially replace nutrients) and **decreased yields** (in the long run and if fertilisers are not used).

'Yield' is the amount of a crop produced.

## ...and Aesthetic Reasons

Some people believe we should conserve biodiversity because it brings **joy** to millions of people.

1) Areas **rich** in biodiversity provide pleasant, **attractive landscapes** that people can enjoy. By maintaining biodiversity we **protect** these beautiful **landscapes**.
2) The more biodiversity in an area the more **visitors** the area is likely to **attract** — this also has economic advantages.

There are lots of aesthetic reasons for maintaining biodiversity... this isn't one of them.

## Practice Questions

Q1 What is meant when we say that organisms in an ecosystem are 'interdependent'?

Q2 What is a genetic resource?

Q3 Give two reasons why it's important to maintain genetic resources.

Q4 Give an economic reason for the conservation of biodiversity.

Q5 Give an aesthetic reason for the conservation of biodiversity.

**Exam Questions**

Q1 Sea otters live in the Pacific northwest. Part of their food web is shown below.

kelp (seaweed) ⟶ sea urchin ⟶ sea otter

Sea otters are described as a keystone species.
a) What is a keystone species? [1 mark]
b) Use the information above to give one reason why the otter is a keystone species. [1 mark]

Q2 Explain why reducing biodiversity through continuous monoculture can come at an economic cost. [4 marks]

## All biodiversity is important — even spider diversity...

*So, it turns out biodiversity is pretty important. Without it, not only would your life lack its little luxuries, like tissues with aloe vera, and designer clothes, just surviving would be tricky — there'd be nothing to eat and fewer drugs to treat you when you're ill. Make sure you learn all the reasons for maintaining biodiversity — they might just crop up in the exam.*

# Conservation and Biodiversity

*Places like zoos and botanic gardens help preserve biodiversity through conservation — they help species that are endangered get out of the woods, or back into the woods, depending how you look at it...*

## In Situ Conservation Keeps Species in Their Natural Habitat

*In situ* conservation means **on site** conservation — it involves protecting species in their **natural habitat**. Conservation is important to **ensure the survival** of **endangered species** — species which are at risk of **extinction** because of a **low** population, or a **threatened habitat**. Methods of *in situ* conservation include:

1) Establishing **protected areas** such as **national parks** and **wildlife reserves** (also known as nature reserves) — habitats and species are protected in these areas by **restricting urban development, industrial development** and **farming**. A similar idea has been introduced to **sea ecosystems** with **Marine Conservation Zones**, where human activities (like fishing) are **controlled**.

2) **Controlling** or **preventing the introduction** of species that **threaten** local biodiversity. For example, grey squirrels are not native to Britain. They **compete** with the native red squirrel and have caused a population **decline**. So they're controlled in some areas.

3) **Protecting habitats** — e.g. controlling water levels to conserve wetlands and coppicing (trimming trees) to conserve woodlands. This allows organisms to **continue living** in their **natural habitat**.

4) **Promoting** particular species — this could be by protecting **food sources** or **nesting sites**.

5) Giving **legal protection** to **endangered species**, e.g. making it illegal to kill them (see next page).

*Jim reckoned he'd seen the last of those red squirrels — but he hadn't counted on their friends turning up.*

One advantage of *in situ* conservation is that often both the **species** and their **habitat** are conserved. **Larger populations** can be protected and it's **less disruptive** than removing organisms from their habitats. The chances of the population **recovering** are **greater** than with *ex situ* methods (see below).

But it can be **difficult to control** some factors that are **threatening** a species (such as poaching, predators, disease or climate change).

## Ex Situ Conservation Removes Species from Their Natural Habitat

*Ex situ* conservation means **off site** conservation — it involves protecting a species by **removing** part of the population from a **threatened habitat** and placing it in a **new location**. *Ex situ* conservation is often a **last resort**. Methods of *ex situ* conservation include:

1) **Relocating** an organism to a **safer area**, e.g. five white rhinos were recently relocated from the Congo to Kenya because they were in danger from **poachers** who kill them for their ivory.

2) **Breeding** organisms in **captivity** then **reintroducing** them to the wild when they are **strong enough**, e.g. sea eagles have been reintroduced to Britain through a captive breeding programme. Breeding is carried out in **animal sanctuaries** and **zoos**.

3) **Botanic gardens** are controlled environments used to grow a variety of **rare** plants for the purposes of **conservation, research, display** and **education**. **Endangered** plant species as well as species that are **extinct in the wild** can be grown and **reintroduced** into suitable habitats.

4) **Seed banks** — seeds can be frozen and stored in seed banks for over a century without losing their **fertility**. Seed banks provide a useful source of seeds if **natural reserves** are **destroyed**, for example by **disease** or other **natural disasters**.

The advantages of *ex situ* conservation are that it can be used to protect individual animals in a **controlled environment** — things like predation and hunting can be managed more easily. It can also be used to **reintroduce** species that have **left an area**.

But, there are disadvantages — usually only a **small number** of individuals can be cared for. It can be **difficult** and **expensive** to create and **sustain** the **right environment**. In fact, animals that are habituated (used to) human contact may be less likely to exhibit natural behaviour and may be more likely to catch a disease from humans. *Ex situ* conservation is usually **less successful** than *in situ* methods — many species can't **breed successfully** in captivity, or don't **adapt** to their new environment when moved to a new location.

# Conservation and Biodiversity

## International Cooperation is Important in Species Conservation

Information about threats to biodiversity needs to be shared and countries need to decide on conservation methods and implement them together. Here are a couple of examples of successful international cooperation:

### Rio Convention on Biological Diversity (CBD)

1) It aims to **develop international strategies** on the conservation of biodiversity and how to use animal and plant resources in a **sustainable** way.

2) The convention made it part of **international law** that conserving biodiversity is **everyone's responsibility**.

3) It also provides **guidance** to governments on how to conserve biodiversity.

### CITES Agreement

1) CITES (**Convention** on **International Trade** in **Endangered Species**) is an agreement designed to increase **international cooperation** in **regulating trade** in wild animal and plant specimens.

2) The member countries all agreed to make it **illegal** to **kill** endangered species.

3) The agreement helps to **conserve** species by **limiting** trade through **licensing**, and by making it **illegal** to trade in products made from endangered animals (such as rhino ivory and leopard skins).

4) It's also designed to **raise awareness** of threats to biodiversity through **education**.

International cooperation is really **important** — it'd be pointless making hunting endangered species illegal in one country if poachers could just go and hunt them in another country.

## Local Conservation Agreements Protect Special Areas in the UK

Whilst international cooperation is important, schemes at the **local** level are vital too. Here is an example from the UK:

### The Countryside Stewardship Scheme (CSS)

1) The **Countryside Stewardship Scheme** was introduced in 1991. Some of its aims were to conserve wildlife and biodiversity, and to improve and extend wildlife habitats by promoting specific management techniques to landowners.

2) The Government offered 10-year agreements to **pay landowners** who followed the **management techniques** they were suggesting. For example, to **regenerate hedgerows**, to leave **grassy margins** around the edges of fields where **wildflowers** could grow, and to **graze upland** areas to keep down **bracken**.

3) In the year 2000, there were 10 000 agreements in England. Since the introduction of the scheme, various **species** have begun to rebuild in numbers, including **birds** such as the **stone curlew**, **black grouse** and **bittern**.

## Practice Questions

Q1 Describe how botanic gardens and seed banks help in the conservation of biodiversity.

Q2 What is CITES and how does it help to conserve endangered species?

Q3 What is the Countryside Stewardship Scheme and how does it help to conserve endangered species?

**Exam Question**

Q1 The hawksbill turtle is an endangered species of sea turtle threatened by hunting and loss of nesting sites. They have slow reproductive, growth and development rates and their numbers are in rapid decline. The hawksbill turtle could be conserved using *in situ* or *ex situ* methods.

a) Suggest how the hawksbill turtle could be conserved by *in situ* methods. [3 marks]

b) Describe the disadvantages of using *ex situ* conservation methods. [4 marks]

## The path of true conservation ne'er did run smooth...

*I'm sure the animals being forcibly removed from their homes are just as bemused as you are right now but I'm afraid it's another case of having to learn the facts. Don't be put off by things like 'in' or 'ex' situ — that's just a way of saying 'on' or 'off' site that makes people feel clever when they say them. In fact, I'm feeling rather clever right now.*

# Classification Basics

*For hundreds of years people have been putting organisms into groups to make it easier to recognise and name them. For example, my brother is a member of the species Idioto bigearian (Latin for idiots with big ears).*

## Classification is All About Grouping Together Similar Organisms

Classification is the act of **arranging organisms** into **groups** based on their **similarities** and **differences**. This makes it **easier** for scientists to **identify** them and to **study** them. **Taxonomy** is the **study** of classification. There are a few different classification systems in use, but they all involve placing organisms into groups in a **taxonomic hierarchy**:

1) There are **eight levels** of groups (called taxonomic groups) used in classification.

*There's more on domains on page 117.*

2) **Similar organisms** are first sorted into one of **three** very **large groups** called **domains**, e.g. animals, plants and fungi are in the Eukarya domain.

3) **Similar organisms** are then sorted into **slightly smaller groups** called **kingdoms**, e.g. all animals are in the animal kingdom.

4) **Similar** organisms from that kingdom are then grouped into a **phylum**. **Similar** organisms from each phylum are then grouped into a **class**, and **so on** down the eight levels of the taxonomic hierarchy.

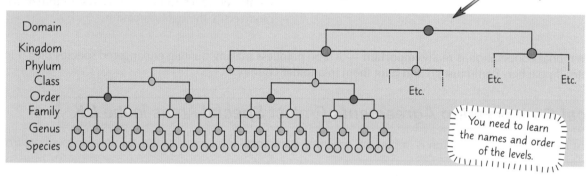

*You need to learn the names and order of the levels.*

5) As you move **down** the hierarchy, there are **more groups** at each level but **fewer organisms** in each group.

6) The hierarchy **ends** with **species** — the groups that contain only **one type** of organism (e.g. humans, dog, *E. coli* and about 50 million other living species).

## Organisms Can be Placed into One of Five Kingdoms

The **five kingdom classification system** is a bit old now (see page 117), but you still need to **learn** these five kingdoms and the **general characteristics** of the organisms in each of them:

| KINGDOM | EXAMPLES | FEATURES |
|---|---|---|
| *Prokaryotae* | bacteria | prokaryotic, unicellular (single-celled), no nucleus, less than 5 µm |
| *Protoctista* | algae, protozoa | eukaryotic cells, usually live in water, single-celled or simple multicellular organisms |
| *Fungi* | moulds, yeasts, mushrooms | eukaryotic, chitin cell wall, saprotrophic (absorb substances from dead or decaying organisms), single-celled or multicellular organisms |
| *Plantae* | mosses, ferns, flowering plants | eukaryotic, multicellular, cell walls made of cellulose, can photosynthesise, contain chlorophyll, autotrophic (produce their own food) |
| *Animalia* | nematodes (roundworms), molluscs, insects, fish, reptiles, birds, mammals | eukaryotic, multicellular, no cell walls, heterotrophic (consume plants and animals) |

*Plants are also known as photoautotrophs — they produce their own food using light.*

# Classification Basics

## The Binomial Naming System is Used in Classification

1) The **nomenclature** (**naming system**) used for classification is called the **binomial system** — all organisms are given **one** internationally accepted scientific **name** in **Latin** that has **two parts**.

2) The **first part** of the name is the **genus** name and has a capital letter. The **second part** is the **species** name and begins with a lower case letter. E.g. using the binomial system humans are *Homo sapiens*. Names are always written in *italics* (or they're <u>underlined</u> if they're **handwritten**).

3) The binomial system helps to avoid the **confusion** of using **common names**. E.g. over 100 different plant species are called **raspberries** and one species of buttercup has over 90 different common names.

## Phylogeny Tells Us About the Evolutionary History of Organisms

1) **Phylogeny** is the study of the **evolutionary history** of groups of **organisms**. Phylogeny tells us **who's related** to whom and how **closely related** they are.

2) All organisms have **evolved** from shared **common ancestors** (relatives). This can be shown on a **phylogenetic tree**, like this one. ⟹

First branch point

Orangutan
Human
Chimpanzee
Bonobo
Gorilla

3) This tree shows the **relationship** between members of the Hominidae family (great apes and humans). The **first branch point** represents a **common ancestor** of **all** the family members. This ancestor is now **extinct**. **Orangutans** were the first group to **diverge** (evolve to become a different species) from this common ancestor.

4) Each of the following branch points represents **another common ancestor** from which a **different group diverged**. Gorillas diverged next, then humans, closely followed by bonobos and chimpanzees.

5) According to phylogenetics, a **species** is the **smallest group** that shares a **common ancestor** — in other words, the **end of a branch** on a phylogenetic tree.

This is known as the phylogenetic species concept.

6) Closely related species **diverged** away from each other **most recently**. E.g. humans and **chimpanzees** are **closely** related, as they diverged very **recently**. You can see this because their branches are **close** together. Humans and orangutans are more **distantly** related, as they diverged longer ago, so their branches are **further** apart.

**Classification** systems now take into account **phylogeny** when arranging organisms into **groups**. Classifying organisms in this way is known as **cladistics**.

## Practice Questions

Q1 List the taxonomic hierarchy in order, starting at the top.

Q2 Give two features of the kingdom Fungi.

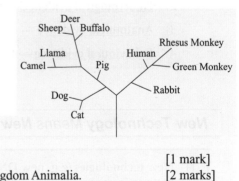

Deer
Sheep   Buffalo
Rhesus Monkey
Llama          Human
Camel       Pig          Green Monkey
Rabbit
Dog
Cat

### Exam Questions

Q1 The brown trout is part of the Salmonidae family. Its Latin name is *Salmo trutta*. It is part of the kingdom Animalia.

a) What genus does the brown trout belong to? [1 mark]

b) Give two features that the brown trout must have to place it in the kingdom Animalia. [2 marks]

Q2 The phylogenetic tree above shows the evolutionary history of some mammalian species.

a) Which species shown on the tree is most closely related to humans? Explain how you know this. [2 marks]

b) On the tree, circle the most recent common ancestor of both camels and deer. [1 mark]

---

## Snozcumber kingdom features — long, thin, green, filled with snot...

*Make sure that you really understand all the basics on these pages before delving any deeper into this section. Learning the order of the levels in the taxonomic hierarchy is about as easy as licking your elbow... try making up a mnemonic to help (like 'Dopey King Prawns Can't Order Fried Green Sausages' for Domain, Kingdom, Phylum, Class, Order, Family, etc).*

# Evolution of Classification Systems

*Classification systems and the groups organisms are placed in aren't set in stone. New technology and new evidence can lead to changes in these systems and the reclassification of organisms.*

## Classification Systems are now Based on a Range of Evidence

### Observable Features aren't Always Enough

1) Early classification systems **only** used **observable features** (things you can see) to place organisms into groups, e.g. whether they lay eggs, can fly or can cook a mean chilli...

2) But this method has **problems**. Scientists don't always agree on the **relative importance** of different features and groups based **solely on physical features** may not show how **related** organisms are.

**EXAMPLE**

**Sharks** and **whales look** quite similar and they both **live** in the **sea**. But they're **not** actually **closely related**. Whales are **mammals** and sharks are **cartilaginous fish** — two completely **different classes**.

It's not all about looks, you know.

### Other Evidence Shows How Similar Organisms are

1) Classification systems are **now** based on observable features **along** with **other evidence**.

2) The **more similar** organisms are, the **more related** they are. We now use a wide range of evidence to see **how similar**, and therefore how related, organisms are.

**EXAMPLES**

1) <u>Molecular evidence</u> — the similarities in **proteins** and **DNA**. **More closely related** organisms will have **more similar** molecules.

   • You can **compare** things like how **DNA** is **stored** and the **sequence** of DNA **bases** (see page 124 for more). E.g. the **base sequence** for human and chimpanzee **DNA** is about 94% the **same**.

   • You can also compare the **sequence** of **amino acids** in **proteins** from different organisms. E.g. **cytochrome C** is a short protein found in many species. The more **similar** the **amino acid sequence** of cytochrome C in two different species, the **more closely related** the species are likely to be.

2) <u>Embryological evidence</u> — the similarities in the **early stages** of an organism's **development**.

3) <u>Anatomical evidence</u> — the similarities in **structure** and **function** of different body parts.

4) <u>Behavioural evidence</u> — the similarities in **behaviour** and **social organisation** of organisms.

### New Technology Means New Discoveries

1) **New technologies** (e.g. new DNA techniques, better **microscopes**) can result in **new discoveries** being made and the **relationships** between organisms being **clarified**.

2) Scientists can share their new discoveries in **meetings** and **scientific journals** (see p. 2). How organisms are **classified** is **continually revised** to take account of any **new findings** that scientists **discover**.

**EXAMPLE**

Skunks **were** classified in the family **Mustelidae** until **molecular evidence** revealed their **DNA sequence** was significantly different to other members of that family. So they were reclassified into the family **Mephitidae**.

# Evolution of Classification Systems

## Five Kingdoms Vs Three Domains

The **five kingdom classification system** shown on page 114 has now been replaced with the **three domain system**:

1) In the older **system** the **largest groups** were the **five kingdoms** — all organisms were placed into **one** of these groups.

2) In 1990, the **three domain system** was proposed. This new system has three domains — **large superkingdoms** that are **above** the kingdoms in the **taxonomic hierarchy** (see p. 114).

3) In the three domain system, organisms that were in the kingdom **Prokaryotae** (which contains unicellular organisms **without a nucleus**) are separated into two domains — the **Archaea** and **Bacteria**.

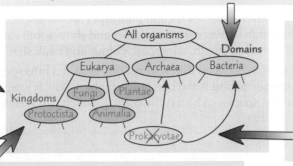

4) Organisms with cells that **contain a nucleus** are placed in the domain **Eukarya** (this includes four of the five kingdoms).

5) The **lower** hierarchy stays the **same** — Kingdom, Phylum, Class, Order, Family, Genus, Species.

## Molecular Evidence Led to the Proposal of the Three Domain System

1) The three domain system was proposed because of **new evidence**, mainly molecular. E.g. the **Prokaryotae** were **reclassified** into **two domains** because new evidence showed **large differences** between the Archaea and Bacteria. The new evidence included:

- Molecular evidence — The enzyme **RNA polymerase** (needed to make RNA) is **different** in Bacteria and Archaea. **Archaea**, but **not Bacteria**, have similar **histones** (proteins that bind to DNA) to **Eukarya**.
- Cell membrane evidence — The **bonds** of the **lipids** (see p. 24) in the **cell membranes** of Bacteria and Archaea are **different**. The **development** and composition of **flagellae** (see p. 13) are also **different**.

2) Most scientists now **agree** that Archaea and Bacteria **evolved separately** and that Archaea are **more closely related** to Eukarya than Bacteria. The three domain system reflects how **different** the Archaea and Bacteria are.

3) The development of the three domain system is an example of how **scientific knowledge** is always **changing** and **improving** (see page 2).

## Practice Questions

Q1 What evidence were the first classification systems solely based on?

Q2 Give three types of evidence currently used to classify organisms.

Q3 What is meant by a domain?

**Exam Questions**

Q1 A gibbon is a type of ape. Describe one way in which scientists could use molecular evidence to determine how closely gibbons are related to humans. [2 marks]

Q2 The three domain system of classification places Cyanobacteria in the domain Bacteria. Describe three differences between organisms in the Bacteria and Archaea domains. [3 marks]

---

## Five kingdoms, three domains — all the makings of a great TV series...

*So there you have it — lots of exciting new discoveries. Molecular evidence in particular has a lot to answer for — imagine thinking you were a Prokaryote, then waking up one morning and discovering you were an archaeon. It's enough to give anyone issues. Make sure you learn why the three domain system was proposed and what it replaced.*

# Variation

*Ever wondered why no two people are exactly alike?  No, well nor have I actually, but it's time to start thinking about it.  This variation is partly genetic and partly due to differences in the environment.*

## Variation Exists Between All Individuals

Here's how I remember which is which — Int-**er** means diff-**er**-ent species.

**Variation** is the **differences** that exist between **individuals**.  Every individual organism is **unique** — even **clones** (such as identical twins) show some **variation**.  It can occur:

1) <u>Within species</u> — Variation within a species is called **intraspecific** variation.  For example, **individual** European robins weigh **between** 16 g and 22 g and show some variation in many other characteristics including length, wingspan, colour and beak size.

2) <u>Between species</u> — The variation between **different species** is called **interspecific** variation.  For example, the **lightest** species of bird is the bee hummingbird, which weighs around 1.6 g on average.  The **heaviest** species of bird is the ostrich, which can weigh up to 160 kg (100 000 times as much).

No matter what anyone said, Malcolm knew size was important.

## Variation can be Continuous...

Continuous variation is when the **individuals** in a population vary **within a range** — there are **no distinct categories**, e.g. **humans** can be **any height** within a range (139 cm, 175 cm, 185.9 cm, etc.), **not just** tall or short.  Here are some more examples:

The categories are <u>not</u> distinct

| Animals |

1) **Milk yield** — e.g. cows can produce any volume of milk within a range.
2) **Mass** — e.g. humans can be any mass within a range.

| Plants |

1) **Number of leaves** — e.g. a tree can have any number of leaves within a range.
2) **Mass** — e.g. the mass of the seeds from a flower head varies within a range.

*Number of people*

*Height*

| Microorganisms |

1) **Width** — e.g. the width of *E. coli* bacteria varies within a range.
2) **Length** — e.g. the length of the flagellum (see p. 13) can vary within a range.

## ...or Discontinuous

Discontinuous variation is when there are two or more **distinct categories** — each individual falls into **only one** of these categories, there are **no intermediates**.  Here are some examples:

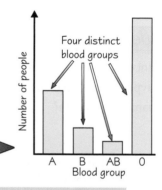

Four distinct blood groups

*Number of people*

A   B   AB   O
Blood group

| Animals |

**Blood group** — e.g. humans can be group A, B, AB or O.

| Plants |

1) **Colour** — e.g. courgettes are either yellow, dark green or light green.
2) **Seed shape** — e.g. some pea plants have smooth seeds and some have wrinkled seeds.

| Microorganisms |

1) **Antibiotic resistance** — e.g. bacteria are either resistant or not.
2) **Pigment production** — e.g. some types of bacteria can produce a coloured pigment, some can't.

# Variation

## Variation can be Caused by Genes, the Environment, or Both

Variation can be caused by **genetic factors**, **environmental factors** or a combination of **both**:

### 1 Genetic factors

1) **Different species** have **different genes**.

2) Individuals of the **same species** have the **same genes**, but **different versions** of them (called **alleles**).

3) The genes and alleles an organism has make up its **genotype**.

4) The differences in **genotype** result in **variation** in **phenotype** — the **characteristics** displayed by an organism.

5) Examples of variation caused **only** by genetic factors include **blood group** in humans (O, A, B or AB) and **antibiotic resistance** in bacteria.

6) You **inherit** your genes from your parents. This means variation caused by genetic factors is **inherited**.

### 2 Environmental factors

1) Variation can also be caused by **differences in the environment**, e.g. climate, food, lifestyle.

2) Characteristics controlled by environmental factors can **change** over an organism's life.

3) Examples of variation caused **only** by environmental factors include **accents** and whether people have **pierced ears**.

### 3 Both

**Genetic factors** determine the characteristics an organism's **born with**, but **environmental factors** can **influence** how some characteristics **develop**. For example:

1) **Height** — genes determine how tall an organism **can grow** (e.g. tall parents tend to have tall children). But **diet or nutrient availability** affect how tall an organism **actually grows**.

2) **Flagellum** — genes determine if a microorganism **can grow** a flagellum, but some will only **start to grow** them in **certain environments**, e.g. if metal ions are present.

## You Can Use the Mean to Look for Variation Between Samples

1) To **investigate variation** you usually take **samples** of a population (see page 106).

2) The **mean** is an **average** of the values collected in a sample. It can be used to tell if there is **variation between samples**. For example:

> The **mean height** of a species of **tree** in woodland A = **26 m**, in woodland B = **32 m** and in woodland C = **35 m**. So the **mean height varies**.

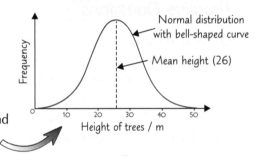

3) Most samples will include values **either side** of the **mean**, so you end up with a **bell-shaped graph** — this is called a **normal distribution**. A normal distribution is **symmetrical** about the mean.

## The Standard Deviation Tells You About Variation Within a Sample

1) The **standard deviation** tells you how much the **values** in a **single sample** vary. It's a measure of the **spread** of values about the **mean**.

2) Sometimes you'll see the mean written as, e.g. **9 ± 3**. This means that the **mean** is **9** and the **standard deviation** is **3**, so most of the **values** are spread between **6** and **12**.

3) A **large standard deviation** means the values in the sample **vary a lot**. A **small standard deviation** tells you that most of the sample data is around the mean value, so **varies little**.

Here, all the values are <u>similar</u> and <u>close to the mean</u>, so the graph is steep and the <u>standard deviation is small</u>.

Here, the values <u>vary a lot</u>, so the graph is fatter and the <u>standard deviation is large</u>.

# Variation

## You Can Find the Standard Deviation Using the Formula

This is the formula for finding the standard deviation of a group of values:

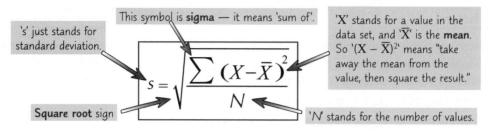

This symbol is **sigma** — it means 'sum of'.

's' just stands for standard deviation.

'X' stands for a value in the data set, and 'X̄' is the **mean**. So '(X − X̄)²' means "take away the mean from the value, then square the result."

$$s = \sqrt{\frac{\sum (X - \bar{X})^2}{N}}$$

Square root sign

'N' stands for the number of values.

### Example:

The table shows the height of four different trees in a forest. To find the **standard deviation**:

| Tree | Height (m) |
|------|-----------|
| A | 22 |
| B | 27 |
| C | 26 |
| D | 29 |

**1** Write out the **equation**. $s = \sqrt{\dfrac{\sum (X - \bar{X})^2}{N}}$

**2** Work out the **mean** height of the trees, $\bar{X}$.    $(22 + 27 + 26 + 29) \div 4 = \mathbf{26}$

**3** Work out $(X - \bar{X})^2$ for each value of X.
For each tree height in the table, you need to take away the mean, then square the answer.

A:  $(22 - 26)^2 = (-4)^2 = \mathbf{16}$      B:  $(27 - 26)^2 = 1^2 = \mathbf{1}$
C:  $(26 - 26)^2 = 0^2 = \mathbf{0}$      D:  $(29 - 26)^2 = 3^2 = \mathbf{9}$

**4** **Add up** all these numbers to find $\sum (X - \bar{X})^2$.    $16 + 1 + 0 + 9 = \mathbf{26}$

**5** **Divide** this number by the number of values, N, then take the **square root** to get the answer.

$26 \div 4 = 6.5$
$\sqrt{6.5} = \mathbf{2.55 \text{ to } 3 \text{ s.f.}}$

## Practice Questions

Q1 What is variation?

Q2 Describe what is meant by continuous variation and give one example.

Q3 Describe what is meant by discontinuous variation and give one example.

Q4 What does the standard deviation of a set of data tell us?

### Exam Question

Q1 The graph shows the results of an investigation into the effects of temperature on the length of time it took for ladybird larvae to emerge as adults. Two species of ladybird were investigated, species A and species B.

a) Describe the results of the study.    [2 marks]

b) Explain what causes the variation within each species.    [1 mark]

---

## *Environmental Factor — the search is on for the most talented environment...*

*It's amazing to think how many factors and genes influence the way we look and behave. It's the reason why every single organism is unique. My parents have often said they're glad they'll never have another child as 'unique' as me.*

# Adaptations

*All the variation between and within species means that some organisms are better adapted to their environment than others...*

## Adaptations make Organisms **Well Suited** to Their **Environment**

1) Being **adapted** to an environment means an organism has features that **increase** its **chances of survival** and **reproduction**, and also the chances of its **offspring reproducing successfully**.

2) These features are called **adaptations** and can be behavioural, physiological and anatomical (see below).

3) Adaptations develop because of **evolution** by **natural selection** (see page 123).

4) In each generation, the **best-adapted individuals** are more likely to survive and reproduce — passing their adaptations on to their **offspring**. Individuals that are less well adapted are more likely to **die before reproducing**.

## Adaptations can be **Behavioural**, **Physiological** and **Anatomical**

**Behavioural adaptations**

Ways an organism **acts** that increase its chance of survival. For example:

- **Possums** sometimes '**play dead**' — if they're being threatened by a **predator** they play dead to **escape attack**. This **increases** their chance of **survival**.

- **Scorpions dance** before **mating** — this makes sure they attract a mate of the **same species**, increasing the likelihood of **successful mating**.

*Bob and Sue were well adapted to hiding in candyfloss shops.*

**Physiological adaptations**

**Processes** inside an organism's body that increase its chance of survival. For example:

- **Brown bears hibernate** — they **lower their rate of metabolism** (all the chemical reactions taking place in their body) over **winter**. This **conserves energy**, so they don't need to look for **food** in the months when it's scarce — **increasing** their chance of **survival**.

- **Some bacteria** produce **antibiotics** — these **kill** other species of bacteria in the area. This means there's **less competition**, so they're **more likely to survive**.

**Anatomical (structural) adaptations**

**Structural features** of an organism's body that increase its chance of survival. For example:

- **Otters** have a **streamlined shape** — making it easier to **glide** through the **water**. This makes it easier for them to **catch prey** and **escape predators**, increasing their chance of **survival**.

- **Whales** have a **thick layer** of **blubber** (fat) — this helps to keep them **warm** in the cold sea. This increases their chance of survival in places where their **food** is found.

## Different Taxonomic Groups May Have **Similar Features**

1) Organisms from **different** taxonomic groups may have **similar** features even though they're **not closely related** — for example, whales and sharks (see page 116).

2) This is usually because the organisms have **evolved** in **similar environments** and to fill **similar ecological niches**.

3) The example you need to learn for your exam is of **marsupial** and **placental moles** — see next page.

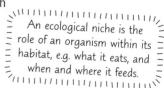
*An ecological niche is the role of an organism within its habitat, e.g. what it eats, and when and where it feeds.*

# Adaptations

## Marsupial and Placental Mammals Have Evolved Separately

1) There are **three different groups** of mammals. Most mammals are **placental mammals**, while some are **marsupials** (and a very few are egg-laying monotremes).

2) Marsupials are found mainly in **Australia** and the **Americas**. They **diverged** from placental mammals many **millions of years ago** and have been **evolving separately** ever since.

**Marsupial** mammals (e.g. kangaroos):
- have a **short gestation period** (pregnancy).
- don't develop a **full placenta**.
- are born **early** in their development and climb into their mother's **pouch**. Here they become attached to a **teat** and receive milk while they **continue** to **develop**.

**Placental** mammals (e.g. humans):
- have a **longer gestation period**.
- develop a **placenta** during pregnancy, which allows the **exchange of nutrients** and **waste products** between the fetus and the mother.
- are born more **fully developed**.

## Marsupial and Placental Moles Look Alike But Aren't Closely Related

1) **Marsupial** moles and **placental** moles **aren't closely related** — they **evolved independently** on different **continents**.

2) They do share **similar anatomical features** though (i.e. they look alike). That's because they've both evolved to live in **similar environments**:

*When two species evolve similar characteristics independently of one another (because they've adapted to live in similar environments) it's called convergent evolution.*

Both types of mole live in **tunnels** in the ground. They **burrow** to reach their **food supply** (e.g. earthworms, insects and other invertebrates). Their **adaptations** to this lifestyle include:
- **Small** or **nonexistent eyes** because they don't need to be able to see underground.
- **No external ears**, to keep a **streamlined head** for burrowing.
- **Scoop-shaped** and **powerful front paws**, which are good for digging.
- **Claws** that are specialised for digging.
- A **tube shaped body** and **cone shaped head**, which makes it easier to push through sand or soil.

## Practice Questions

Q1 What is meant by the term adaptation?

Q2 Describe the differences between behavioural, physiological and anatomical adaptations.

Q3 Explain why marsupial moles and placental moles share similar anatomical features, even though they are not closely related.

Q4 Give two anatomical features marsupial and placental moles have in common.

**Exam Question**

Q1 a) Both whales and sharks have developed a streamlined body and fins, despite being from different taxonomic groups. Suggest why. [1 mark]

b) Like humans, whales are mammals. This means they can't breathe underwater and have to come to the surface for air. However, whales have developed the ability to exchange up to 90% of the oxygen in their lungs compared to the human average of 10-15%.

Suggest why humans haven't developed the same oxygen-exchanging ability as whales. [1 mark]

## I'm perfectly adapted — for staying in bed...

*Adaptations are features that make an organism more likely to survive and reproduce. Repetitive? Yes, but that's why it's so easy to learn. Adaptations develop because of evolution by natural selection, which is on the next page. Lucky you.*

# The Theory of Evolution

*Evolution is the slow and continual change of organisms from one generation to the next. It explains how advantageous adaptations become common within a population of organisms...*

## Darwin Published his Theory of Evolution by Natural Selection in 1859

Darwin made **four** key observations about the world around him.

**Observations:**
1) Organisms produce **more offspring** than **survive**.
2) There's **variation** in the characteristics of members of the **same species**.
3) Some of these characteristics can be **passed on** from one generation to the next.
4) Individuals that are **best adapted** to their environment are more likely to **survive**.

Darwin wrote his theory of **evolution by natural selection** to **explain** his observations:

*Natural selection is one process by which evolution occurs.*

**Theory:**
1) Individuals within a population **show variation** in their **phenotypes** (their characteristics).
2) **Selection pressures** (environmental factors such as **predation**, **disease** and **competition**) create a **struggle for survival**.
3) Individuals with **better adaptations** (characteristics that give a selective advantage, e.g. being able to run away from predators faster) are **more likely** to **survive** and have **reproductive success** — in other words, they **reproduce** and **pass on** their advantageous adaptations to their **offspring**.
4) Over time, the **proportion** of the population possessing the **advantageous adaptations increases**.
5) Over generations this leads to **evolution** as the favourable adaptations become **more common** in the population.

*The opposite is also true — organisms without these adaptations are less likely to survive and have reproductive success.*

1) We now know that **genes** determine many of an organism's **characteristics** and that individuals show variations in their **phenotypes** partly as a result of **genetic variation**, i.e. the different **alleles** they have.
2) When an organism with advantageous characteristics **reproduces**, the **alleles** that determine those characteristics may be passed on to its **offspring**.

## Wallace Contributed to the Theory of Evolution

**Alfred Russel Wallace**, a scientist working at the **same time** as Darwin, played an important part in developing the **theory of evolution by natural selection**.
- He **independently** came up with the idea of **natural selection** and wrote to Darwin about it.
- He and Darwin **published** their **papers** on evolution **together** and acknowledged each other's work — although they **didn't always agree** about the mechanisms involved in natural selection.
- Wallace's **observations** provided lots of **evidence** to **support** the theory of evolution by natural selection. For example, he realised that **warning colours** are used by some species (e.g. butterflies) to deter predators from eating them and that this was an example of an **advantageous adaptation** that had evolved by natural selection.

1) Unfortunately for Wallace, it wasn't until Darwin published his famous book **'On the Origin of Species'** that other **scientists** began to pay **attention** to the theory.
2) In this book Darwin gave lots of **evidence** to support the theory and expanded on it. For example, he wrote about all the **species** that he had **observed** during his voyage to South America and the Galápagos Islands in the 1830s.
3) The book is partly why **Darwin** is usually **better remembered** than Wallace — even though **Wallace helped** to come up with the **theory**.

# The Theory of Evolution

## There's *Plenty of Evidence* to *Support Evolution*

### Fossil Record Evidence

Fossils are the **remains** of organisms **preserved in rocks**.
By arranging fossils in chronological (date) order, **gradual changes** in organisms can be observed that provide **evidence** of evolution.

**Example** — The fossil record of the **horse** shows a **gradual change** in characteristics, including increasing **size** and **hoof** development.

### DNA Evidence

1) The theory of evolution suggests that all organisms have **evolved** from shared **common ancestors**.
2) Closely related species **diverged** (evolved to become different species) **more recently**.
3) Evolution is caused by **gradual changes** in the **base sequence** of an organisms' DNA.
4) Organisms that diverged away from each other more recently, should have **more similar DNA**, as **less time** has passed for changes in the DNA sequence to occur. This is exactly what scientists have found.

See p. 38 for more on the DNA base sequence.

Chimps   Humans
Mice
Common ancestor

**Example** — Humans, chimps and mice all evolved from a common ancestor. Humans and mice diverged a **long time ago**, but humans and chimps diverged **quite recently**. The DNA base sequence of humans and chimps is 94% the same, but human and mouse DNA is only 85% the same.

In **eukaryotes**, most DNA is found in the **cell nucleus**. But scientists don't just analyse **nuclear DNA** to find out about **evolutionary relationships**. Eukaryotic organisms also have **DNA** in their **mitochondria**, so scientists can also look at **differences** in **mitochondrial DNA** to see how **closely related** organisms are.

### Molecular Evidence

In addition to DNA, the similarities in **other molecules** provide evidence. Scientists compare the **sequence** of **amino acids** in **proteins**, and compare **antibodies**. Organisms that diverged away from each other **more recently** have **more similar molecules**, as **less time** has passed for changes in proteins and other molecules to occur.

## *Populations* of *Insects* can *Evolve Resistance* to *Pesticides*

**Pesticides** are chemicals that **kill pests** (e.g. insects that damage crops). Scientists have observed the evolution of **pesticide resistance** in many species of insect.

For example, some populations of **mosquito** have **evolved resistance** to the pesticide **DDT**. Some populations of **pollen beetles** (which damage the crop oilseed rape) are resistant to **pyrethroid** pesticides.

Janet was resistant to DDT but not to Malcolm's smooth talking.

The evolution of **pesticide resistance** can be explained by **natural selection**:
1) There is **variation** in a population of insects. **Genetic mutations** create **alleles** that make some insects naturally **resistant** to a pesticide.
2) If the population of insects is exposed to that pesticide only the individuals with resistance will **survive** to **reproduce**.
3) The **alleles** which cause the pesticide resistance will be **passed on** to the next generation, and so the population will **evolve** — more individuals will carry the allele than in the previous generation.

The pesticide acts as a selection pressure — without a selection pressure, natural selection won't take place.

# The Theory of Evolution

## The Evolution of **Pesticide Resistance** has **Implications** for **Humans**

1) **Crop infestations** with **pesticide-resistant** insects are **harder** to **control** — some insects are resistant to **lots of different pesticides**. It takes farmers a while to figure out which pesticide will kill the insect and in that time **all** the crop could be **destroyed**. If the insects are resistant to specific pesticides (ones that only kill that insect), farmers might have to use **broader pesticides** (those that kill a range of insects), which could kill beneficial insects.

2) If **disease-carrying** insects (e.g. mosquitoes) become pesticide-resistant, the **spread of disease** could **increase**.

3) A population of insects could **evolve resistance** to **all** pesticides in use. To prevent this **new pesticides** need to be **produced**. This takes **time** and costs **money**.

## The Evolution of **Drug Resistance** Has **Implications** for **Humans** Too

1) You might remember from page 104 that scientists have observed the **evolution** of **antibiotic resistance** in many species of **bacteria**, e.g. **MRSA**.

2) **Other pathogens** have **evolved resistance** to specific **drugs** too. For example, some of the **protoctista** that cause **malaria** (see page 94) are **resistant** to several drugs used to treat malaria.

3) **Infections** caused by drug-resistant microorganisms are **harder** to **treat** — especially if the microorganism is resistant to **lots of different drugs**. It can take doctors a while to figure out which drugs will get rid of the infection, and in that time the **patient** could become **very ill** or **die**.

4) There could come a point where a pathogen has become resistant to **all the drugs** we currently use against it. To prevent this, **new drugs** need to be **developed**. This takes **time** and costs a lot of **money**.

## Practice Questions

Q1 What four key observations did Darwin make?

Q2 Give one way in which Wallace contributed to the theory of evolution.

Q3 Briefly describe how fossil evidence supports the theory of evolution.

Q4 Describe how DNA evidence supports the theory of evolution.

### Exam Questions

Q1 Tawny owls show variation in colour. There are light grey owls and darker brown owls. Before the 1970s there were more grey owls than brown owls in Finland. Since then, climate change has been causing a decrease in the amount of snowfall in Finland. During this period, the darker brown owls have become more common.

a) Suggest why the brown owls are better adapted to living in an area with less snowfall than the grey owls. [2 marks]

b) Explain how the brown owls have become more common. [3 marks]

Q2 The diamondback moth is a pest of many crops. In 1953 it became resistant to the pesticide DDT and by 1981 it had become resistant to 36 other pesticides.

a) Explain how the diamondback moth populations could have developed DDT resistance. [4 marks]

b) Describe two possible implications of the diamondback moth developing resistance to pesticides. [2 marks]

## The fossil record — it rocks...

*Evolution by natural selection isn't that bad really... just remember that any adaptation that increases the chances of an organism surviving (e.g. by avoiding being killed by antibiotics) or reproducing will increase in the population due to the process of natural selection. Now I know why mullets have disappeared... so unattractive...*

# Answers

## Module 1 — Development of Practical Skills

### Page 9

1 a) Any three from: e.g. the concentration of amylase solution used. / The concentration of starch solution used. / The volume of amylase solution used. / The volume of starch solution used. / The procedure used to mix the amylase and starch solutions together. / The volume of the sample added to the spot tile. / The volume of iodine solution added to each sample.
*[1 mark for each correct answer.*
*Maximum of three marks available.]*

 b) It is an anomalous result *[1 mark]*.

 c) Any two from: e.g. the solutions of amylase and starch were mixed together before they were placed in the water bath, so the reaction started before the test temperature was reached *[1 mark]*. This could be improved by putting the solutions in the water bath and bringing them both to the desired temperature before they are mixed together *[1 mark]*. / The samples were only tested every minute which means the results may not be very accurate *[1 mark]*. This could be improved by testing the samples at more regular intervals *[1 mark]*. / The colour change depends heavily on personal judgement so the results may not be reproducible *[1 mark]*. This could be improved by making sure the same person determines the colour change each time/using a colorimeter to record the colour change *[1 mark]*.

 d) Between 10 °C and 40 °C the time taken for amylase to break down starch decreases slowly *[1 mark]*. From 40 °C to 60 °C the time taken for amylase to break down starch increases rapidly *[1 mark]*.

## Module 2: Section 1 — Cell Structure

### Page 13 — Eukaryotic Cells and Organelles

1 B *[1 mark]*
2 a) i) mitochondrion *[1 mark]*
 ii) Golgi apparatus *[1 mark]*
 b) Mitochondria are the site of aerobic respiration *[1 mark]*. The Golgi apparatus processes and packages new lipids and proteins / makes lysosomes *[1 mark]*.

### Page 15 — Prokaryotic Cells

1 a) Ribosomes *[1 mark]* because this is where protein synthesis occurs *[1 mark]*.
 b) The rough endoplasmic reticulum *[1 mark]* and some vesicles *[1 mark]*.
 c) Vesicles transport substances in and out of the cell and between organelles *[1 mark]*.
2 Any three from: supports the cell's organelles *[1 mark]*. / Strengthens the cell/maintains its shape *[1 mark]*. / Transports materials around the cell *[1 mark]*. / Enables cell movement *[1 mark]*.

### Page 17 — Studying Cells — How Microscopes Work

1 Magnification = image size ÷ object size
 = 80 mm ÷ 0.5 mm *[1 mark]*
 = × 160 *[1 mark]*
 Always remember to convert everything to the same units first — the insect is 0.5 mm long, so the length of the image needs to be changed from 8 cm to 80 mm.
2 Image size = magnification × object size
 = 100 × 0.059 mm *[1 mark]*
 = **5.9 mm** *[1 mark]*
 Hint: To convert 59 µm into mm, divide by 1000.
3 a) mitochondrion *[1 mark]* and nucleus *[1 mark]*
 The resolution of light microscopes is not good enough to show objects smaller than 0.2 µm *[1 mark]*.

 b) All of the organelles in the table would be visible *[1 mark]*. The resolution of SEMs is good enough to resolve objects down to about 0.002 µm in size *[1 mark]*.

### Page 19 — Studying Cells — Using Microscopes

1 a) 10 ÷ 6.5 = **1.5 µm** *[2 marks for the correct answer or 1 mark for the correct calculation]*
 b) 14 × 1.5 = **21 µm** *[1 mark for multiplying 14 by answer to part a), 1 mark for an answer of 21 or 22 µm.]*

## Module 2: Section 2 — Biological Molecules

### Page 21 — Water

1 As the water evaporates from the surface of the elephant's body *[1 mark]*, some of the elephant's heat energy is used to break the hydrogen bonds which hold the water molecules together *[1 mark]*. This cools the surface of the elephant's body *[1 mark]*.

### Page 23 — Carbohydrates

1 B *[1 mark]*
 Remember a hexose monosaccharide is one with six carbon atoms and carbohydrates don't contain nitrogen, so the chemical formula must be $C_6H_{12}O_6$.

2 Glycogen is a polysaccharide of alpha-glucose, which is used to store excess glucose in animals *[1 mark]*. It has a branched structure, meaning glucose can be released quickly *[1 mark]*. It's also a very compact molecule, so it's good for storage *[1 mark]*.

### Page 25 — Lipids

1 They arrange themselves into a (phospholipid) bilayer/double layer *[1 mark]*, with fatty acid tails facing towards each other *[1 mark]*. This is because the fatty acid tails are hydrophobic (water-repelling), forcing them to face inwards, away from the water on either side of the membrane *[1 mark]*.

2 a) The flattened shape allows the cholesterol molecules to fit in between the phospholipids, causing the phospholipids to pack together more tightly *[1 mark]*, which makes the membrane less fluid and more rigid *[1 mark]*.

 b) The hydrophobic tails force triglycerides to clump together in the cytoplasm as insoluble droplets *[1 mark]*. This means they can be stored in cells without affecting the cell's water potential *[1 mark]*.

### Page 28 — Proteins

1 keratin *[1 mark]*
2 *5-6 marks:*
 The answer fully describes four different bonds that may be in the tertiary structure and explains clearly how the structure of HSA makes it suited to its role.
 The answer has a clear and logical structure.
 The information given is relevant and detailed.
 *3-4 marks:*
 The answer describes two or three of the bonds that may be in the tertiary structure and explains briefly how the structure of HSA makes it suited to its role.
 The answer has some structure. Most of the information given is relevant and there is some detail involved.
 *1-2 marks:*
 The answer briefly describes one of the bonds that may be in the tertiary structure and there is an attempt to link the structure of HSA to its role.
 The answer has no clear structure. The information given is basic and lacking in detail. It may not all be relevant.
 *0 marks:*
 No relevant information is given.

# Answers

**Here are some points your answer may include:**
The tertiary structure may contain ionic interactions.
These are weak attractions between negatively-charged R
groups and positively-charged R groups on different parts of the
molecule. It may also contain disulfide bonds, which form when
the sulfur atoms in two nearby cysteine molecules bond.
There may also be hydrogen bonds, which are weak bonds
between slightly positively-charged hydrogen atoms in some
R groups, and slightly negatively-charged atoms in other R groups
on the polypeptide chain. The tertiary structure will also contain
hydrophobic and hydrophilic interactions. Hydrophobic R groups
clump together, meaning that hydrophilic R groups are more
likely to be pushed to the outside. This will make HSA soluble in
water, which makes it suited for its role of transporting molecules
in the blood.

## Page 29 — Inorganic Ions

1   hydrogencarbonate *[1 mark]*, $HCO_3^-$ *[1 mark]*
    *If a $H_2CO_3$ molecule loses a hydrogen ion ($H^+$) it will become $HCO_3^-$.*
    *(You're told in the question an anion is made, so you should definitely know*
    *to add the minus sign.)*

## Page 31 — Biochemical Tests for Molecules

1 a) Solution C *[1 mark]*
    *Solution C has the lowest absorbance. It therefore has the least amount*
    *of Benedict's reagent* left *— so it had the most reducing sugar* before *the*
    *Benedict's test.*
  b) Any two from, e.g: the amount of Benedict's reagent used in each
    test tube *[1 mark]*. / The concentration of Benedict's reagent used
    *[1 mark]*. / The length of time each solution is left for *[1 mark]*.

## Page 33 — Biochemical Tests and Separating Molecules

1 a) A concentrated spot of the sugar solution was placed on the line
    at the bottom of the paper *[1 mark]*. The bottom of the paper was
    then dipped in a solvent *[1 mark]*. The paper was taken out when
    the solvent had nearly reached the top of the paper *[1 mark]*.
  b) The substances in the sugar solution travel different distances in
    the mobile phase *[1 mark]*.
  c) $R_f$ value = $\dfrac{\text{distance travelled by spot}}{\text{distance travelled by solvent}}$

    = 2.5 cm ÷ 10.4 cm = **0.24** *[2 marks for 0.24 or*
    *1 mark for the correct calculation]*
    The carbohydrate in spot X is fructose *[1 mark]*.
    *Fructose has a $R_f$ value of 0.24 in the table of $R_f$ values,*
    *so the carbohydrate in spot X is fructose.*

# Module 2: Section 3 — Nucleotides and Nucleic Acids

## Page 35 — Nucleotides

1 a) A is cytosine and B is adenine *[1 mark]*. Cytosine is a pyrimidine
    base, so it only has 1 (carbon-nitrogen) ring *[1 mark]*. Adenine is
    a purine with 2 (carbon-nitrogen) rings *[1 mark]*.
  b) Any one from: hydrogen / oxygen / carbon *[1 mark]*.
    *The carbon atoms aren't labelled in the diagrams on the page, but they're*
    *present at each corner of the rings (except where there's a N atom there*
    *instead).*
2 a) AMP consists of a ribose sugar *[1 mark]*, an adenine base
    *[1 mark]* and a single phosphate group *[1 mark]*.
    *Be specific with your answer here — make sure you write 'ribose' and*
    *'adenine' instead of just 'sugar' and 'base' or you won't get the marks.*
  b) phosphorylation *[1 mark]*
3   ATP contains the sugar ribose *[1 mark]* so increasing the heart's
    supply of ribose could help it to produce ATP faster *[1 mark]*.

## Page 37 — Polynucleotides and DNA

1 a) Nucleotides are joined between the phosphate group of one
    nucleotide and the (deoxyribose) sugar of the next *[1 mark]*
    by phosphodiester bonds *[1 mark]*. This is catalysed by DNA
    polymerase *[1 mark]*.
  b) Two polynucleotide strands join through hydrogen bonding
    between the base pairs *[1 mark]*. Base pairing is complementary
    (e.g. A always pairs with T and C always pairs with G) *[1 mark]*.
    The two (antiparallel) polynucleotide strands twist to form a DNA
    double helix *[1 mark]*.
2 a) The detergent breaks down cell membranes *[1 mark]*.
  b) He could have added an enzyme/RNase to the mixture before
    adding the ethanol *[1 mark]* to break down any RNA present
    *[1 mark]*.
3   **5-6 marks:**
    The answer describes the full process of DNA replication with
    correct references to the enzymes involved and bonding.
    The answer has a clear and logical structure.
    The information given is relevant and detailed.
    **3-4 marks:**
    The answer describes most of the process of DNA replication
    with some references to the enzymes involved or bonding.
    The answer has some structure. Most of the information
    given is relevant and there is some detail involved.
    **1-2 marks:**
    One or two steps involved in the process of
    DNA replication are referenced.
    The answer has no clear structure. The information given
    is basic and lacking in detail. It may not all be relevant.
    **0 marks:**
    No relevant information is given.
    **Here are some points your answer may include:**
    DNA helicase breaks the hydrogen bonds between the two DNA
    strands. The DNA helix unzips. Each strand acts as a template
    for a new strand. Individual free DNA nucleotides join up
    along the template strand by complementary base pairing.
    DNA polymerase joins the individual nucleotides together, so that
    the sugar-phosphate backbone forms. Hydrogen bonds then form
    between the bases on each strand and the strands twist to form a
    double-helix. Two identical DNA molecules are produced.
    Each of the new molecules contains a single strand from the
    original DNA molecule and a single new strand.

## Page 39 — Genes and Protein Synthesis

1   C *[1 mark]*
2 a) 4 *[1 mark]*
  b) GUG = valine
    UGU = cysteine
    CGC = arginine
    GCA = alanine
    Correct sequence = **valine, cysteine, arginine, alanine**.
    *[2 marks for all 4 amino acids in the correct order. 1 mark for*
    *a minimum of 3 correct amino acids in the correct order.]*
3 a) The mRNA sequence is 18 nucleotides long and the protein
    produced is 6 amino acids long *[1 mark]*. 18 ÷ 6 = 3, suggesting
    three nucleotides code for a single amino acid *[1 mark]*.
  b) E.g. The sequence produced began leucine-cysteine-glycine.
    This would only be produced if the code is non-overlapping, e.g.
    UUGUGUGGG = UUG-UGU-GGG = leucine-cysteine-glycine
    *[1 mark]*.
    *If the code was overlapping, the triplets would be, e.g. UUG-UGU-GUG-*
    *UGU, which would give a sequence starting leucine-cysteine-valine-cysteine.*
    Also, this part of the DNA sequence produces 6 amino acids. This
    is only correct if the code is non-overlapping — the sequence of
    amino acids would be longer if the code overlapped *[1 mark]*.

# Answers

## Page 41 — Transcription and Translation

1 a) CGCUUCAGGUAC *[1 mark]*
   b) GCGAAGUCCAUG *[1 mark]*
2 The drug binds to DNA, preventing RNA polymerase from binding, so transcription can't take place and no mRNA can be made *[1 mark]*. This means there's no mRNA for translation and so protein synthesis is inhibited *[1 mark]*.
3 $(10 \times 3 =)$ 30 nucleotides long *[1 mark]*. Each amino acid is coded for by three nucleotides (a codon), so the mRNA length in nucleotides is the number of amino acids multiplied by three *[1 mark]*.

# Module 2: Section 4 — Enzymes

## Page 43 — Action of Enzymes

1 Dextran binds to the active site of the dextranase enzyme *[1 mark]*. As it does so, dextran makes the active site change shape slightly to fit more closely around it *[1 mark]*. Amylose is not able to fit into dextranase's active site and make it change shape in the right way, so dextranase won't catalyse its breakdown *[1 mark]*.

## Page 46 — Factors Affecting Enzyme Activity

1 C *[1 mark]*
2 a) She could add a buffer solution of a different pH to each of the test tubes containing the milk powder solution *[1 mark]*.
   b) E.g. the volume of milk powder solution used in each test tube / the concentration of milk powder solution used in each test tube / the volume of trypsin used / the concentration of trypsin used / the temperature *[1 mark]*.
   c) Any four, valid points from: above the optimum pH, the OH⁻ ions in the alkaline solution *[1 mark]* will interfere with the ionic/ hydrogen bonds that hold trypsin's tertiary structure in place *[1 mark]*. This will make the active site change shape *[1 mark]*, so the rate of reaction will decrease *[1 mark]*. The enzyme will eventually denature *[1 mark]*. *[Maximum of 4 marks available.]*

## Page 47 — Cofactors and Enzyme Inhibition

1 C *[1 mark]*
   Galactose is a product inhibitor of ß-galactosidase. This means it's reversible, so it must bind to the enzyme via weak hydrogen or ionic bonds. Galactose is a competitive inhibitor because it binds to the active site of ß-galactosidase.
2 a) Magnesium ions are a cofactor for hexokinase *[1 mark]*. They help the enzyme and substrate bind together *[1 mark]*.
   b) Aluminium ions are an enzyme inhibitor for hexokinase *[1 mark]*. They bind to the enzyme and prevent the enzyme-substrate complex from forming *[1 mark]*.
   c) Because they inhibit respiration, which is a metabolic reaction *[1 mark]*.
3 Ritonavir will prevent the HIV virus from replicating *[1 mark]*, because the virus will not be able to break down the proteins and use the products to make new viruses *[1 mark]*. The Ritonavir molecules are a similar shape to the protease enzyme's substrate so it will act as a competitive inhibitor *[1 mark]* / it will bind to the active site of the enzyme and block it so the substrate cannot fit in *[1 mark]*. *[Maximum of 3 marks available.]*

# Module 2: Section 5 — Biological Membranes

## Page 51 — Cell Membranes

1 The membrane is described as fluid because the phospholipids are constantly moving *[1 mark]*. It is described as a mosaic because the proteins are scattered throughout the membrane like tiles in a mosaic *[1 mark]*.

2 Any two from: Proteins form channels in the cell membranes which allow small or charged particles through *[1 mark]*. / Carrier proteins transport molecules and ions across the cell membrane *[1 mark]*. / Proteins can act as receptors for molecules, e.g. hormones, which are important in cell signalling *[1 mark]*.

## Page 53 — Cell Membranes

1 a) Cut five equal-sized pieces of beetroot and rinse them to remove any pigment released during cutting *[1 mark]*. Make up five test tubes with alcohol concentrations 0, 25, 50, 75 and 100% *[1 mark]*. Place a piece of beetroot in each test tube for the same length of time *[1 mark]*. Remove the piece of beetroot from each tube and use a colorimeter to measure how much light is absorbed by each of the remaining solutions *[1 mark]*.
   b) As the concentration of alcohol increased the absorbance also increased *[1 mark]*. This means that more pigment was released by the beetroot as the alcohol concentration increased, which suggests that the cell membrane became more permeable *[1 mark]*.
   c) E.g. Increasing the concentration of alcohol increases the permeability of the cell membrane because the alcohol dissolves the lipids in the membrane causing it to lose its structure *[1 mark]*.

## Page 55 — Transport Across Cell Membranes

1 a) Any two from: e.g. the concentration of hydrochloric acid solution *[1 mark]*. / The temperature of the hydrochloric acid and gelatine cubes *[1 mark]*. / The concentration of cresol red in each gelatine cube *[1 mark]*.
   b) As surface area to volume ratio decreases, rate of diffusion decreases *[1 mark]*. *[Opposite explanation also gets 1 mark.]*
   You can see from the results of the experiment that as the surface area to volume ratio of the cubes gets smaller, the time taken for the gelatine cubes to turn yellow gets longer. Therefore the rate at which the hydrochloric acid is diffusing through the gelatine blocks is decreasing.
   c) Any one from: e.g. observing the colour change is a matter of opinion *[1 mark]*. / It is hard to say exactly when the colour change has occurred *[1 mark]*. / It would be difficult to cut the blocks to exactly the same size every time *[1 mark]*.

## Page 57 — Transport Across Cell Membranes

1 Facilitated diffusion involves channel proteins, which transport charged molecules across the membrane *[1 mark]* and carrier proteins, which transport large molecules across the membrane *[1 mark]*. Both types of protein transport molecules down a concentration gradient *[1 mark]*.
2 Endocytosis takes in substances from outside the cell *[1 mark]* via vesicles formed from the plasma membrane *[1 mark]*. Exocytosis secretes substances from the cell *[1 mark]* via vesicles made from the Golgi apparatus *[1 mark]*.
   Make sure you don't get these two processes mixed up — try to remember endo for 'in' and exo for 'out'.

## Page 59 — Transport Across Cell Membranes

1 a) The water potential of the sucrose solution was higher than the water potential of the potato *[1 mark]*. Water moves by osmosis down a water potential gradient / from a solution of higher water potential to a solution of lower water potential *[1 mark]*. So water moved into the potato, increasing its mass *[1 mark]*.
   b) The water potential of the potato and the water potential of the solution was the same *[1 mark]*.
   c) − 0.4 g *[1 mark]*. The difference in water potential between the solution and the potato is the same as with the 1% solution, so the mass difference should be about the same, but negative / mass should be lost not gained *[1 mark]*.
   A 5% sucrose solution has a lower water potential than the potato. This means that water will move out of the potato into the sucrose solution, decreasing the mass of the potato.

# Answers

## Module 2: Section 6 — Cell Division and Cellular Organisation

### Page 61 — The Cell Cycle and Mitosis

1 a) C *[1 mark]* because the centromeres have divided and the chromatids are moving to opposite ends of the cell *[1 mark]*.
   b) X = Nuclear envelope *[1 mark]*.
      Y = Cell membrane *[1 mark]*.
      Z = Centriole *[1 mark]*.

### Page 63 — Sexual Reproduction and Meiosis

1 a) Meiosis I because the homologous pairs have separated, halving the chromosome number *[1 mark]*.
   b) During meiosis I/prophase I, homologous pairs of chromosomes come together *[1 mark]*. The chromatids twist around each other and bits swap over *[1 mark]*. The chromatids now contain different combinations of alleles *[1 mark]*. This means each of the four daughter cells will contain chromatids with different combinations of alleles *[1 mark]*.
   c) Independent assortment means that the separation of homologous pairs of chromosomes (in anaphase I) is random/can happen in any way *[1 mark]*. So, the daughter cells produced by meiosis can contain any combination of maternal and paternal chromosomes with different alleles *[1 mark]*.

### Page 65 — Stem Cells and Differentiation

1 It has many chloroplasts to absorb light for photosynthesis *[1 mark]*. It has thin cell walls, so carbon dioxide can easily enter *[1 mark]*.
2 Stem cells divide to make new, specialised cells *[1 mark]*. In animals, adult stem cells are used to replace damaged cells *[1 mark]*, e.g. stem cells in the bone marrow differentiate/ become specialised to make erythrocytes (red blood cells)/ neutrophils (white blood cells) *[1 mark]*.

### Page 67 — Tissues, Organs and Systems

1 It's best described as an organ *[1 mark]* as it is made of many tissues working together to perform a particular function *[1 mark]*.
2 B *[1 mark]*

## Module 3: Section 1 — Exchange and Transport

### Page 69 — Specialised Exchange Surfaces

1 Any two from, e.g. they have thin walls *[1 mark]*. / They have a good blood supply *[1 mark]*. / They're well-ventilated *[1 mark]*. / They have a large surface area to volume ratio *[1 mark]*.
2 The microvilli give the cells a large surface area *[1 mark]*, so nutrients can be absorbed faster *[1 mark]*.

### Page 71 — The Gaseous Exchange System in Mammals

1 a) The trachea will contain large C-shaped pieces of cartilage in its walls *[1 mark]*. The walls of the bronchi will contain smaller pieces of cartilage *[1 mark]* and the large bronchiole will not contain any cartilage *[1 mark]*.
   b) E.g. the student will be able to see goblet cells / ciliated epithelium / smooth muscle in the tissue sample from the largest bronchiole, but not the sample from the smaller bronchiole *[1 mark or opposite argument accepted for 1 mark.]*
2 a) If the elastic fibres are destroyed, the walls of the alveoli may not recoil properly on breathing out *[1 mark]*. This may make it difficult for the person to exhale/breathe out fully *[1 mark]*.
      Destruction of the elastic fibres means the alveoli can't recoil to expel air as well, so more air than normal remains trapped in the lungs.

b) Any two from, e.g. it could cause mucus to build up in the lungs/ airways *[1 mark]*. / It could prevent dust/microorganisms from being cleared out of the lungs/airways *[1 mark]*. / It could increase the chances of a lung infection developing *[1 mark]*.

### Page 73 — Ventilation in Mammals

1 The external intercostal muscles contract *[1 mark]*, making the ribs move up and out *[1 mark]* and the diaphragm contracts/ flattens *[1 mark]*. This increases the volume of the thorax *[1 mark]*, so the pressure inside decreases, drawing air into the lungs *[1 mark]*.

### Page 75 — Ventilation in Fish and Insects

1 a) E.g. the liquid preservative has entered the grasshopper's tracheae, so they are no longer filled with air (and they would appear silver in colour if filled with air) *[1 mark]*.
   b) To provide support *[1 mark]*.
2 The fish opens its mouth, which lowers the floor of the buccal cavity *[1 mark]*. This increases the volume of the buccal cavity *[1 mark]*, decreasing the pressure *[1 mark]*. Water then flows into the buccal cavity *[1 mark]*.

## Module 3: Section 2 — Transport in Animals

### Page 77 — Circulatory Systems

1 The blood flows through the body in vessels *[1 mark]*.
2 Beetles are insects, so they have an open circulatory system *[1 mark]*. The blood is pumped into the body cavity where it circulates freely *[1 mark]*.
3 a) It is a closed system *[1 mark]*.
   b) It is a single circulatory system, not a double one *[1 mark]*.

### Page 79 — Blood Vessels

1 D
2 The hydrostatic pressure in the capillary is greater than the hydrostatic pressure in the spaces around the cells *[1 mark]*, so fluid moves out of the capillary and into spaces around the cells *[1 mark]*.

### Page 81 — The Heart

1 a) i) D *[1 mark]*
      The semi-lunar valve will only open if the pressure in the ventricle is higher than the pressure in the aorta (or pulmonary artery, if you're looking at the right side of the heart).
   ii) C *[1 mark]*
      The atrioventricular valve will be forced closed when the pressure in the ventricle becomes higher than the pressure in the atrium.
   b) The graph should increase and decrease at the same times as the graph for the left side (because both ventricles contract together) *[1 mark]*. The pressure should be lower than for the left side of the heart at all times *[1 mark]*. E.g.

The left ventricle of the heart has thicker, more muscular walls than the right ventricle because it needs to contract powerfully to pump blood all the way round the body. The right side only needs to get blood to the lungs, which are nearby — this is why the pressure will always be lower in the right ventricle than the left.

# Answers

## Page 83 — Heart Activity

1 a) The sino-atrial node acts as a pacemaker/initiates heartbeats *[1 mark]*.
   b) The Purkyne tissue conducts electrical impulses through the ventricle walls *[1 mark]*.
2   The ventricles are not contracting properly *[1 mark]*. This could be because of muscle damage / because the AVN is not conducting impulses to the ventricles properly *[1 mark]*.

## Page 85 — Haemoglobin

1   B *[1 mark]*
    You know that the Bohr effect means that as $pCO_2$ increases, more $O_2$ is released from the blood, so this removes A and C. If the curve shifts right this means that at a particular $pO_2$ the haemoglobin will be less saturated with $O_2$ at higher $pCO_2$. (This is true so the curve shifts right and the correct answer is B.) Try doing a sketch of the $O_2$ dissociation curve and experiment with the movement of the curve to help you remember this.

# Module 3: Section 3 — Transport in Plants

## Page 87 — Xylem and Phloem

1   Any two from: e.g. xylem vessel cells have no end walls *[1 mark]*, so they form an uninterrupted tube that allows water to pass through easily *[1 mark]*. / The vessel cells are dead and contain no cytoplasm *[1 mark]*, which allows water to easily pass through *[1 mark]*. / Their walls are thickened with a woody substance called lignin *[1 mark]*, which helps support the xylem vessels/stop them collapsing inwards *[1 mark]*. / The vessel walls have small holes called pits *[1 mark]*, which allow substances to pass in and out of the vessels *[1 mark]*.

## Page 89 — Water Transport

1   When water evaporates from the leaf this creates tension that pulls more water molecules into the leaf *[1 mark]*. This then causes water to move through the xylem and into the leaf to replace water that has been lost from the plant *[1 mark]*. Cohesive forces between water molecules mean that they are attracted to each other *[1 mark]*. This means that when water molecules move through the xylem, they move as a continuous column *[1 mark]*.
2   Blocking the plasmodesmata would prevent water from travelling between cells via the symplast pathway *[1 mark]*. This would mean that water would only be able to travel via the apoplast pathway *[1 mark]*.

## Page 91 — Transpiration

1   'Hairs' on the epidermis *[1 mark]* trap moist air round the stomata, which reduces the water potential gradient and so reduces transpiration *[1 mark]*. A thick waterproof cuticle *[1 mark]* stops water evaporating through it *[1 mark]*.

## Page 93 — Translocation

1 a) Water enters at point A/the source by osmosis *[1 mark]*. This increases the pressure at the source end of the top tube *[1 mark]*, causing the sugar solution to flow along the tube from the source to the sink *[1 mark]*.
   b) i) phloem *[1 mark]*
      ii) xylem *[1 mark]*

# Module 4: Section 1 — Disease and the Immune System

## Page 95 — Pathogens and Communicable Diseases

1   C *[1 mark]*
2 a) Indirect transmission, because the virus is being transferred via an intermediate (the gardeners' hands/tools) *[1 mark]*.

   b) E.g. they could wash their hands after handling infected plants/ between handling one plant and another plant *[1 mark]*. / They could wash/disinfect their tools after using them on infected plants *[1 mark]*.
3 a) bacteria *[1 mark]*
   b) Any two from: e.g. more overcrowding (in low-income country) *[1 mark]* / more limited access to drugs (in low-income country, compared to wealthier country) *[1 mark]* / less likely to be diagnosed/treated (in low-income country) *[1 mark]*.

## Page 97 — Defence Against Pathogens

1 a) Plant cells are surrounded by a cell wall, which forms a physical barrier against pathogen entry *[1 mark]*. When the cell wall is damaged, the barrier is broken and the virus can enter the cells *[1 mark]*.
   b) E.g. callose deposition at the plasmodesmata *[1 mark]*.

## Page 101 — The Immune System

1   D *[1 mark]*
2   IgG can bind two pathogens at the same time, so the pathogens become agglutinated/clump together *[1 mark]*. This makes phagocytosis easier, so IgG also acts as an opsonin *[1 mark]*.
3   Any three from: e.g. the nucleus of the neutrophil will have three lobes *[1 mark]*. / The nucleus of the B lymphocyte will not have lobes and will take up most of the cell *[1 mark]*. / The neutrophil's cytoplasm will be grainy/contain granules, but the B lymphocyte's won't *[1 mark]*. / The B lymphocyte will be smaller than the neutrophil *[1 mark]*.
4   When the person caught chickenpox for the first time, her B and T lymphocytes produced memory cells *[1 mark]*. When she was exposed to the virus for a second time, the memory B lymphocytes divided into plasma cells *[1 mark]* to produce the right antibody to the virus *[1 mark]*. The memory T lymphocytes divided into the correct type of T lymphocyte to kill the virus *[1 mark]*. The secondary response was quicker and stronger, so got rid of the pathogen before she showed any symptoms *[1 mark]*.

## Page 103 — Immunity and Vaccinations

1   Memory cells produced from vaccination with one strain of the influenza virus will not recognise other strains with different antigens *[1 mark]*. So a new vaccine is made every year to protect against the most recently circulating strains of influenza *[1 mark]*.

## Page 105 — Antibiotics and Other Medicines

1   There was genetic variation in the *Staphylococcus aureus* population that meant some of the bacteria were resistant to meticillin. / Some *Staphylococcus aureus* developed a mutation that made them more resistant to meticillin *[1 mark]*. This made them more likely to survive and reproduce in a host being treated with meticillin *[1 mark]*. The bacteria passed the allele for meticillin resistance on to their offspring *[1 mark]*, so meticillin resistance became more common in the population over time *[1 mark]*.

# Module 4: Section 2 — Biodiversity

## Page 107 — Studying Biodiversity

1 a) Species richness is the number of different species in an area *[1 mark]*. Species evenness is a measure of the relative abundance of each species in an area *[1 mark]*.
   b) Field A, D = $1 - ((80/400)^2 + (110/400)^2 + (210/400)^2)$
              = $1 - 0.39 =$ **0.61** *[1 mark]*
      Field B, D = $1 - ((20/400)^2 + (50/400)^2 + (330/400)^2)$
              = $1 - 0.70 =$ **0.30** *[1 mark]*

# Answers

## Page 109 — More on Biodiversity

1   36/80 = **0.45** *[1 mark]*

2   **5-6 marks:**
The answer describes a variety of the impacts of population growth and monoculture on global biodiversity levels.
The answer has a clear and logical structure.
The information given is relevant and detailed.
**3-4 marks:**
The answer describes some of the impacts from population growth and monoculture.
The answer has some structure. Most of the information given is relevant and there is some detail involved.
**1-2 marks:**
One or two points are given relating to either population growth or monoculture.
The answer has no clear structure. The information given is basic and lacking in detail. It may not all be relevant.
**0 marks:**
No relevant information is given.
**Here are some points your answer may include:**
Human population growth leads to more human development, which destroys habitats, decreasing habitat diversity. There is a greater demand for resources, which can lead to over-exploitation / resources being used up faster than they can be replenished, decreasing genetic diversity and species diversity. Urbanisation can isolate species, meaning populations are unable to interbreed, decreasing genetic diversity. High amounts of pollutants can kill species or destroy habitats, decreasing biodiversity.
Monoculture leads to loss of habitats and habitat diversity as land is cleared for large fields. Local and naturally occurring plants and animals are destroyed with pesticides and herbicides, reducing species diversity. Heritage varieties of crops are lost because they don't make enough money and so aren't planted any more, decreasing species diversity.

## Page 111 — Importance of Biodiversity

1 a) A keystone species is a species on which many of the other species in an ecosystem depend and without which the ecosystem would change dramatically *[1 mark]*.
  b) Because it is a predator *[1 mark]*.

2   Continuous monoculture is growing a single variety of a single crop in an area without interruption *[1 mark]*. Over time this leads to soil depletion, where the nutrients in the soil are used up and not replaced *[1 mark]*. This results in increased spending on fertilisers *[1 mark]* and decreased yields in the long run *[1 mark]*.

## Page 113 — Conservation and Biodiversity

1 a) In situ methods could include protecting the turtles from hunters *[1 mark]* and protecting their nesting sites *[1 mark]*. A national park/protected area could also be established to restrict human usage of the area *[1 mark]*.
  b) It's only possible to conserve a limited number of individuals with ex situ methods *[1 mark]*. They can be very expensive *[1 mark]*. It may be difficult to sustain the environment for the turtle *[1 mark]*. They don't protect the habitat of the turtle *[1 mark]*.

# Module 4: Section 3 — Classification and Evolution

## Page 115 — Classification

1 a) *Salmo* *[1 mark]*
   *Remember that the genus is always the first part of the Latin name.*
  b) Any two from: e.g. it must be eukaryotic *[1 mark]*. / It must be multicellular *[1 mark]*. / It must have no cell walls *[1 mark]*. / It must be heterotrophic/consumes plants or other animals *[1 mark]*.

2 a) Green monkey *[1 mark]* because it's the closest to humans on the tree *[1 mark]*.

  b) The following branch point should be circled:

*[1 mark]*

## Page 117 — Evolution of Classification Systems

1   E.g. scientists could compare the DNA base sequences of gibbons and humans *[1 mark]*. The more similar the sequences, the more closely related they are *[1 mark]*. / Scientists could compare the amino acid sequences of a protein found in both humans and gibbons (e.g. cytochrome C) *[1 mark]*. The more similar the amino acids sequences of the protein, the more closely related they are likely to be *[1 mark]*.

2   Any three from: e.g. RNA polymerase is different in the Archaea and Bacteria *[1 mark]*. / Archaea, but not Bacteria, have histones similar to Eukarya *[1 mark]*. / The bonds of the lipids in the cell membranes of Archaea and Bacteria are different *[1 mark]*. / The development and composition of flagellae are different in the Archaea and Bacteria *[1 mark]*.

## Page 120 — Variation

1 a) For species A and species B, as the temperature increases the development time decreases *[1 mark]*. The development time of species B is less affected by temperature than species A *[1 mark]*.
  b) Individuals within a species have different forms of the same genes (alleles), which causes genetic variation *[1 mark]*.

## Page 122 — Adaptations

1 a) Whales and sharks live in a similar environment (water) so have evolved similar adaptations to help them survive in that environment *[1 mark]*.
  b) E.g. humans don't need to be as efficient at exchanging oxygen as whales because they spend most of their time on land, where oxygen is readily available in the air *[1 mark]*.

## Page 125 — The Theory of Evolution

1 a) E.g. the brown owls may be better camouflaged/blend in with the landscape better than the grey owls when there's no snow cover *[1 mark]*. This makes them less likely to be eaten by predators *[1 mark]*.
   *Snow makes everything white, so lighter coloured owls blend in better when there's snow around. They stick out more when there's no snow though.*
  b) The brown owls are more likely to survive and reproduce when there's less snow cover *[1 mark]* and pass on the allele for darker/brown colouring to their offspring *[1 mark]*. Over time, the allele for darker/brown colouring will become more common in the population *[1 mark]*.

2 a) Genetic mutations/variation would have resulted in some moths having alleles for DDT-resistance/being resistant to DDT *[1 mark]*. When the population was exposed to DDT (a selection pressure), only those individuals who were resistant would survive to reproduce *[1 mark]*. The alleles which code for resistance would be passed on to the next generation *[1 mark]*. Over time, the number of individuals with DDT resistance would increase and it would become more common within the population *[1 mark]*.
  b) Any two from: e.g. moth infestations would be harder to control *[1 mark]*. / Broader pesticides might be used, which could kill beneficial insects *[1 mark]*. / New pesticides might need to be developed if the moth develops resistance to all pesticides in use *[1 mark]*.

# Index

# Index

# Index